LEGEND OF THE CHINESE *LUNG*

— THE CHINESE "DRAGON"

LEGEND OF THE CHINESE *LUNG*

— THE CHINESE "DRAGON"

Dr. Ong Hean-Tatt

EASTERN Dragon PRESS

Published in Malaysia by:
Eastern Dragon Press
A Publishing Division of
S.Abdul Majeed & Co.,
7, Jalan 3/82,
Bangsar Utama,
59000 Kuala Lumpur
Malaysia.

1996

ISBN 983-899-596-7

Printed in Malaysia by
Percetakan Sooriya

PREFACE

Of all the delightful animals in Chinese animal symbolism, the ***"Lung"***, alias the Chinese dragon, must be the most fabulous. The legend of the ***"Lung"*** permeates the ancient Chinese civilisation and culture even up to today. It was the Imperial emblem of China, the Emperor and the nation proudly referred to themselves as the descendants of the ***"Lung"***.

The ***"Lung"*** is a very auspicious creature and has several layers of powerful significance in Chinese culture. Its auspiciousness is associated with aspects like the Heraldic position of ***"Lung"***, the **Double Dragons**, the Dragon Boat Festival, ***"Lung*-Phoenix"** pair and, the Dragon-Pearl. Several of these significances are also found in other cultures.

Even though there are many references, notes and comments about the ***"Lung"***, no one seems to know how the significance of the ***"Lung"*** came about. Despite the inherently difficult and controversial task of trying to examine the past, this book makes an analytical study of several ancient references about the ***"Lung"***, including its etymology and references to the past through ancient Chinese sources, as well as from sources of other cultures.

The ability of the ***"Lung"*** to move through water, land and air and to appear and disappear at will appears to point to the Chinese regard of the ***"Lung"*** as primarily a spirit creature. In the world today, filled with "modern" scientific technology, strange things still happen which baffle science. Hence, it is narrow-minded to ignore the existence of a spirit world and to dismiss the spirit ***"Lung"*** as an imaginary creature.

The deeper meanings of ***"Lung"*** are rooted in the Chinese ***Ganzhi*** system, of which the ***Pakua*** or **"Eight Diagrams**, showing ***"Lung"*** as one of the **Four Heraldic Animals**, is only one facet and the ancient Chinese mystical classic, the ***I Ching***, another facet.

However, the true significance of the magnificent ***"Lung"*** goes back even earlier, to the time when mankind radiated and migrated from Mesopotamia to form new nations away from the ancient Middle East.

This book compares information from various ancient cultures, ranging from the Double-Horned, Bearded, Fish-tailed ***"Lung"*** mentioned in ancient Middle East to Biblical lore where this creature is always depicted as the **"Angel of the East"** as opposed to the "serpent", which is the creature of the north. ***"Lung"*** is also linked with the Biblical Cherubim with the "flaming sword" blocking the east entrance into the Garden of Eden.

The book clarifies the confusion of the benevolent ***"Lung"*** with the malevolent serpent and shows that the ***"Lung"*** is actually among the highest of the holy angels of God. The Greek word **"drakon"** means **"serpent"** and, while this is a proper term for the Biblical "Serpent, the Old Dragon", it has been wrongly applied to the Chinese ***"Lung"***. The Chinese ***"Lung"***, never the dragon, has been wrongly and misleadingly called the **"dragon"**. There is also evidence that there were ancient attempts to convert the ***"Lung"***, originally a creature oriented along a north-south axis, into a lunar dragon oriented along an east-west axis, and hence made responsible for eclipses, which are regarded as bad omens. These misconceptions have transformed the auspicious ***"Lung"*** into a fearsome malignant creature.

Readers are taken on some ancient historical journey especially to the time of Emperor Huang Ti of 2688 B.C., Emperor Ta Yu of 2205 B.C. and even further back to that of Emperor Fu Hsi of 2945 B.C. It was the glorious feats of these three Emperors which determined most of the layers of significance of the ***"Lung"***. Therein occurred great events, which connect the Chinese people with ***"Lung"***. They form the historical reasons why the World First Emperor, Fu Hsi, and World Third Emperor, Huang Ti, are respectively called **Azure *"Lung"*** and **Golden *"Lung"***. These events, ever since, have determined the fundamental auspiciousness of ***"Lung"*** in ancient Chinese culture.

The legend of the ***"Lung"*** has hidden secrets about the dim distant history of ancient China. There will be a number of surprising revelations in the book. One is that the ***"Lung"*** is originally not an animal but a human being. The ***"Lung"*** was that ancient emperor acting as the King-Priest of ***Shang Ti***, the One Supreme Formless-Imageless God.

TABLE OF CONTENTS

LIST OF TABLES

LIST OF ILLUSTRATIONS

Part A:

TRADITIONAL AUSPICIOUS MEANINGS OF "*LUNG*"

CHAPTER 1

THE "*LUNG*": BENEVOLENT SYMBOL OF CHINA

INTRODUCTION

A fabulous, colourful, serpentine creature with bearded, doubled horned head, fish-tail and four limbs with eagle claws, threading the clouds and riding the foams of the seas; that is the striking image often portrayed of the Chinese ***"Lung"***.

From very ancient times, the ***"Lung"*** shared with the ***Pakua,*** (or **Eight Diagrams)** the role as characteristic symbols of Chinese culture. The ***"Lung"*** is a popular motif in Chinese art and artifacts. The Chinese proudly referred to themselves as the "descendants of the ***'Lung'***" (Hsu and Ward 1984 p.459).

Among several cultures, the ancients spoke widely of this fabulous being. Venerated among the religions of the earliest people and particularly that of the Chinese nation, it has become a central object of their mythology as the minister of the will of gods and the guardian of sacred treasures (Williams 1931 p.112).

The ***"Lung"*** is the symbol of ancient China. The Chinese Emperor is the ***"Lung"***, sitting on the ***"Lung"*** throne and wearing the ***"Lung"*** robes of gold. In the Chinese classic ***I Ching***, ***"Lung"*** is the **Great Man.** In Chinese ***Feng Shui***, the energy forces affecting the environment and human destiny are called **"dragon lines"** (***"Lung chi"***).

Only one other ancient symbol is as important in the Chinese culture; that is the ***Pakua,*** or **Eight Diagrams**, which, like the ***"Lung"***, is a symbol of blessings and safeguard against evil. The pre-eminence in Chinese culture of these two great symbols, the

THE MAJESTIC
□*LUNG*□

RIDING THE CLOUDS AND THREADING THE WAVES OF THE SEAS

IT CONTROLS STREAMS, FLOODS, SEAS AND RAINS. IT ALSO BRINGS THE RAIN CLOUDS TO NOURISH THE HARVEST.

FU HSI
PAKUA

THE *"PAKUA"* IS THE SYMBOL OF CHINESE CULTURE.

IT IS USED TO WARD OFF EVIL & ALSO ACTS AS AN AUSPICIOUS SYMBOL OF GOOD FORTUNE, HAPPINESS AND LONGEVITY.

"Lung" and the ***Pakua***, is an indication that they have deep interrelated meanings and origins.

BENEVOLENCE OF THE *"LUNG"*

China is the home of ***"Lung"*** worship. The ***"Lung"*** is basically a benevolent being whose auspicious influence could be summed up as the Chinese saying goes:

"Good fortune in the Lung-Phoenix."

In the East, the ***"Lung"*** is a venerated being and harbinger of blessings. The ***"Lung"*** is regarded as the leader among all animals which swim or crawl. It can be visible or invisible and assume many sizes. It ascends to heaven in spring and descends into the waters in autumn. It is not malicious nor poisonous like the dragon pictured by the Westerners but is generally a benevolent creature particularly associated with the bringing of rains (Wu 1982 p.5). There are several other layers of significance of ***"Lung"*** in the Chinese culture:

- The ***"Lung"*** is distinctly the Imperial symbol of ancient China and the Chinese Emperor. The Imperial significance of ***"Lung"*** is often associated with **"Nine *Lungs*"**, which are motifs worn on Imperial robes.

- In Chinese philosophy, like in the ***I Ching***, the ***"Lung"*** is the symbol of the Great Man.

- The ***"Lung"*** represents the benevolent influences of water in the form of rivers and rains.

- The ***"Lung"***, particularly the Double Dragons, signify the "Guardian" power of angels watching over the Universe and the World, including Man.

- In Chinese ***Feng Shui***, the energy forces affecting human destiny are called ***"Lung chi"***, "dragon breath or lines". The ***"Lung"*** occupies important central meanings in ancient Chinese religious culture.

"Lung" is the essence of strength, goodness and blessings. These are several sayings reflecting the auspicious meanings attributed to the ***"Lung"***. Only one other symbol may also sum up the essence of Chinese culture: this is the ***Pakua***, or **Eight Diagrams.**

"*LUNG*", THE IMAGE OF WATER AND CLOUDS

"Lung" has been commonly linked to the beneficent influences of water and its multiple forms like the clouds and winds. The mysterious home of the ***"Lung"*** is among the clouds or waters and it remains hidden in the caves of high, inaccessible, mysterious mountains, or deep in the unfathomable, unexplored depths of the sea. At proper times, it would slowly wake up and enter into activity. Moving majestically among the storm clouds; it unfolds and washes its mane in the dark whirlpools of heaven and earth. Its claws are like lightning forks, its scales glisten in the rains. Its voice is like thunder winds which scatter the withered forest leaves and renew the spring. The ***"Lung"*** signifies the essence of flux and change, therefore of life itself (Williams 1931 p.109).

The ancient Chinese believe the water-spout to be a living ***"Lung"*** and regard swelling waves as enchanted. The ***"Lung"*** is said to have the power to raise huge waves to injure men and boats (Williams 1931 p.112). One writer wrote:

> **Shen Lung controls the streams, floods, seas and rains, he can be either a blessing or a curse to man. We find him**

LUNG AS AN EMBLEM OF GREATNESS

DRAGON PRINCE OF THE SEA: *A very rich and elegant person or place.*

THE DRAGON'S PRESENCE, NOT THE DEPTH, MAKES THE WATER EFFECTIVE: *The reputation of a place depends on its men, not its size.*

A DRAGON COILED AND A TIGER READY TO SPRING: *An impregnable position.*

THE DRAGON IS THE CHIEF OF THE FOUR SPIRITUAL ANIMALS: *The leader (Dragon is also chief of all scaly animals).*

RISING DRAGON AND SOARING PHOENIX: *A man rising in status.*

DRAGON'S STEPS AND TIGER'S GLANCE: *Dignified (also Dragon's walk and tiger's pace).*

FLYING DRAGONS IN THE SKY: *One who has won power.*

A DRAGON AMONG MEN: *A famous man.*

A PEN MOVING LIKE DRAGON AND SNAKE: *Exquisite penmanship.*

DRAGON-TIGER LIST: *The list of successful examination candidates.*

GOD OF THE SOIL EATS EARTHWORMS; THAT WHICH ONE LOVES IS A GOLDEN DRAGON: *Precious things.*

CONDITIONS THE "*LUNG*" ABIDES BY

THE MIGHTY DRAGON IS NO MATCH AGAINST THE LOCAL SERPENT: *The local who is familiar with his environment is a match for the stranger who is more able.*

THE WICKED DRAGON FINDS IT DIFFICULT TO TRIP LOCAL SNAKES: *An evil ruler cannot escape public disfavour.*

KEEPING A DRAGON IN A POND: *Limiting the scopes of able men.*

A DRAGON OUT OF WATER: *Moment of power not yet arrive.*

THE *CHIAO* DRAGON GAINS CLOUDS AND RAINS BUT NOT THE POND: *One who is not yet powerful.*

A DRAGON RETURNS TO THE SEA, A TIGER TO THE MOUNTAIN: *The powerful one in his element.*

A DRAGON WILL NOT LEAVE HIS POOL, THE PHOENIX, HIS NEST: *A person knowing he would be helpless out of his element.*

THE TIGER AND LEOPARD ANXIOUS LEST THEY MEET THE UNICORN; THE DRAGON IS AFRAID OF THE CENTIPEDE: *No matter how powerful, one has someone to fear.*

SEEING THE TAIL BUT NOT THE HEAD OF THE DRAGON: *A great man does not reveal everything - the Dragon never exposes his whole body to the gaze.*

DRAGON-TIGER DAYS: *There is a different day in each month when the tiger and dragon rule over.*

LUNG A SYMBOL OF HIGH ASPIRATIONS

MAN CAN ACHIEVE WEALTH, FOR THE DRAGON GOVERNS THE WATER: *A hint to someone who hesitates to do anything because of a lack of money.*

THE THIRD AND FOURTH MONTHS BRING NO WEALTH, SPENT FIFTH AND SIXTH MONTHS CURSING THE DRAGON: *Procrastination brings trouble.*

WISHING TO EAT DRAGON'S FLESH, ONE HAS TO GO TO SEA: *Asking others to do things but finally having to do these oneself.*

TO CATCH THE TIGER'S THREE OUNCES OF SILVER AND GRASP THE DRAGON'S FIVE OUNCES: *Lucky man or person who uses wealth righteously.*

DESPISE NOT THE SNAKE WHICH MAY BECOME A DRAGON: *Blindly despising someone who may become great.*

DRAGON'S HEAD BUT SNAKE'S TAIL: *A pretentious beginning but small results.*

DRAGON'S HEAD BELONGS TO THE OLD: *When several are seeking the same position it is usually the old who will win it.*

IN GREATNESS, HE COVERS THE SUN AND THE HEAVENS, IN SMALLNESS, HE HIDES IN THE MUSTARD SEED: *One who can do a small or a great thing equally well.*

SEIZING A DRAGON IN THE OCEAN: A brave deed.

THE "DARK" SIDE OF THE "*LUNG*"

TO VOMIT CLOUDS AND SPIT MIST LIKE THE DRAGON: *Boasting.*

THE TONGUE IS A DRAGON'S DEN: *"Dragon's den" refers to the sword - thus, the saying testifies to the danger of an unbridled tongue.*

ANGER OF FIVE DRAGONS: *Ungovernable anger.*

Mr Yeh, claiming to love dragons, was always painting them. The Heavenly Dragon heard about this and wanted to see Mr Yeh. But Mr Yeh, on knowing of his coming, fled. *Moral: Mr Yeh is a hypocrite.*

GREAT FLOODS WASH AWAY THE TEMPLE OF THE DRAGON KING: *One fails to recognise another family member.*

A DRAGON BLOCKS A THOUSAND RIVERS: *One obstructs many.*

TWO DRAGONS AND THE PEARL: *Fighting for supremacy (also, One pool cannot have two dragons).*

PLUCKING THE BLACK PEARL FROM THE DRAGON: *One who immediately gains power through working for another.*

Many people, confusion; many dragons, drought; many daughters-in-law, mother cooks; many roosters, morning unannounced, many hens, no eggs: *Too many cooks spoil the soup.*

LEAVING 100,000 FEET HIGH DRAGON CAVE AND MEETING 3,000 CRUEL SOLDIERS: *Experiencing one difficulty after another (also, Out of the tiger's den into the dragon's pool).*

YOUNG SWALLOWS SEEK THE OLD NEST, OLD DRAGON RETURNS TO HIS OLD DEN: *Leaving the employment of a master without trouble, one yearns to return to it.*

SHRIMPS DISTURB DRAGONS IN SHALLOW WATERS, CANINE IMPS LAUGH AT TIGERS ON PLAINS: *A great man in trouble through the actions of inferiors.*

WITH MONEY, A DRAGON, WITHOUT MONEY, A WORM: *Children of rich men are looked upon but children of the poor are despised.*

THE LUNG SIGNIFIES AUSPICIOUSNESS

DRAGON'S BREATH BECOMES CLOUDS: *Auspicious event.*

WHEN THE DRAGON RETURNS TO SEA CAVES, CLOUDS RETAIN THEIR MOISTURE; WHEN THE MUSK DEER CROSSES THE GREEN HILLS, THE GRASS AND TREES RETAIN THEIR PERFUME: *Auspicious events.*

MAN DEPENDS ON THE DRAGON KING; A TIGER DEPENDS ON THE MOUNTAIN; A WIFE - ON THE HUSBAND: *Each has something to depend on.*

A DRAGON DRAWING WATER: *Raining.*

NINE DRAGONS PLAYING IN THE WATER: *About to rain.*

THE DRAGON BEARS NINE VARIETIES: *A man will have different descendents.*

DRAGONS BEGET DRAGONS, TIGERS BEGET LEOPARDS, THE DONKEY BEGET A UNICORN, THE PIG - AN ELEPHANT: *Mean parents may yet have noble sons.*

DRAGON BEARS THE DRAGON; THE PHOENIX BEARS THE PHOENIX; THE SON OF A BEGGAR HANDLES THE STICK: *Like beget like.*

acting both ways. He moves his head and blows out the clouds that the earth may be nourished. At other times he returns to his sea home and the clouds retain their moisture. Under normal circumstances his worship takes place on the first and fifteenth of each month. During a drought he is most earnestly sought by all classes of the people. A large paper dragon is made and borne in a procession, while prayers are continually offered to secure his help. So as it is to him that the people must look for the rains which give the harvests, he is considered man's friend. He constantly does things for which the people should bless him. On the other hand, he is blamed for the floods, obstructed rivers, and many of the cataclysms of nature. So although he gives prosperity and happiness to his people, within his mouth there is also a sword ready to strike at a moment's notice. With a god of such power watching one's actions, man should be most careful so that later there will be nothing for which he can be blamed. He exerts his power in protecting the places of those he likes from evil influences and demons. For this reason any spot where he will dwell in peace is fortunate. But when he is not permitted to live in his chosen home, he becomes a menace to the community. He may be either the friend or enemy of man, as he chooses (Plopper 1935 pp.45-47).

The ancient people of the East depict the dragon as possessing life-giving powers through the agency of water. In most ancient concepts the dragon controls water on earth in the form of rivers, streams, seas, pools, wells and in the sky as clouds, thunder and lightning. It is essentially life-giving and is venerated even though it has its angry menacing moods in the form of storms (Whittick 1960 pp.176-178). The many manifestations of storm clouds are the swirling motions of the moving ***"Lung"***. Lightning forks are the claws of the ***"Lung"***. The ***"Lung"*** signifies the essence of flux and change, therefore of life itself.

AUGUST

□*SHEN LUNG*□

JUST AS *"LUNG"* IS THE RAIN-MAKER BRINGING WELCOMED RAINS,THE EMPEROR PROVIDES BLESSINGS TO THE PEOPLE.

Shen Lung, the **Divine *"Lung"***, regulates the streams, floods, seas and rains, and can be a blessing or a curse to man. He moves his head and blows out the clouds that the earth may be nourished. At other times he returns to his sea home and the clouds retain their moisture. During a drought he is most earnestly sought by all classes of the people. It is to him that the people must look for the rains which give the harvests, he is considered man's friend. He constantly does things for which the people should bless him.

The popular colourful Chinese Dragon Boat Festival, on the 5th day of the 5th Moon, exemplifies the natural element of ***"Lung"*** in water. It also reflects the influence of ***"Lung"*** in providing water.

On the other hand, he is blamed for the floods, obstructed rivers, and many of the cataclysms of nature.

But, the ***"Lung"*** is a righteous being. Though he gives prosperity and happiness to his people, within his mouth there is also a sword ready to strike at a moment's notice usually when there has been an offence committed against Heaven. With a god of such power watching one's actions man should be most careful, so that later there will be nothing for which he can be blamed (Plopper 1935 pp.45-47). In some ancient Middle East cultures, ***"Lung"*** is actually their "Storm God"; a most powerful of gods, administering justice against evil.

However, historical evidence indicates that ***"Lung"*** assumed its water roles only in the later Shang period and after. For Hsu and Ward (1984 p.462) note:

> ***..the Shang seldom prayed to the Lung for rain...***

CHAPTER 2

ASTROLOGICAL AUSPICIOUSNESS OF THE *"LUNG"*

FENG SHUI AUSPICIOUSNESS OF THE *"LUNG"*

The ***"Lung"*** also exerts its benevolence through means other than water. ***"Lung"*** is the very essence of vitality and the ***"Lung chi"***, or "dragon's breath" permeates to vitalise the land.

All hills and rivers are inhabited by dragons and when a house is built the ***Feng Shui*** master would be consulted about the dragon spirits. The shrine dedicated to the house deity is really put up for the local dragon which protects the family house. The virtue of the house dragon lasts about one hundred years after which, the powers of the dragon need to be reinvigorated with more elaborate ceremonies. Three days are spent in preparations and on the fourth day, the exorcism of evil influences are carried out. The ***Feng Shui*** master would then go to the nearest hill and invoke the dragon spirit to return (Dennys 1968 p.108).

He exerts his power in protecting the places of those he likes from evil influences and demons. For this reason any spot where he will dwell in peace is fortunate. But when he is not permitted to live in his chosen home, he becomes a menace to the community. He may be either the friend or enemy of man, as he chooses (Plopper 1935 pp.45-47).

In ***Feng Shui***, the ***"Lung"*** is one of the **Four Animals of the Four Cardinal Directions** and resides in the East. The basis of ***Feng Shui*** is related to the different manifestations of the ***Ganzhi*** system

THE *GANZHI* SYSTEM

IS THE INTERACTION OF THE CELESTIAL STEMS (4 HERALDIC ANIMALS) WITH THE TERRESTRIAL BRANCHES (12 ZODIAC ANIMALS).

Celestial Stems

Terrestrial Branches

THE *"LUNG"* IS DIFFERENTIATED FROM THE SNAKE IN BOTH THE CELESTIAL STEMS AND THE TERRESTRIAL BRANCHES.

TERRESTRIAL BRANCH SIGNIFICANCE OF THE *"LUNG"*

Order of Animals:	**5th**
Time ruled by *"Lung"*	**5th Hour, Ch'en (0700 to 0900)**
Season	**End of Spring**
Month	**5th astronomical moon**
Direction	**S60E**
Western constellation	**Aries**
Ruling Planet*	**Mars**
Lucky Gemstone	**Amethyst**
Shade	**Yang**
Year	**1904, 1916, 1928, 1940, 1952, 1964, 1976, 1988**
Associated Immortal*	**Fu-Hsi (Azure *"Lung"*), Huang Ti (Golden *"Lung"*)**
Symbol:*	**Good augury and luck. Also symbolise powers of destiny.**
Good points:	**Determined, strong, fighter. Not cunning or guileful. Lively, full of vitality. Follow own judgment but just and magnanimous. Admired, highly intelligent. Filial.**
Bad points:	**Seldom agree with elders. Blunt and rough. Risk making mistakes through error of judgment. Eccentric and egoistic.**
Others:	**Can be successful if he can check his impulses and improve his ways.**
Compatible	**Monkey, Rat, Snake.**
Incompatible	**Ox, Dog.**

***These features are those of the Ten Celestial Stems level.**

CELESTIAL STEM SIGNIFICANCE OF THE *"LUNG"*

The "tiangan" factor predisposes the *"Lung"* along the following trends:

Metal	**Most strong willed and intense** **Bright, open, expressive** **Honest, unbending, critical** **Action oriented, combative** **Little patience, intimidating** **Exaggerate, undiplomatic, foolhardy**
Water	**Inhibited but progressive** **Witty, strong in will** **Calm, democratic, liberal minded** **Fast, reliable, good negotiator** **Over-optimistic** **Try to do too many difficult tasks by oneself**
Wood	**Creative, magnanimous** **Likes to explore and be logical** **Generous, moderate, accomodative** **Condescending, egoistic** **Outspoken, proud, fearless**
Fire	**Most righteous, open, impartial** **Outgoing, inspiring, competitive** **Critical, demanding, aggressive** **Bad air of superiority and authority** **Overzealous, overgeneralise** **Short temper, inconsiderate**
Earth	**Sociable, hardworking, executive type** **Fair, reasonable, appreciative** **Realistic, solid, stable, impersonal** **Autocratic** **Quiet, brave, strong**

of the **Ten Celestial Stems** and **Twelve Terrestrial Branches**. The position of the "***Lung***" being the animal in the East in this ***Ganzhi*** system, provides an important clue as to its ancient origins of which we shall discuss further.

ZODIAC SIGNIFICANCE OF THE "*LUNG*"

The majestic ***"Lung"*** is the fifth of the twelve Zodiac Animals.

The ***"Lung"*** has two different sets of significance as it is not only the 5th of the Zodiac Animals, but also one of the **Four Heraldic Animals of the Four Directions.** The two different sets of significance is reflective of the Chinese ***Ganzhi*** system of chronology and directions. The ***Ganzhi*** system has two main levels viz.:

1. **Ten Celestial Stems**.

   These are the **Five Elements** of Wood, Fire, Metal, Water and Earth. They are also represented by the **Four Heraldic Animals**, with the **Azure *"Lung"*** in the East, Phoenix in the South, Tiger in the West, Snake-Tortoise in the North and the central Earth position occupied by another ***"Lung"***, the **Golden *"Lung"***.

   They are essentially the highest angels controlling the four spheres of Heaven. Each of the **Four Heraldic Animals** also appear to have under it, seven other animals thus forming the 28 constellations.

2. **Twelve Terrestrial Branches**.

   They are the Twelve Zodiac Animals, including the ***"Lung"***, or the 12 years in the Jupiter Cycle. They can also represent the twelve points of the compass as well as the twelve divisions of the day and year. They are the twelve areas of angelic influences on Earth.

The **Celestial Stems** are the angelic forces of Heaven, while the **Terrestrial Branches** are the angelic forces on Earth; their interactions, as postulated by the ***Ganzhi*** system, regulates the whole Universe. Hence, the ***"Lung"*** would have a set of meanings associated with the Heavenly ***"Lung"*** and another set of meanings associated with the Earthly ***"Lung"***.

Most of the beneficial auspiciousness ascribed to the ***"Lung"*** are those of the **Celestial Stems** level. They represent the powers and manifestations of the Heavenly ***"Lung"***. The Zodiac ***"Lung"*** is really the characteristic of the terrestrial guardian angel of the man it is associated with; its attributes are terrestrial and may determine major features upon the behaviour and destiny of the man born under the ***"Lung"*** sign.

There are seven animals to each of the **Four Heraldic Animals**, making up to the total of the **Twenty-Eight Constellations**. The ***"Lung"*** in the East also forms two of these 28 constellations of which the ***Tong Shu*** describes:

o **Earth Dragon** (sometimes known as Crocodile) is the 1st lunar Constellation of ***Chiao***, the Horn, a cross-like four stars in **Virgo.** It falls on a Thursday under the influence of Jupiter and is auspicious:

To build today will bring prosperity and glory. Men of letters will approach the Emperor. Marriages will lead to many offsprings. But repairing a tomb or going to a funeral would bring a new grief.

ANIMALS OF THE 28 CONSTELLATIONS

No.*	Hsiu	Object	Animal	Element	Auspiciousness
	EAST AZURE DRAGON SECTOR:				
1.	Chiao	Horn	Crocodile Earth Dragon	Wood	auspicious
2.	K'ang	Neck	Sky Dragon	Metal	inauspicious
3.	Ti	Root	Badger	Earth	inauspicious
4.	Fang	Room	Hare	Sun	auspicious
5.	Hsin	Heart	Fox	Moon	auspicious
6.	Wei	Tail	Tiger	Fire	auspicious
7.	Chi	Basket	Leopard	Water	auspicious
	NORTH BLACK TURTLE SECTOR:				
8.	Nan tou	Ladle	Unicorn, Griffion	Wood	auspicious
9.	Niu	Buffalo	Buffalo	Metal	inauspcious
10.	Nu	Woman	Bat	Earth	inauspicious
11.	Hsu	Void	Rat	Sun	inauspicious
12.	Wei	Roof	Swallow	Moon	inauspicious
13.	Shih	House	Pig, Bear	Fire	auspicious
14.	Pi	Wall	Porcupine	Water	auspicious
	WEST WHITE TIGER SECTOR:				
15.	K'uei	Legs	Wolf	Wood	inauspicious
16.	Lou	Link	Dog	Metal	auspicious
17.	Wei	Stomach	Pheasant	Earth	auspicious
18.	Mao	Lights	Cock	Sun	inauspicious
19.	Pi	Thread	Crow, Raven	Moon	inauspicious
20.	Tsui	Turtle	Monkey	Fire	inauspicious
21.	Shen	Three associates (3 stars)	Gibbon	Water	auspicious
	RED PHOENIX SECTOR:				
22.	Ching	Well	Tapir	Wood	auspicious
23.	Kuei	Ghost	Goat,Sheep	Metal	inauspicious
24.	Liu	Willow	Buck	Earth	inauspicious
25.	Hsing	Star	Horse	Sun	inauspicious
26.	Chang	Fishing net	Stag	Moon	auspicious
27.	I	Wings	Snake	Fire	inauspicious
28.	Chen	Chariot	Earthworms	Water	auspicious

*1 to 7 and their multiples correspond to the seven days of the week, starting with Thursday, and the seven planets Jupiter, Venus, Saturn, Sun, Moon, Mars and Mercury.

o **Sky Dragon** is the 2nd lunar Constellation of ***K'ang***, the Neck, four stars in the feet of **Virgo**. It falls on a Friday under the influence of Venus and is inauspicious:

Do not build today; do not let the eldest lead. Anything undertaken the following ten days will bring disaster. Funeral and marriages will lead to untimely death of husbands.

RELATED AUSPICIOUSNESS IN OTHER CULTURES

The dragon does not arise independently in various civilisations but has a common origin probably in the ancient Sumerian civilisation which may have derived its ideas from or passed them to Egypt. One of the earliest representations of dragons is on an archaic cylinder-seal from Susa and depicts a lion or lioness combined with an eagle or falcon. The ancient Chinese dragon is more complicated, with a camel head, deer horns, ox ears, elephant tusks, serpentine body, fish scales, ridge-shaped horny spine, long serpentine fish-tail, four legs with the feet of a tiger and eagle claws (Whittick 1960 pp.176-178).

As the beneficent life-giving element of water, the ***"Lung"*** is the national symbol of Imperial China and also the emblem of the Japanese Emperor. The Romans adopted it as their standard (along with the eagle) and it also appeared as the emblem of West Saxon and English-Welsh kings like Henry VII, Henry VIII, James I. The dragon is further represented as a guardian of treasure. The golden apples in the Garden of Hesperides were guarded by Ladon, the hundred-headed dragon (Whittick 1960 pp.176-178).

While the dragon is a benevolent creature in a number of cultures, it was only in the Bible that the dragon was associated with the evil serpent (Whittick 1960 pp.177-178). It appears that Indian Buddhism introduced some confusion, for the Lamas and Chinese

Buddhists, not daring to call the mythical Indian serpents (Naga) "serpents" as what they really are, termed these Nagas as ***"Lung"*** in their translations of the Sankrit Buddhist scriptures (Williams 1931 p.109).

DIFFERENCES FROM THE TYPICAL VIEW OF WESTERNERS

The Chinese ***"Lung"*** is the essence of strength, goodness and blessings and is therefore unlike the one pictured by Europeans as a terrible, evil, medieval monster. In the West, the dragon seems deemed as the incarnation of the Devil:

> **One of the most famous mythological creations in the history of human thought is the horrid serpentine monster called the dragon. Together with the serpent and other things of the same repulsive and dangerous class, this is the universal symbol of evil — of some living power inimical to God and all good and the just terror of all men. The Serpent stands for that form of the Evil One in which cunning, artifice, deceit and malignant subtlety are the characteristics. The Dragon represents the same power armed, defiant, and putting forth in imperial forms and devastating by force. The Serpent is the sly and creeping deceiver, smoothly gliding in to betray, insinuating his poison and destroying by stealth. The Dragon is the terrific oppressor, assailing with teeth and claws, armed all over with spikes, lifting speary wings and tail, spouting fire and fury, and rushing upon its prey with every vehemence of malignant energy. The Serpent and the Dragon are one and the same, only in different modes of manifestation. Hence the Devil is called "the Dragon, that old Serpent". Whenever the power of evil is clothed in political sovereignty, persecuting, tyrannising, and oppressing, it is always the Dragon, or some rampant figure of destruction answering to it** (Seiss 1972 p.58).

Westerners, especially Christians, may wonder why the Chinese consider themselves the children of the ***"Lung"***, when the dragon is supposed to be the evil symbol of Satan the Devil. The Chinese ***"Lung"*** would be considered out of place in a Christian home. But, is the Chinese ***"Lung"*** so bad as that?

The oriental ***"Lung"*** differs from the "western" dragon in a number of important aspects: in appearance, in disposition, and in regard to which it is held. In the West, the dragon is usually regarded as a huge cruel monster, the personification of evil, and the terrible enemy of man. The Chinese ***"Lung"*** is however, the opposite. It augurs the rains which water the crops that, in turn, supply the food of man. It is a benevolent being, a friend who brings blessings to man (Plopper 1935 p.47).

Why is there a remarkable difference between western and eastern beliefs in regard to the **"dragon"**?

The truth may surprise many people! The surprising truth is that the Chinese ***"Lung"*** is not the same as the "Biblical Dragon"! The Bible mentions several angelic beings and actually shows that, unlike the "Biblical Dragon", the Chinese ***"Lung"*** is among the highest holy creatures of God!

The ***"Lung"*** has been misleadingly called the "dragon" by Westerners. In fact, the Westerners applied the term "dragon" to various mythical animals in different religions and mythologies, while these animals are actually different! For the time being, we will use the western term "dragon" for the Chinese ***"Lung"***.

This book will describe many benevolent significance of the ***"Lung"***. We will examine the thoughts given to the problems of the significance of ***"Lung"***. Then, we will discover the original reasons why the Chinese people have purposefully immersed their culture with the glory of the ***"Lung"***.

CHAPTER 3

VARIETIES OF "*LUNGS*"

MYTHOLOGICAL IMAGES OF THE "*LUNG*"

The current serpentine ***"Lung"*** is a composite image, its body drawn from the parts of nine different natural animals (Plopper 1935 pp.47-49; Williams 1931 pp.109-110):

1. A head like a camel, with a pearl in his forehead, with a long beard, and with a sharp sword as a tongue.

   On each side of its mouth are whiskers, and a beard hangs under its chain, where also is placed a bright pearl; Its breath proceeds from the mouth like a cloud; which sometimes changes into water, at other times into fire; its voice is like the jingling of copper pans striking each other.

2. Horns of a deer.

3. Eyes of a rabbit.

4. Ears of a cow. It cannot hear, which is the reason why deaf persons are called ***"Lung"***.

5. Neck of a snake.

6. Belly of a frog.

7. Scales of a carp. There is also a ridge of scales along its back, eighty-one in number; the scales on its throat lie towards the head, and those on the head are disposed like the ridges in a chain of mountains.

8. Legs and claws of a hawk.

9. Paws of a tiger.

"Lung", being a divine animal, dies of its own accord. It eats swallows' flesh, for which reason, when people pray to the ***"Lung"*** for rain they throw swallows into the water (Williams 1931 p.110). An author wrote:

> **"As he passes from place to place, he is royal in his stride and appearance and receives the homage of all living beings. He has the power of altering his size, becoming exceedingly large or infinitesimally small at will. He can also make himself visible or invisible as he chooses."** (Plopper 1935 pp.47-49).

The ***"Lung"*** is not a natural animal known to Man. This is despite attempts to link it to giant lizards like the huge monitor lizards, the crocodiles-alligators and the Indonesian Komodo Dragons. (Williams 1931 pp.109-110) notes:

> **"The Shou Wen dictionary, A.D. 200, states that of the 369 species of scaly reptiles, such as fishes, snakes and lizards, the *'Lung'* is the chief; it wields the power of transformation and the gift of rendering itself visible or invisible at pleasure. In the spring it ascend to the skies, and in autumn it buries itself in the watery depths. It covers itself with mud in the autumnal equinox and emerges in**

THE SERPENTINE
「LUNG」

POSSESSES THE BODY PARTS OF 9 DIFFERENT ANIMALS, REPRESENTING THE 9 EXTRAORDINARY ABILITIES OF THE *"LUNG"*.

the spring; thus announcing by its awakening the return of nature's energies, it became naturally the symbol of the productive force of moisture, that is of spring, when by means of genial rains and storms all nature renew itself. It may be noted that the crocodile was worshipped by the ancient Egyptians, and the theory had been advanced that the Chinese *'Lung'* is merely a modified form of the alligator found occasionally to the present day in the Yangtze River, for the emergence of the latter from hibernation synchronises with the coming of spring, when the *'Lung'* is believed to be exerting its beneficent influence; it is, however, difficult to trace an analogy between this fabulous animal and any other natural species, for the body of this *'Lung'* seems to be distinctly serpentine, its head is made up of parts of various other animals, the teeth are those of a mammalian carnivore, while the legs and claws are those of a bird. Moreover, as it is a beneficent creature, it cannot be compared with the ferocious dragon of heraldry and medieval mythology. The dragon seems to perpetuate the tradition of primeval flying saurians of geologic times, now known only through their fossilised remains. The Lamas and Chinese Buddhists have assimilated them with the mythical serpents (Naga) of Indian myth."

The only reason why the ***"Lung"*** has not been linked with the dinosaurs could be because the giant reptiles were supposed to have been extinct out before the coming of Man.

Fossil remains of the stegodon, mastodon, elephant, etc. are occasionally unearthed in various parts of Northern China. The bones are called Dragon's Bones and the fossil ivory is termed Dragon's Teeth. They are powdered and used medicinally in the treatment of various ailments such as chorea, spermatorrhaea, ague and haemorrhages (Williams 1931 p.109).

THE MAIN DIFFERENT KINDS OF "*LUNGS*"

There are several varieties of ***"Lung"***; some horned and others hornless, some have no scales, and one type has no wings. There is the Winged Dragon; the Coiling Dragon which inhabits the waters; and the Yellow Dragon which emerged from the River Lo to present the elements of writing to the legendary Emperor Fu Hsi (Williams 1931 pp.110-111). The Chinese cosmogonist has classified four chief kinds of ***"Lung"*** (Plopper 1935 p.45):

- o The Celestial Dragon, ***Tien Lung***, which guards the mansions of the gods and support them so that they would not fall.

- o The Spiritual Dragon, ***Shen Lung***, which causes the wind to blow and produces rain for the benefit of mankind.

- o The ***"Lung"*** of the earth, ***Ti Lung***, which marks out the courses of rivers and streams.

- o The ***"Lung"*** of the hidden treasures ***Fu Tsang Lung*** which watches over the wealth concealed from the eyes of mortals.

A rather fabulous ***"Lung"*** is the God of Mount Zhong called ***Zhu Lung***, "Illuminating Dragon" (Walls and Walls 1984 p.12). It is supposed to be 300 ***li*** long and has a red, snake-like body. Day would dome when its eyes are open and night when closed. His breath is the wind and it would be cold in winter and hot in summer. It takes no food and needs no rest.

There also appears to be other main fabulous species of ***"Lungs"***:

- o ***"Lung"*** proper, which is the most powerful and inhabits the sky.

- o ***Li***, which is hornless and lives in the ocean.

- o ***Chiao***, which is scaly and resides in marshes and dens in the mountains.

The ***Chiao***, which inhabits the marshes and dens, differs but little from the ***"Lung"*** of the sky. It is described as having "a small head and neck, without horns, a breast of a crimson colour, back striped green and sides yellow, has four legs; but is otherwise like a snake and is about thirteen feet long" (Williams 1931 p.110).

- o A primitive form, akin to the ***"Lung"***, is known as ***K'uei***. It is a beneficent creature, said to exert a restraining influence against the sin of greed, and it generally occurs in conventional form on ancient Chinese bronzes (Williams 1931 pp.110-111).

The Winged ***"Lung"*** is the highest form of ***"Lung"***

THE NINE OFFSHOOTS

According to legend, a certain ***"Lung"*** gave rise to nine distinct offshoots, which are distinguished by special characteristics (Hsu and Ward 1984 p.465). These creatures, according to the ***Ch'ien Chu'eh Lei Shu*** by Chen Jen-hsi, are as follows (Williams 1931 pp.111-112):

1. ***P'u lao***, carved on the tops of bells and gongs, in token of its habit of crying out loudly when attacked by its arch-enemy the whale.

2. ***Ch'iu niu***, carved on the screws of fiddles, owing to its taste for music.

THE NINE □*LUNG* s□

AS DEPICTED ON THE TSING BANNER

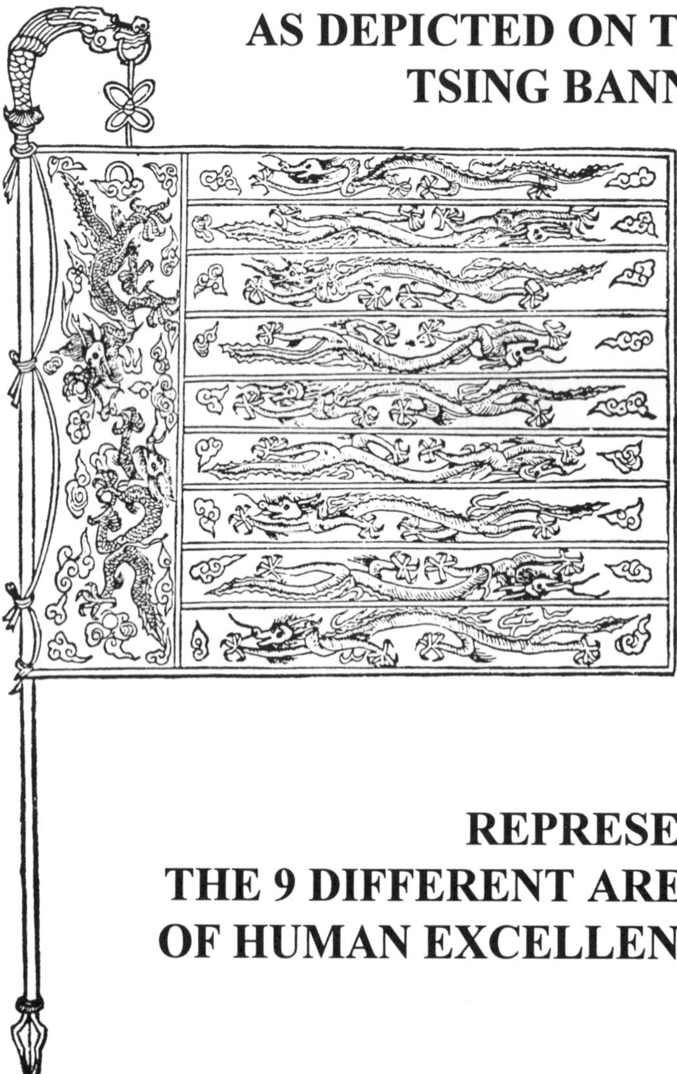

REPRESENT THE 9 DIFFERENT AREAS OF HUMAN EXCELLENCE.

3. ***Pa-hsia***, carved on top of stone tablets, since it is fond of literature; it is also said to represent a male and female tortoise bowed down by grief, and is largely used as a pedestal for tombstones, one head looking each way. It is a river god and is believed to be endowed with supernatural strength.

4. ***Pu-hsia***, carved at the bottom of stone monuments, as it is able to support heavy weights.

5. ***Chao-feng***, carved on the eaves of temples, owing to its liking for danger.

6. ***Chih-wen***, carved on the beams of bridges, because of its fondness for water. It is also placed on the roofs of buildings to keep off fire. It likes to gaze and look out and is sometimes symbolised by the figure of a fish with uplifted tail.

7. ***Suan-ni***, carved on Buddha's throne, on account of its propensity for resting. It has also been identified with the ***Shih tzu*** or symbolic lion.

8. ***Yai tzu***, carved on sword-hilts, and where the blade joins the handle, in memory of its lust for slaughter.

9. ***Pi-kan***, carved on prison gates, as it is addicted to litigation and quarrelling and love to use its energy and strength, being very fierce. It is a scaly beast with one horn.

There must be some link between these "nine offsprings" of the ***"Lung"*** with the "nine animals" whose body parts make up the composite image of the ***"Lung"***, as well as to the **"Nine *Lungs*"** motif. They could be symbolic of the nine divisions of ancient China attributed to Emperor Ta Yu, as described in the ***Shu King*** (Gorn 1902). This ancient event must have been so significant that this symbolic act linked with the number "nine", took a number of forms in Chinese memory.

Other variants of the ***"Lung"*** are given in publications like the ***Sheng An Wai Chi***:

- The ***Chiao-t'u*** carved on door-handles because it likes to close things.

- The ***T'ao-t'ieh***, carved on covers and sides of food-vessels as a warning against its gluttonous nature; and the ***Cha-yu*** which has the head of a ***"Lung"***, tail of a horse and claws of a tiger; this monster is 4 ***chang*** (40 feet) long, and loves to eat men; it appears in the world if the ruling sovereign shows a lack of virtue.

- The ***Lang-pei***, said to be amphibious and supposed to have short hind legs unsuitable for locomotion, so that one animal rides upon another of the species, the latter making use of its long fore legs. This combination is a symbol of two persons joined together for evil purposes (Williams 1931 p.112).

THE DEVELOPMENT OF CREATURES INTO "*LUNGS*"

The Chinese believe that various creatures could develop into ***"Lungs"***. Both, the snake and the fish through patient exertion and much suffering may ascend to this exalted state. The sea-serpent after a period of five hundred years may become a scaly ***"Lung"***; after another one thousand years it may become a hornless ***"Lung"***. After another five hundred years it may become a horned ***"Lung"***. Again, after a period of a thousand years he may become a winged ***"Lung"*** (Plopper 1935 pp.49-50).

The most popular motif of a creature becoming a ***"Lung"***, and a very auspicious one, is that of the **"Golden Carp leaping over the Dragon Gate"**:

> **"The carp leaping the dragon gate"**, i.e. to gain a degree (Proverb 230 quoted by Plopper 1935 p.49).

> The **Dragon Gate** or ***"Lung-meng"*** is said to be a cataract of the yellow River in the district of Ho Ching in Shansi. The fish go up the river and those which leap the barrier become dragons. Their tails are burned off by lightning as they go over it. If they do not succeed, they fall onto the rocks and die or thunder kills them. Only a few escape and they have a mark left on their foreheads. There are also a number of other places called the Dragon Gate (Plopper 1935 p.49).

A number of ***"Lung"*** proverbial sayings encourage people to be diligent, in imitation of the fish striving to become a ***"Lung"***:

> ***Fish becoming Dragon***: Success in literary examination.

Also with similar meanings as the above:

> ***Carp leaping the Dragon's Gate.***

> ***Any man of ability may leap the Dragon Gate.***

> ***Once scale the Dragon Gate, one's reputation is tenfold more.***

> ***The Dragon leaps the celestial gate***: Rise to a very high position.

GOLDEN CARP LEAPS
□*LUNG-MENG*□

TO BECOME A *"LUNG"*
IT IS A SYMBOL OF WISDOM

"*LUNG*", THE LEADER, CAN ARISE ONLY FROM AN INDUSTRIOUS PERSO AS SYMBOLISED BY THE CARP.

KUEI HSING
GOD OF LITERATURE

RIDING THE "DRAGON-FISH", WHICH SEEKS TO LEAP *"LUNG-MENG"*.

SYMBOLISES THAT THE GREATEST RESOURCE FOR SUCCESS & WEALTH IS WISDOM.

Bamboo sprouts shed their sheath; fish tossed by waves become dragons: No perfection without trials.

THE JAPANESE DRAGON

The Japanese version of the ***"Lung"*** absorbs almost all the features and significance of, and is therefore derived from the Chinese. The Japanese ***"Lung"*** is always pictured with three claws, whereas the Chinese see it as having four or five claws.

The Japanese word for ***"Lung"*** is ***"Tatsu"***. One standard work describes the Japanese viewpoint of the ***"Lung"***:

> **Chief among the ideal creatures in Japan is the dragon. The word "dragon" stands for a genus of which there are several species and varieties. To describe them in full, and to recount minutely the ideas held by the Japanese rustics concerning them would be to compile an octavo work on dragonology... In the carvings on tombs, temples, dwellings and shops — on the government documents — printed on the old and the new paper money, and stamped on the new coins — in pictures and books, on musical instruments, in high relief on bronzes, and cut in stone, metal and wood, — the dragon (*tatsu*) everywhere "swings the scaly horror of his folded tail," whisks his long moustaches, or glares with his terrible eyes. The dragon is the only animal in modern Japan that wears hairy ornaments on the upper lips...**
>
> **There are many kinds of dragons, such as the violet, the yellow, the green, the red, the white, the black and the flying dragon. When the white dragon breathes the breath of its lungs goes into the earth and turns to gold. When the violet dragon spits, the spittle becomes a ball of pure crystal, of which gems and caskets are made. One kind of dragon**

> has nine colours on its body, and another can see everything within a hundred *ri*; another has immense treasures of every sort; another delights in killing human beings. The water dragon causes floods through rain; when it is sick the rain has a fishy smell. The fire-dragon is only seven feet long, but its body is of flame. The dragons are all very lustful, and approach beasts of every sort. The fruit of a union of one of these monsters with a cow is the kirin; with a swine, an elephant; and with a mare a steed of the finest breed. The female dragon produces at every parturition nine young. The first young dragon sings and likes all harmonious sounds, hence the tops of Japanese bells are cast in the form of this dragon; the second delights in the sound of musical instruments, hence the koto or horizontal harp, and suzumi, a girl's drum, struck by the fingers, are ornamented with the figure of this dragon; the third is fond of drinking and likes all stimulating liquors, therefore goblets, and drinking-cups are adorned with representatives of this creature; the fourth likes steep and dangerous places, hence gables, towers, and projecting beams of temples and pagodas have carved images of this dragon upon them; the fifth is a great destroyer of living things, fond of killing and bloodshed, therefore swords are decorated with golden figures of this dragon; the sixth loves learning and delights in literature, hence on the covers and titles of books and literary works are pictures of this creature; the seventh is renowned for its power of hearing; the eighth enjoys sitting, hence the easy chairs are carved in its images; the ninth loves to bear weight, therefore the feet of tables and *hibachi* are shaped like this creature's feet (Ingersoll 1928 pp.101-102).

The sea gods are often female water snakes, while the river gods are the four footed dragons like the Chinese ***"Lung"***.

There are four types of "dragon kings":

- o ***Sui Riu*** — the rain dragon which, when in pain, causes the rain to turn red, coloured by its blood.
- o ***Han Riu*** — striped with nine different colours; forty feet long; can never reach heaven.
- o ***Ka Riu*** — scarlet; fiery; only seven feet long.
- o ***Ri Riu*** — has wonderful sight; able to see more than 100 miles away.

Children are told of the dragon with fish scales called ***"maketsugo"***. This is apparently a version of the Chinese **"Golden Carp leaps Lung-meng"** to become a ***"Lung"***. It is impressed on children during the 5th Moon to inspire the children to aim for success in life.

Another peculiar but rare feature of the Japanese traditions about these animals is the bird like features of some of the ***"Lungs"***. These look like half-dragons, half-birds and are called ***"hai riu"***. They appear to be Japanese renderings of the Chinese ***"Ying Lung"***, which is the "Winged Cloud Dragon". These have dragons' heads, plumrose wings and birds' claws.

THE KOREAN DRAGON

Korea came under the influence of the Chinese culture very early and, like Japan, absorb much of the Chinese traditions about ***"Lung"***. The Korean traditions about ***"Lung"*** could be summarised as follows:

The *"riong"* is one of the four supernatural or spiritually endowed creatures. He is an embodiment of all the forces of motion, change and power for offence and defence in animal life, with the mysterious attributes of the serpent. There are many varieties of the genus Dragon... In the spring it ascends

to the skies, and in the autumn buries itself in the watery depths. It is this terrific manifestation of movement and power which the Korean artist loves to depict — always in connection with waters, clouds, or the sacred jewel of which it is the guardian. (Ingersoll 1928 p.88).

Mountains in Korea tend to be personified and associated with dragons. The terrestrial dragon is believed to preside over mines and gems. For this reason the Koreans fear to work in mines, as this could disturb the dragon which may retaliate in anger. Every river and stream was formerly the abode of dragons. So each village would make the appropriate adoration of its power.

Like the Chinese, the Koreans also believe that animals like fish and snakes could turn into dragons. The Koreans also adopted several of the Chinese sayings about the ***"Lung"***, such as the fish transformed into a dragon, the dragon child, dragon horse, etc.

The ***"Lung"*** is usually regarded as divine and righteous in Korea. It appears that the gentle belief in the ***"Lung"*** was corrupted by the Buddhist introduction of naga-cobra worship. The cheerful dragons of the past became fearful horrid snakes, filling the land and seas with fear.

CHAPTER 4

THE CHANGING IMAGES OF THE "*LUNG*"

HISTORICAL RELICS AND RECORDS OF "*LUNG*"

The Chinese gods are known to be introduced into Chinese history through at least three or four stages of canonisation (Ong 1991 pp.204-207), viz.:

- o Gods who existed before the time of Hsien Yang, circa before 2698 B.C.
- o Canonisation by Hsien Yang (Yellow Emperor Huang Ti), circa 2698 B.C.
- o Canonisation by Chiang Tzu-ya, circa 1100 B.C.
- o Ming dynasty, circa A.D. 1400

Before the time of Yellow Emperor Huang Ti, 2698 B.C., the ancient Chinese worshipped only ***Shang Ti***, the One Supreme Imageless Formless God. Associated with ***Shang Ti*** were the four ***Chinkangs***, representing the **Four Cardinal Directions** and also a few stellar deities. The ***Chinkangs*** are ***"Lung"*** spirits. ***"Lung"***, therefore, like ***Shang Ti***, had existed very long in Chinese cultural history, going back virtually to the dawn of Chinese history.

The evolution on the images of the ***"Lung"*** could be traced through several picture records of the ancient Chinese historical periods. These historical images show that the present image of the ***"Lung"*** evolved from something very different.

The Shang Dynasty's record of the ***"Lung"*** is viewed as a **"Double-Horned, Two-Limbed, Fish-tailed, non-serpentine"** being, alike to a half-man, half-fish and not the present serpentine four-legged animal. During the late Shang and Chou dynasties, the ***"Lung"*** was still alike to the image featured of early Shang. It was only around the time of the Han dynasty and after that the ***"Lung"*** began to assume the traditional image of a **"Doubled-Horned, Bearded, Four-Legged, Fish-tailed Serpentine"** creature.

EVOLUTION OF THE WATER ROLES AFTER SHANG PERIOD

The ***"Lung"*** was thus known in China from very ancient times. Inscriptions of the word for ***"Lung"*** appeared on the Shang oracle bones, placing the ***"Lung"*** in the very beginning of Chinese civilisation in China around 1400 B.C. The Shang graph for ***"Lung"*** appeared on the oracle bone as the name of a state (Hsu and Ward 1984 p.459). The ***"Lung"*** was part of ancient Shang ceremonies:

> ***Will there be rain if a "Lung" is constructed in (such and such) a field?*** (Shang oracle bone)

This custom of praying to the Dragon and placing a dragon statute in the rice field still exists in Japan today (Hsu and Ward 1984 p.462).

There are some ancient records of ***"Lung"*** being found in nature. In 513 B.C., Duke Chao of Lu (in his 29th Year of rule) noted a man in the time of Emperor Shun known as Tung-Fu, who was fond of dragons and reared them. Consequently, Emperor Shun conferred on the man the name Tung and his clan the name Huan-Tung. The Duke also noted that Kung-chia of the Hsia Dynasty was given two teams of dragons by God, one team from the Ho River and the other from the Han. But Kung-chia was unable to feed and rear them until Liu Lei learnt the art from the Huan-Tung clan and helped Kung-chia. These stories indicate that some amphibious animal might have been taken as the ***"Lung"***.

□*LUNG*□ DESIGNS ON SHANG OBJECTS

1700-1120 B.

NOTE THE *"LUNG"* HAS DOUBLE HORNS ON THE HEAD AND ONLY TWO LIMBS.

"*LUNG*" DESIGNS ON CHOU OBJECTS

1120-220 B.C.

DURING THE CHOU PERIOD, THE "*LUNG*" WAS ALSO DOUBLE HORNED AND STILL MAINLY HAVING TWO LIMBS.

□*LUNG*□ DESIGNS DURING HAN AND LATER PERIOD.

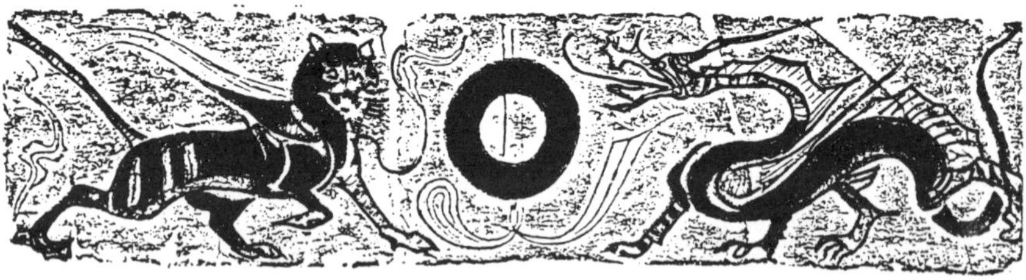

HAN DYNASTY TILES WITH *"LUNG"* AND TIGER

NORTHERN & SOUTHERN

SUI DYNASTY

FIVE DYNASTIES

THE *"LUNG"* ASSUMED SERPENTINE FORM WITH FOUR LIMBS DURING THE HAN DYNASTY (220 B.C. - A.D. 220).

In fact, a Shang bronze wine mixer actually carries a Yangtze alligator together with a ***"Lung"*** design. This may seem to support the theory that some kind of similar reptile was taken as a common representation of the ***"Lung"***; however, this very same bronze mixer may be proof that the alligator and the ***"Lung"*** were two different creatures.

This link to water leads to speculations to connect its real origins with some kind of water animal. As reflected by these ancient descriptions, some have thought the ***"Lung"*** to be allied to the crocodile:

- o The ***"Lung"*** of the earth ***Ti Lung***, which marks out the courses of rivers and streams;

- o The snake-like ***Chiao***, which is scaly and resides in marshes and dens in the mountains.

The crocodile, as one of the animal symbols of the ***Ganzhi's*** 28 constellations, is also called ***Ti Lung*** or Earth Dragon. The crocodile, perhaps, come closest but is still not exactly alike to the physical look of the ***"Lung"***; for the typical ***"Lung"*** is a composite illustration with parts taken from at least nine different natural animals and also the ***"Lung"*** could fly. Despite its superficial similarities to the crocodile or alligator, the ***"Lung"*** is a fabulous mythological creature.

Williams (1931 p.109) notes:

> **It may be noted that the crocodile was worshipped by the ancient Egyptians, and the theory had been advanced that the Chinese *"Lung"* is merely a modified form of the alligator found occasionally to the present day in Yangtze River, for the emergence of the latter from hibernation synchronises with the coming of spring, when the *"Lung"* is believed to be exerting its beneficent influence; it is, however, difficult to trace an analogy between this fabulous**

□*LUNG*□ AND THE ALLIGATOR

TOP: YANGTZE ALLIGATOR
BOTTOM: YANGTZE ALLIGATOR AND *"LUNG"* DESIGNS ON SHANG BRONZE WINE MIXER.

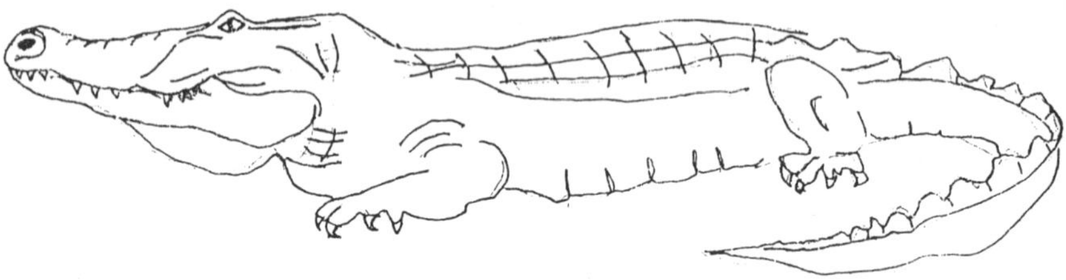

CONTRARY TO BELIEF, THE ABOVE SHANG DESIGN SHOWS THAT *THE ALLIGATOR AND THE "LUNG" ARE TWO DIFFERENT THINGS!*

> **animal and any other natural species, for the body of this *"Lung"* seems to be distinctly serpentine, its head is made up of parts of various other animals, the teeth are those of a mammalian carnivore, while the legs and claws are those of a bird.**

The ***"Lung"*** is capable of flying. Hence, this amphibious creature may be one which could fly; though modern science knows no such natural creature. Hsu and Ward (1984) postulate that the ***"Lung"*** is related not only to the Yangtze alligator but also the tornado and rains whose seasons coincide with the appearance of the river alligator. ***"Lung"*** is thus regarded as a merging of the alligator with the features of the accompanying rains and tornado; thereby the flying part.

It has also been postulated that ***"Lung"***, whose beneficial influences centre around water, is a symbol of the Hwang Ho River. This river is the cradle of Chinese civilisation and its waters are so important to the crops that feed the millions of people. Hence, the sinuous river is revered in the form of the ***"Lung"***. This theory, however, merely reflects the characteristic of only one of the four types of ***"Lung"***:

- o The ***"Lung"*** of the earth ***Ti Lung***, which marks out the courses of rivers and streams;

But, the historical evidence is that ***"Lung"*** assumed its water roles only in late Shang period and after. For Hsu and Ward (1984 p.462) note:

> ***..the Shang seldom prayed to the Lung for rain...***

Thus, originally the ***"Lung"*** has none of the auspicious water roles, for which the present ***"Lung"*** is associated with. The water roles came in the later part of the Shang dynasty and after. Theories on the origins of the ***"Lung"*** from water and water-related objects (like the Hwang Ho river, crocodile etc.) are questionable.

The different interpretations mentioned above may be because the ***"Lung"*** have several layers of significance, of which the well known water-regulating roles are not original roles and compose merely one, albeit prominent, facet. The ancient origins of the ***"Lung"*** must be related to more fundamental event(s) which not only account for the later emergence of water roles but also for the other significances of the ***"Lung"***, particularly the association with "divine power", the "Emperor" and the role of being the "guardian of sacred things"

THE FIRST *"LUNG"*: HALF-MAN, HALF-FISH

The earliest original Shang image of the ***"Lung"*** is that of a half-man, half-fish. This image is also seen in the early motifs of the World First Emperor, Fu Hsi, who is also known as the **Azure *"Lung"***.

Emperor Fu Hsi, and his wife Nu Hwa, are often depicted in a half-man, half-fish form. The tails of the two images are distinctly those of the fish. The image of Fu Hsi also has two horns.

The ***"Lung"***, as we shall see later, is also the symbol of the emperor. Hence, the close similarities between the early Shang image of ***"Lung"*** and the half-man, half-fish Fu Hsi are striking.

This mighty character is not unknown to the West. For, it is the very striking image of the sea god King Neptune! The ***"Lung"*** very likely belonged to that group of creatures legends refer to as call the mermen and mermaids.

The Fu Hsi images indicate that the ***"Lung"*** was originally a biped creature, being man himself! Later, other significances evolved,

FU HSI, the FIRST □*LUNG*□

WORLD FIRST EMPEROR, FU HSI, ALSO CALLED THE "AZURE *LUNG*", IS THE FIRST *"LUNG"*. NOTE HIS TWO HORNS, FISH-TAIL AND TWO LIMBS.

SHANG *"LUNG"*   FU HSI   NEPTUNE-JUPITER

THE HALF-MAN, HALF-FISH, TWO HORNED FIGURE IS ALSO THAT OF THE HALF-MAN, HALF-FISH, SEA GOD NEPTUNE!

making the ***"Lung"*** in the image of what it is today.

As we shall see, this half-man, half-fish image of the ***"Lung"*** is found in the earliest legends of many cultures. Furthermore, the subsequent evolution in the image of the ***"Lung"*** is also preserved in many ancient cultures.

CHAPTER 5

THE FOUR HERALDIC ANIMALS

THE "*LUNG*" LINK WITH THE PAKUA

The ancient Chinese culture is not only strongly associated with the ***"Lung"***. Another equally important symbol is the mystical Chinese ***Pakua,*** or **Eight Diagrams.** These two symbols, the ***"Lung"*** and the ***Pakua***, are deeply inter-related and this relationship constitute the original fundamental meanings of ***"Lung"***.

The ***Pakua*** is a circular arrangement of eight trigrams according to the four cardinal points and the four corners. Like the ***"Lung"***, the ***Pakua*** has several layers of significance. It is the cardinal points that link the ***"Lung"*** to the ***Pakua.*** These cardinal points of North, West, South and East are associated with the Chinese **Four Heraldic Animals**, the snake, tiger, phoenix and ***"Lung."***

The Chinese consider the ***"Lung"*** to be the "chief of the **Four Spiritual Animals**". The **Four Spiritual Animals** are 1. The ***Ling*** or unicorn 2. The phoenix 3. The tortoise 4. The dragon. "The unicorn, the phoenix, the tortoise, and the dragon are the four spiritually endowed creatures" (Plopper 1935 pp.47, 113). The **Four Supernatural Animals** and the **Four Spiritual Animals** are not essentially different. This is because the snake is often replaced by the tortoise (Black Warrior). The hairy animal representing the West could be the tiger, the bear or the unicorn (Hsu and Ward 1984 p.467).

The position of the ***"Lung"*** among the **Four Heraldic Animals** of the **Four Cardinal Directions** of the ***Pakua*** system is an important clue to its real original significance.

THE "*LUNG*" AS ONE OF THE FOUR HERALDIC ANIMALS

Chinese Taoism regard the **Four Heraldic Animals** as the **Four Heavenly Kings** (or **Buddhist Chinkangs**) (Williams 1931):

- o Guardian of the East. Mo Li-Ching. Land Bearer. White faced. He has a ferocious appearance and copper coloured beard, he carries a jade ring, a spear, and a magic sword.

- o Guardian of the West. Mo Li-Hai. Far-Gazer. Blue-faced. He carries a four-stringed guitar.

- o Guardian of the South. Mo Li-Hung. Lord of Growth. Red faced. He holds an umbrella.

- o Guardian of the North. Mo Li-Shou. Well-famed. Black faced. He has two whips, a bag, and a snake.

These four beings are associated in the worship of the **Nine Emperor Gods**; the East, West, South, North and Centre are guarded by the Green, White, Red, Black and Yellow Dragons or Generals (Cheu 1988). Thus, the four guardians of the **Four Cardinal Directions** are also ***"Lungs"***.

The association of these four animals with the four directions is also seen in Chinese astrology:

> **STARS: ..Seven of those stellar 'mansions' were allocated to each of the four quadrants of the vault of heaven. The quadrants are associated with four animals... The Azure Dragon presides over the eastern quarter, the Vermilion Bird, i.e. the Chinese phoenix over the southern, the White Tiger over the western and the Black Warrior, i.e. the**

4 HERALDIC ANIMALS

FENG SHUI ARRAY

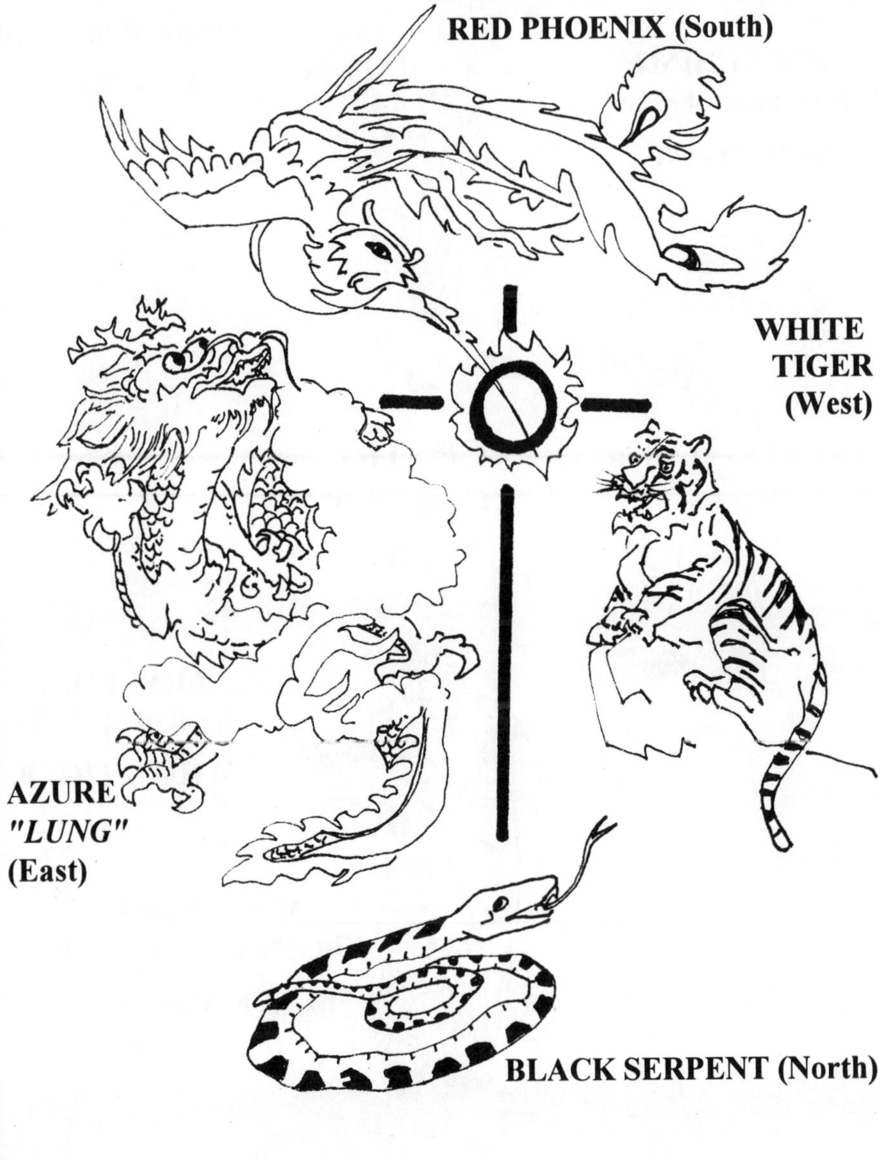

4 BUDDHIST *CHINKANGS*

ALSO TAOIST HEAVENLY KINGS

MO-LI-HUNG
Guardian of the South
RED PHOENIX

MO-LI-CHING
Guardian of theEast
AZURE *"LUNG"*

CENTRE
GOLDEN
"LUNG"

MO-LI-HAI
Guardian of the Wes
WHITE TIGER

MO-LI-SHOU
Guardian of the North
BLACK SERPENT

4 HERALDIC ANIMALS

TONG-SHU, THE CHINESE ALMANAC.

TOP, SOUTH: PHOENIX

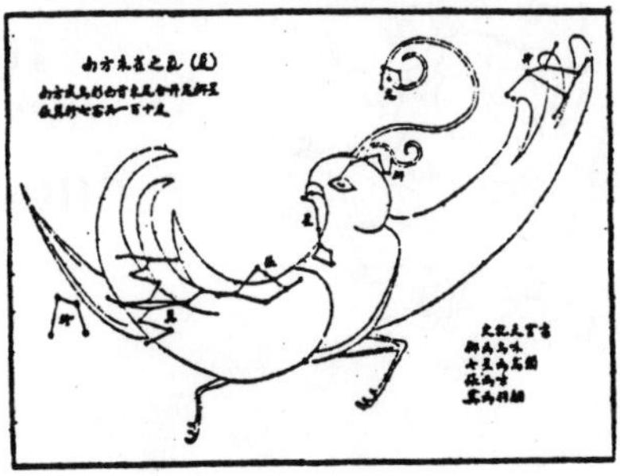

南官

LEFT, EAST: *"LUNG"*

RIGHT, WEST: TIGER

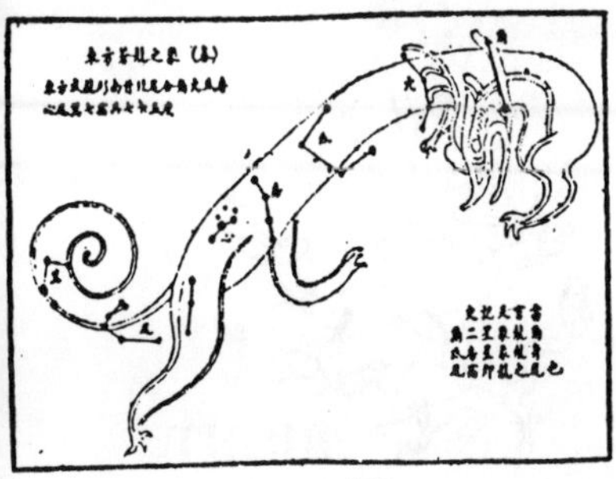

東官

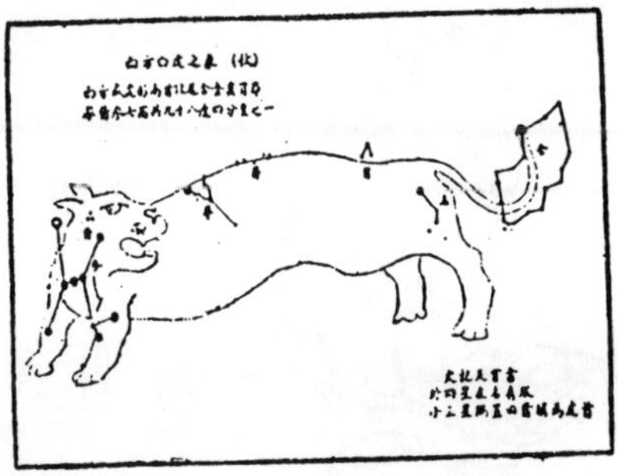

西官

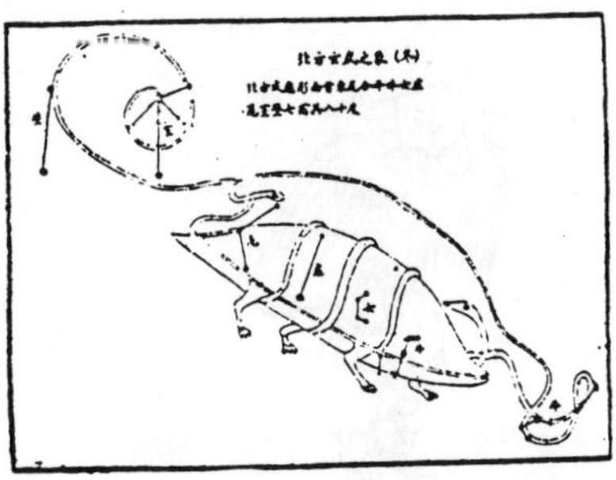

北官

BOTTOM, NORTH: SERPENT

4 HERALDIC BEINGS

from SHAN HAI KING

TOP, SOUTH:

CHU-JUNG

LEFT, EAST:

KOU-MANG

RIGHT, WEST:

JU-SHOU

BOTTOM, NORTH:

YU-CHIANG

> **tortoise over the northern... The morning sun is in the east, which hence corresponds to Spring; at noon it is in the south which suggests Summer. By similar parallelism the west corresponds to Autumn and the north to Winter..... The Great Bear occupies a prominent position in the Taoist heavens as the aerial throne of their supreme deity, Shang Ti, around whom all the other star-gods circulate in homage. The Northern Dipper, a group of stars in Ursa Major ..together with the Southern Dipper in the southern heavens. They are also styled Shou Hsing and Lu Hsing.... and represent the Gods of Longevity and Wealth.... The "Mother of the Measure" or the Queen of Heaven the Buddhist Goddess Maritchi...who dwells among the stars that form the Dipper in the Constellation of the Great Bear is also worshipped...** (Williams 1931 pp.336-340).

When the **Five Emperors**, Fu Hsi, Shen Nung, Huang Ti, Shao Hao and Chuan Hsu were canonised as the **Five Emperor Gods** they were associated with the **Four Heraldic Animals**:

> **In The Five Elements according to the Former Heaven Sequence, the five elements of wood, fire, earth, metal, water correspond respectively to east, south, centre, west and north. They are also connected respectively to the five animals azure dragon, red phoenix, yellow dragon, white tiger and black snake-tortoise and the five emperors Fu Hsi, Shen Nung, Huang Ti, Shao Hao and Chuan Hsu** (Skinner 1982, Table 5 pp. 58-59).

As we recall that in the worship of the **Nine Emperor Gods**, the East, West, South, North and Centre are guarded by the Green, White, Red, Black and Yellow Dragons or Generals (Cheu 1988). That is, the spiritual animals the phoenix, tiger and snake-tortoise are also represented by ***"Lungs"***.

The ***Shan Hai Ching*** (early 1st millennium B.C.) provides another version of the **"Four Heraldic Animals"**, where the Red Phoenix, **Azure *"Lung"***, Black Serpent and White Tiger correspond to human beings named Chu Jung, Kou Mang, Yu Chiang and Ju Shou.

THE DRAGON-PEARL MOTIF

The round red object which seems to be the constant appurtenance of the ***"Lung"*** is variously described as the sun, the moon, the symbol of thunder rolling, the egg emblem of the dual influences of nature, the peak of potentiality (the loss of which betokens deficient power), or the "night-shining pearl" which some define as a carbuncle. The Chinese Imperial coat of arms from the Han to the Ch'ing dynasty consisted of a pair of dragons fighting for a pearl (Williams 1931 p.112).

Two lions playing with an embroidered ball is a common design, which may have the same significance as two dragons fighting for the pearl of supremacy (Williams 1931 p.218).

The significance of this "pearl" is discussed in a later chapter.

THE *"LUNG"* IS ONE OF THE BIBLICAL FOUR ANGELIC BEASTS

The arrangement of **Four Heraldic Animals**, with the ***"Lung"*** in the East, is a significant concept in other ancient cultures. The Bible mentions these four angelic beasts around the throne of God:

> ***And before the throne..were four beasts full of eyes before and behind. And the first beast was like a lion and the second beast like a calf, and the third beast had a face as a man and the fourth beast was like a flying eagle. And the four beasts had each of them six wings about him and they were full of eyes within and they rest not day and night***

4 KABALIC BEINGS

THE TENTH KEY OF TAROT.

FOUND IN HEBREW AND ASSYRIAN-BABYLONIAN PHILOSOPHY.

NOTE THE SIMILARITIES TO CHINESE HERALDIC ARRAYS: SPHINX = PHOENIX, HORNED, FISH-TAILED MAN = "LUNG", DOUBLE SNAKES = SERPENT, DOG = TIGER.

4 HERALDIC BEINGS

THE KEY OF WILLIAM POSTEL

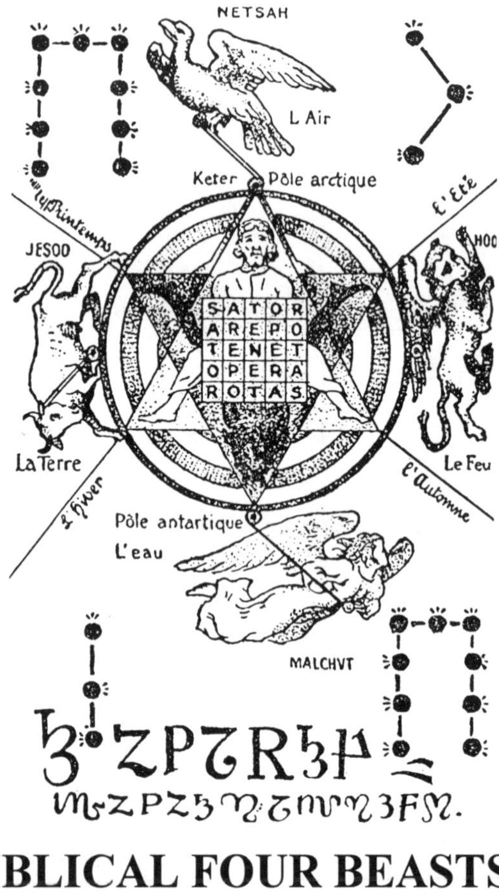

THE BIBLICAL FOUR BEASTS, FOUND IN HEBREW PHILOSOPHY.

NOTE THE SIMILARITIES TO CHINESE HERALDIC ARRAYS: EAGLE = PHOENIX, BULL = "LUNG", CHERUBIM = SERPENT, LION = TIGER.

saying Holy, holy, holy, Lord God Almighty which was, and is, and is to come (Revelation 4:6-8).

Now the cherubim stood on the right side of the house when the man went in and the cloud filled the inner court...And when I looked behold the four wheels by the cherubim, one wheel by one cherub and another wheel by another cherub: and the appearance of the wheels was as the colour of a beryl stone...And every one had four faces: the first face was the face of a cherub, and the second face was the face of a man, and the third the face of a lion and the fourth the face of an eagle...And the cherubim...stood at the door of the east gate of the Lord's house... (Ezekiel 10:3,9, 14, 19 - verse 9 indicates there were four cherubim).

The figures in adjoining pages illustrate these Ezekiel's **Four Heraldic Animals** in Biblical and Jewish Kabalic symbolism, and also another Kabalic arrangement of the Four Heraldic Animals which is also found in the ancient Babylonian-Assyrian culture. These winged angelic creatures include the lion, the calf and the eagle.

A host of angelic creatures compose those marvellous creatures known as "cherubs or cherubim". These cherubim have many forms. Peloubet (1947) wrote:

> **Cherub, Cherubim. The symbolical figure so called was a composite creature-form which finds a parallel in the religious insignia of Assyria, Egypt and Persia, e.g. the sphinx, the winged bulls and lions of Nineveh, etc. A cherub guarded paradise. Gen 3:24. Figures of cherubim were placed on the mercy seat of the ark. Ex. 25:18. A pair of colossal size overshadowed it in Solomon's temple with the canopy of their contiguously extended wings. 1 Kings 6:27...It is remarkable that with such precise directions as**

to their position, attitude and material, nothing, save they were winged, is said concerning their shape. On the whole it seems likely that the word "cherub" meant not only the composite creature-form, of which the man, lion, ox and eagle were the elements, but, further, some peculiar and mystical form. Ezekiel 1:6....

The Biblical, Middle East and Kabalic philosophy thus describe angels as looking like animals. A fundamental basis of Chinese animal symbolism is that the animals are actually images of angels and the ***"Lung"*** is such an angelic animal.

The ***Shan Hai Ching*** (from early 1st millennium B.C.) associates the Double ***"Lungs"*** with carrying agents bringing messages back and forth between heaven and earth. Oracle bones inscriptions show that ***Shang Ti*** the Supreme God was believed to have been served by many officials including the "messenger phoenix". (Chang 1983 pp. 65, 68). The ***"Lung"*** and the Phoenix are therefore regarded as the messengers of God. So, they are really the same as the "angels" in the Bible — for the word "angel" means "messenger of God".

THE FOUR DIRECTIONS AND THE KABALIC ANGELIC BEASTS

In its Tenth Key of the Tarot, the Kabala associates four animals with the cardinal points (Levi 1825-1875):

- Top, South — Woman headed Sphinx — The front of a woman with a lion's forebody and claws; eagle's wings and the backbody and tail of an ox.

  (Chinese parallel — phoenix)

o	Left, East	Kerub — A Sphinx of a bull-horned, bearded man. The front of a bull-horned, bearded man with the backbody and tail of a fish. (Chinese parallel — ***"Lung"***)
o	Bottom, North	Typhon — The double serpents. (Chinese parallel — snake)
o	Right, West	Dog-headed Sphinx — The head of a dog with a man's body. (Chinese parallel — tiger)

These Kabalic arrangements of the four animals are very similar to the Chinese ***Pakua*** arrangement of the **Four Supernatural Animals**. They could not have come about independently.

WHY IS THE *"LUNG"* SO COMMON IN MANY CULTURES?

All these cultures see the ***"Lung"*** as a symbol of divine power and as Heaven's guardian of sacred things. Only in some cultures, does the ***"Lung"*** assume a role in water regulation. This indicates that the original primary significance of the ***"Lung"*** is in being the power-guardian of sacred things. The fact that the ***"Lung"*** is the heraldic animal in the East in a number of different cultures means that the legend of the ***"Lung"*** is far wider than just its significance in ancient Chinese culture.

It is very difficult to see how the different cultures could independently conjure up such an overall similar image of the ***"Lung"***. It means that at some time in the dim past, these different people were of the same culture with some common concepts about ***"Lung"***:

> **The dragon does not appear to arise independently in various civilisations but have a common origin probably in the ancient Sumerian civilisation which may have derived its ideas from or, passed them to Egypt** (Whittick 1960 pp. 176-178).

These similarities are very strong evidence that there must be common origins to the development of the arrangement of the **Four Heraldic Animals** among the different cultures. As the Chinese civilisation is newer as compared to the older Middle East civilisations, the **Four Heraldic Animals** symbol must have migrated from the Middle East into China. There is a Middle East origin to the legend of the ***"Lung"***

The legend must have been triggered by some important event(s) involving all these cultures. Something spectacular happened in the distant past which left lasting impressions in the memory of Man in many cultures about ***"Lung"***. As we shall see, this legend is at least connected to the Dragon Boat Festival.

CHAPTER 6

"DOUBLE *LUNGS*" AND DOOR GODS

Symbol of the New Year

INTRODUCTION

Chinese folklores have many stories connected with the ***"Lung"***. Popular stories include the Monkey God defeating the Dragon King and seizing the Magic Staff of Yu from the Dragon Palace. There is the famous story about the fire-wheel boy-god, Na Cha or Lo Cha, slaying the son of the Dragon King.

There are many stories linking the ***"Lung"*** with the Emperor. One is about Kao Tsu, founder of the Han dynasty. Madam Llu was restlng on the bank of a large pool when she dreamt of a god who came to her. The sky suddenly grew dark and thunder pealed away while lightning struck across the sky. Kao Tsu's father went to look for his wife and saw a scaly ***"Lung"*** hovering over her. After this incident she became pregnant and Kao Tsu was born. When Kao Tsu grew up he became successful in the Imperial examinations. He became an official and was the head of the village of Ssu River. He treated all others wlth dlsdaln and famllIarlty. He drank wine and was fond of women. He often went to Madam Wang or old lady Wu to drink on credit. When he was drunk and asleep the old lady Wu would always witness a wondrous sight — that of a dragon hovering over the place. The ladies found that whenever Kao Tsu was in their shops their business would prosper.

TANG EMPEROR TAIZONG AND THE DRAGON KING

A most famous and significant tale about the ***"Lung"*** and the

Emperor is that of Emperor Tai Tsiung (Taizong) who helped his father to set up the Tang Dynasty (A.D. 618-906). A number of Chinese customs are reflected in this story, including that of the **Two Door Gods** and the **Double Dragons.**

The story of the Tang Emperor Taizong and the Dragon King is a well known story elaborated in the story of the Monkey God escorting the Buddhist priest Sanzang in **"Journey to the West"** (Wu Cheng'En, Ming dynasty).

During the Tang dynasty, the Dragon God of rain was annoyed because the fishermen knew where to trap the fishes which were his subjects owing to predictions by a fortune-teller. So he wanted to show that the fortune teller was wrong about being able to predict things so that the fishermen would no longer believe in him. The Dragon King thought he could confound the fortune teller by making him predict about the time, location and amount of rains and spread the news among the people. He then set out to scatter rains not according to the prediction, despite the fact that a messenger from Heaven announced the Supreme God's instructions about sending rains just as the fortune teller foretold.

The Dragon King's disobedience of the instructions of the Supreme God was a serious offence and the heavenly prime minister was delegated to behead him at a specific time. The Dragon King ran to the fortune-teller to beg for mercy and to seek his help to avoid being executed. The fortune-teller told him to approach the Emperor as the Dragon was after all, the representation of the Imperial family.

So the Dragon King appeared to the Tang Emperor Taizong in a dream and begged the Emperor to influence the minister Wei Zheng and save him. The Emperor called up the minister and purposely played chess with him hoping to make him forget the time and thus save the dragon. During the game, the minister became sleepy. But the latter suddenly woke up and cried he had to do a beheading. The dragon's head fell from the sky and landed right between them.

THE DOUBLE □*LUNG* s□

ARE FOUND EACH ON ONE SIDE OF DOUBLE DOORS AND ON ROOF TOPS OF TEMPLES.

HEY ACT AS GUARDIANS OF ENTRANCES and are equivalent to the TWIN DOOR GODS.

The dragon's ghost appeared before the Emperor and threatened him for breach of promise and insisted on bringing up the case in the nether-world. The Emperor fell sick as the haunting occurred every night. Eventually, two generals, Yu Chih Kung and Ch'in Ch'iung, agreed to take turns to guard the Emperor's front doors. The demon did not come and the Emperor slept peacefully. After a few nights, the Emperor, in consideration for the two generals, had pictures of them pasted onto the doors to frighten off the demon.

However the Emperor's condition deteriorated. The minister Wei Zheng then devised a scheme for the Emperor's soul to be in Hell and there obtain the help of one of his friends, Judge Cui to help save him. Judge Cui resolved the case in favour of the Emperor as it was written in the books of Fate that the Dragon King was destined then to die at the hands of a personal minister.

The Emperor begged forgiveness and made a new promise for the Dragon King. The Emperor instructed that honour was to be given to the dragon by having the officers and the people carry the dragon above their heads. The dragon's image was placed on every palace roof and this was the origin of the images of ***"Lung"*** on the roofs of temples (Dennys 1968 p.92).

According to Jenner (1986) who translated the story, Wu Cheng'En wrote the many stories around a real event that happened. That event was the mission Tang Emperor Taizong appointed to the Buddhist priest Sanzang to fetch Buddhist scriptures from India. Jenner (1986) notes that the many tales Wu wove around the journey of the priest Sanzang are actually earlier legends before the Tang Dynasty. The figures of the Monkey God etc. were legends which existed before the Tang Dynasty.

THE TWO DOOR GODS AND THE DOUBLE DRAGONS

In parallel to the significance of what happened to Emperor Taizong, these two mighty generals protect the doors of every farmer's house, pictured wearing heavy armour with weapons like bows and arrows and halberds and axes (Eberhard 1972 p.21). This is the origin of the custom of placing the **Two Door Gods**.

According to Eberhard (1972 pp.20-21) the two generals, Yu Chih Kung and Ch'in Ch'iung, have a long history of more than two millennium behind them. The two generals were descendants whose ancestors were of the company of demon-exorcists and were supposed to originally live under a magic peach tree on a fairy mountain on an island in the ocean.

Often, instead of the **Two Door Gods**, the two sides of the doors were decorated with slips of red paper or cloth, on which may be written auspicious inscriptions like (Eberhard 1972 p.21):

> ***May wealth and glory become complete.***
>
> ***Wealth, high rank and good salary.***

Some families place philosophical writings on them. Other forms of luck-promising inscriptions may be written, depending on one's ingenuity.

These **Two Door Gods** are at times replaced by **Two Dragons** ornamented onto the doors. This is the real significance of the **Double Dragons** or the **"Double *Lungs*"** reflecting the "guardian nature" of these powerful angelic creatures. This "guardian nature" of the **"Double *Lungs*"** is in line with the significance of this creature in other cultures where the dragon "guards" the sacred treasures of Heaven. In Chinese culture, different types of ***"Lungs"*** also guard different things and places.

The ***"Lung"*** is thus a powerful guardian. The placing of the **"Double *Lungs*"**, usually by the main doors, is an invocation of the help of these angelic creatures to guard the place. The **"Double *ungs*"** are sometimes placed on either side of the altar to signify

THE TWIN DOOR GODS

THE TWIN DOOR GODS, SHEN T'U (DIVINE BITTER HERB), AND YU LEI (LUXURIANT GROWTH)

ARE ALSO FOUND EACH ON ONE SIDE OF DOUBLE DOORS OF TEMPLES AND THEY ACT AS GUARDIANS OF ENTRANCES.

that the way to the deity is guarded by the two ***"Lungs"***

During Taoist magical rites, including those of the **Nine Emperor Gods**, the **Four Dragon-Generals of the Four Directions** would be summoned to assist the invoker. The "guardian" powers of these beings are actually being sought by the invoking priest to help solve difficult problems believed to be caused by powerful malevolent spirits.

THE CONNECTION OF THE DOOR GODS TO NEW YEAR CELEBRATIONS

Eberhard (1972 pp.18-21) notes that the **Two Door Gods** would be put up during the sealing of the house on New Year Eve to double ensure that no evil would enter the premises for the coming whole year. Instead of the **Two Door Gods**, slips or pieces of red paper or cloth could be put up, which is the more acceptable modern practice. The placing of these red cloths and the firing of fire-crackers during the New Year are to scare off the ***"Nien"*** Beast. The homes of those who do not perform these precautions would be entered by the ***"Nien"*** Beast and misfortune would befall the household.

The malevolent influence of the ***"Nien"*** Beast (which is often illustrated as a Dragon-Horse like creature) is quite alike to the malevolent Dragon-demon who disturbed Emperor Taizong. The ***"Nien"*** Beast or "Year Beast" is related to the "Year Star" Jupiter. Jupiter, the "Year Star" (Hsu and Ward 1984 pp. 434-435), is the most important planet and its movement is used to determine times of sacrifices. The Shang named Jupiter after the symbol of an execution axe. The planet Jupiter appeared linked to punishments of the Shang dynasty; it is also the planet thought to be controlled by the highest god, and to show the Mandate of Heaven.

This connection of the guardian **"Double *Lungs*"** with the ***"Nien"*** Beast and the planet "Jupiter" has more implications than realised.

We shall see later how this really reflects the true ancient original significance of ***"Lung"*** as the symbol of "divine guardian power".

We do have a puzzling case where the ***"Lung"*** appears to be capable of being malevolent as well as being a beneficial guardian against entry of evil. However, there are a number of ways to resolve the apparent contradiction. For example, the moral is that the ***"Lung"*** protects those who know how to follow the ancient rituals. These people are usually the good who are ever willing to obey the rules of Heaven. Those who do not perform the rites are deemed as wanting in behaviour and deserve punishments. The ***"Lung"*** is thus not only the harbinger of Heaven's blessings on the good but also of punishment on the wicked.

Confucius stated that those who follow and thus honour the ancient rites would be blessed. These ancient rites are intimately linked to ancestral memorials, the essence of family honour, dignity and filial piety and Heaven rewards those who remember. There is something worthy in the performance of ancestral rites during the New Year period.

"DOUBLE *LUNGS*" AS CARRIERS OF HEAVEN'S MESSAGES

The **"Double *Lungs*"** is a very old motif as the phrase **"a pair of *Lungs*"** appears repeatedly in the ***Shan Hai Ching.*** The term is invariably associated with agents bringing messages back and forth between heaven and earth. ***Shan Hai Ching*** was composed in the earlier part of the 1st millennium B.C. (Chang 1983 pp.48, 65).

The ***Shan Hai Ching***, in its chapter ***"Ta-huang hsi ching"***, tells of K'ai (or Ch'i), the second Emperor of the Hsia Dynasty:

> **"Beyond the sea in the southwest, south of the Red River and west of the shifting sands, a man wears two green snakes on his ears and rides on two *Lung*-dragons, and his**

name is Kai, the Lord of Hsia. K'ai ascended to heaven three times to have an audience [with God] and he descended with the Chiu-pien and Chiu-ko. The same figure is seen also in the 'Hai-wai hsi ching' chapter, where he is again described as riding on two *Lung*-dragons. Clearly K'ai was a hero who brought heavenly music and poetry to the world, and in that role he was a shaman helped by two snakes and two dragons." (Chang 1983 pp.65-66).

Another document referring to the **"Double *Lungs*"** is ***Ch'u Tz'u***, a late Chou work also tied to shamanistic tradition. The ***Shan Hai Ching*** and ***Ch'u Tzu*** are believed to contain earlier traditions from early Chou and Shang times (Chang 1983 p.68).

The ***Chiu-ko*** said of the God of the Yellow River, Ho Po (Chang 1983 p.68):

> **I wander with you by the Nine Mouths of the river**
> **When the storm wind rises and lashes up the waves**
> **I ride a water chariot with a canopy of lotus**
> **Two *"Lung"* draw it, between two water-serpents.**

The ***Shan Hai Ching*** depicts the **"Double *Lungs*"** as assisting the **Four Heraldic Beings**:

East: Kou Meng with the body of a bird and face of a human, riding two ***"Lungs"*** (Hai-wai tung ching).

West: Ju Shou, wearing a snake on his left ear, riding two ***"Lungs"*** (Hai-wai hsi ching).

South: Chu Jung with the body of a beast and face of a human, riding two ***"Lungs"*** (Hai-wai nan ching).

North: Yu Chiang, with the face of a human and body of a bird. He wears two green snakes on his ears and has two green snakes under his feet. Another version reads: with a black body, hands and feet, riding two ***"Lungs"*** (Hai-wai pei ching).

Chu Jung was a minister of Emperor Huang Ti (2698-2598 B.C.) who ordered him to destroy Hui Lu (Werner 1922). Chu Jung was also canonised as the Fire Emperor.

These early motifs indicate that ***"Lung"*** is involved in the transmission of messages between Heaven and Earth. It seems to be the creature carrying the Agents of Heaven in this transmission of messages. This may be another significance of the **"Double *Lungs*"**, whose illustrations as two creatures by the altars, doors and roofs of temples reflect their roles in the transmission of messages between Heaven and Earth.

CHAPTER 7

THE DRAGON BOAT FESTIVAL

THE SUMMER SOLSTICE FESTIVAL

Near the time of the Summer Solstice (around June 21st) when the day is longest is the Dragon Boat Festival, held officially on the 5th Day of the 5th Moon. The Dragon Boat Festival emphasizes the connection of the ***"Lung"*** with the element of Water and its various aspects of rains, clouds and floods.

It is a very popular and much coloured animated festival. Crowds in gay colourful clothes would come to the rivers, lakes and seas. Different guilds and groups would bring their long, narrow colourful boats each capable of holding sixty or more rowers, to race up and down the river in pairs with much clamour, as if searching for someone who has been drowned. A dragon boat could measure over 100 feet in length, 2 1/2 feet in depth, and 5 1/2 feet in width. The bow of the boat is ornamented or carved into a dragon's head, and the stern as a dragon's tail. Red is the dominant colour as it is the colour of fire and of the male. The boat would carry men beating gongs and drums and waving flags to inspire the rowers. The festival may also be connected with the **"Chingay"** procession which follow the boat races. This procession, usually accompanied by brightly decorated "boats", would parade along the streets. There would be huge flags tied to tall poles and the young men would try to show off their acrobatic skills by manoeuvring the flags along the streets of the towns.

Accidents frequently occur during these races and some local authorities have accordingly restricted or banned the practice. It is said that an accident has to happen so that there would be a human sacrifice to appease the spirits. This human sacrifice is the true significance of the festival.

IN MEMORY OF CHU YUAN OF THE WARRING STATES

The festival is now popularly connected with the memory of a statesman named Ch'u Yuan, a native of Ying who drowned himself in the River Mi-lo in 295 B.C. During these Warring States Period some 2,300 years ago Ch'u Yuan was a minister and councillor to the king of Ch'u. He was also a patriotic poet whose motherland was the State of Chu in the southern part of China. He was born around 340 B.C. at a time when Chinese society was in the throes of cataclysm. He frowned upon the corruptness of the aristocrats in the state. After having been falsely accused by one of the petty princes of the state, and as a protest against the corrupt condition of the government, he drowned himself in the river.

The people, who loved the unfortunate courtier for his virtue and fidelity, sent out boats in search of the body, but to no purpose. They threw rice into the river for his soul. But his ghost appeared and said that the fish ate up all the rice. So, the people prepared a peculiar kind of rice called ***"tsung"*** made of glutinous rice and wrapped in silk (which were later replaced by leaves) and set out across the spot of tragedy to offer to the spirit of the loyal statesman. This mode of commemorating the event has been carried down to posterity as an annual holiday. (Williams 1931 p.114). The boatmen continue to honour the memory of Chu Yuan, hence the boat races and the Dragon Boat Festival.

Eberhard (1972 pp.83-85) postulates that Chu Yuan's family might have descended from the Tai tribe of Ch'u as his poems contained several allusions to Tai's sacrificial and ceremonial songs. What is significant is that the Tai tribe of ancient times used to trap strangers, especially bearded ones (and therefore often scholars), to be sacrificed on this day. The stranger would be well treated but he would know his role preserved for that day. It sometimes happen that some girl from the tribe may fall in love with the stranger and the couple might escape.

Chu Yuan's act might have been a voluntary human sacrifice. The

Dragon Boat Festival is strongly connected to the ancient rites of human sacrifices:

- It is said that the equivalent to this festival in some parts of China is stone throwing between two groups of people wading in the waters (Eberhard 1972 p.85). There would be songs and dancing until a person got killed by the stones.

- There are links to this festival, tales of young girls being sacrificed to the "river god" on this day. There was one story of sorcerers dressing up a young girl and sending her down the river on a raft to be married to the river god. She naturally got killed in the rapids and waterfalls. A wise governor then sent the sorcerers down the river in the same manner first to ask if the river god approve of the chosen bride. As the sorcerers did not return, the intended victim was saved and the custom stopped ever since.

- There is also the legend of the rich girl Meng Chiang pining for her dead lover at the Great Wall of China which is also connected to this day (Eberhard 1972). Emperor Shih Huang Ti had conscripted thousands of men to build the Great Wall and innumerable numbers died and their bones were buried into the walls. Han Chi Liang was the only son in a family and tried to escape the conscription. During his hiding, he met the girl and both were married. But the police chief took him away to the Great Wall. The girl managed to locate her husband's bones with her tears which turned the bones red.

  This legend is sometimes connected with the famous **"Keng Hua"** (the desert Christmas cactus) whose lovely blooms opened only during deep nights, poignantly reminding one of the delicate forlorn love. Once, a king was walking in the garden during the mourning for his later father. He heard crying in the garden and saw a beautiful girl weeping. The girl too was crying for her dead father. The king wanted to marry her but both found that they were brother and sister and the match was forbidden. The king insisted on the marriage and locked the girl up in a desert fortress to be readied for the marriage. On the wedding eve, the girl escaped into the desert. When the soldiers found her, she was dead, surrounded by the desert cacti which were blooming in the night.

The Chinese ceremonial fertility bath of iris broth for both men and women is said to be connected to the river sacrifice of this day. Instead of bathing in an orchid bath or drinking wine seasoned with iris, one could hang up the ***artemesia*** (Eberhard 1972 pp.90, 92). The 5th Day of the 5th Moon and the Dragon Boat Festival appears to have a strong connection with an ancient concept of tragedy in love.

"*TSUNG*" THE RICE DUMPLING

The festival is associated with a special type of glutinous rice dumpling called ***"tsung"***. This ***"tsung"*** is a triangular shaped dumpling wrapped during ancient times using silk and in more recent times with the use of leaves.

These dumplings are wrapped in sharp edged reed leaves to form sharp edges and points to scare off the demons. Thus, to perform such a function, the dumplings were originally tied with strings of five colours, viz. red, yellow, blue, black and white (i.e. the five colours of the five cardinal directions).

AN ANCIENT FESTIVAL TO BRING RAINS

The festival has an even earlier origin, and may be inaugurated with the object of propitiating the beneficent dragon, in the hope that he would send down sufficient rain for the crops (Williams

1931 p.114). The reasoning is logical as this is the period when the day is longest and therefore the hottest time of the year.

This 5th Moon Festival or Summer Festival or Dragon Boat Festival is **"one of the three main folk festivals of China, apart from the Spring Festival and the Mid-Autumn Festival...falls on the 5th day of the 5th month and is an age-old festival. According to Wen Yido, a noted contemporary scholar this festival had been observed long before Qu Yuan was born and the many customs observed on that day had something to do with *'Lung'* ..glutinous rice wrapped up in reed leaves on the Dragon Boat Festival was originally done to offer to the dragon as a sacrifice. In many places in the country there was the custom of collecting rain water on that day. It was supposed to be the holy water spread on earth by the heavenly *'Lung'* and it had the reputation of preventing diseases. In some places in ancient times, bronze mirrors with designs of crouched *'Lungs'* on them were cast on a river on the festive day. With these mirrors on hand, it is said, rain would come if one prayed to heaven for it"** (Xing 1988 pp.36-37).

THE CONNECTION WITH DEMON EXORCISM, CHANG TAO LING, *PAKUA* MAGIC AND ARTEMESIA

As Eberhard (1972 pp.78-79) notes, despite the superficial gaiety of the festival, there is **"an element of fear and horror hidden in every ceremony.... Man is on the defensive against dangerous enemies, overwhelming dark powers."** It is curious but significant to note that the 5th Day of the 5th Moon which is most popularly associated with the colourful Dragon Boat Festivities, is also the date for other important Chinese customs associated with the warding off of evil:

- It is the time when the Taoist Pope Chang Tao Ling would ride out on his tiger to quell demons.

THE 〔PAKUA〕

CHANG TAO-LING RIDING THE TIGER ON THE 5TH DAY OF THE 5TH MOON

IT IS HUNG OVER THE MAIN DOOR OF HOUSES TO WARD OFF EVIL.

THE □*PAKUA*□

FIVE POISONOUS ANIMALS CHARM.

T IS SUSPENDED FROM THE ROOF OF HOUSES ON THE 5TH DAY OF THE 5TH MOON.

PAI AI
ARTEMESIA ARGYI

**THE DIVINE BITTER HERB OF SHEN
T'U, ONE OF THE TWIN DOOR GODS,
(THE OTHER BEING YU LEI
LUXURIANT GROWTH)**

IT IS HUNG OVER THE MAIN DOOR OF HOUSES ON THE 5TH DAY OF THE 5TH MOON TO WARD OFF EVIL.

The ***Pakua*** or **Eight Diagrams** is often placed outside the main door to ward off evil. This ***Pakua*** is often illustrated with Chang Tao Ling riding the tiger. Or the illustrations may depict in the place of the ***Pakua***, a huge red cock busy killing the poisonous animals. The red cock is believed to be the essence of male ***yang*** force and hence capable of destroying the evil. The illustrations would in red print on yellow coloured paper.

- o Or, the ***Pakua*** may be illustrated with the **Five Poisonous Animals**, viz. snake, scorpion, toad, centipede and spider, also to ward off evil. This symbol would be placed on the roofs of houses on the 5th Day of the 5th Moon to ward off the evil influences of these **Five Poisonous Animals**. It is a general charm against evil as a whole.

- o Sometimes the five animals are placed in a jar till one is left alive. That survivor would be killed and dissolved in wine or food. It is said that taking this preparation would ward off evil.

  One drinking the preparation would also fall in love with the server. In fact, several love charms could be prepared on the 5th Day of the 5th Moon such as using small stones taken from magpies' nests.

- o During the initial few days of the 5th Moon, the Demon-Queller, Chung Kuei, is sometimes invoked.

- o ***Artemesia***, a plant believed to ward off evil is also placed outside the main doors to ward off evil on this 5th Day of the 5th moon. Several sayings connected to this are:

  If on the 5th of the 5th Month Festival you do not wear artemesia you will die away from home.

On the 5th of the 5th Moon, if you do not stick up artemesia you will hardly eat any new wheat.

On the 5th of the 5th Month stick it in the gourd or fire will come.

If on the 5th of the 5th Month you do not stick up artemesia you will become a clam-shell when you die.

The 5th Day of the 5th Moon, indeed the whole 5th Moon, is a time of danger. One should not climb a roof, beds and mattresses must not be exposed to the sun on this day (Eberhard 1972 pp.96-97).

The ***"Lung"*** would be called upon not only to provide rains for the crops but also to protect the people against diseases. This could be linked to diseases which come in the wake of the lack of water for washing and bathing as well as diseases which come with the hot weather conditions of rainless times.

A UNIVERSAL FESTIVAL KNOWN IN MANY ANCIENT CULTURES

It is very significant to realize that this period of the 5th Day of the 5th Moon, the summer solstice, is also known in several cultures even in the West as the time of the Harvest Festival and is equivalent to the time of the May Pole Dance. The indigenous people of South East Asia, like the Kadazans of East Malaysia, also have harvest festivals around the same period; which in ancient times was connected with head-hunting. Just as the ancient Chinese associated this day with human sacrifices, the ancient western Harvest Festival is also associated with human sacrifices.

This day is evidently steeped into some very ancient memory among the many cultures of a universal event of great evil. The element of human sacrifice is strong. It is an ancient event where the tradition of a tragedy of a great love is also featured. In some ways, the ***"Lung"*** was involved. As Xing (1988) speculates, the many customs observed on that day have something to do with the ***"Lung"***; some ancient event in which it participated. This memory of the ***"Lung"*** must have migrated into China from somewhere. Just, who is this fabulous creature?

THE "*LUNG*" OF THE DRAGON BOAT FESTIVAL AND *PAKUA* THUNDER MAGIC

The Dragon Boat Festival is linked to evil aspects such as human sacrifices, water shortages, evil influences of poisonous animals as well as the opposing remedial aspects of the ***"Lung"*** bringing the water and the use of ***Pakua*** magic to destroy the evil influences.

Pakua magic is especially used to counter black magic. In order to counter evil black magic, the serious Taoist has to know about the art first. The Taoist lores always identify the epitome of black magic as ***Mao Shan*** magic. ***Mao Shan*** magic, using a horizontal array with a moving changeable and highly flexible powerful serpent head (the trigram ***Chen***), is also known as "serpent magic" (Saso 1978 pp.235, 260), a clue to its source as one of the **Four Heraldic Animals**. For ***Mao Shan*** or "serpent magic" is the manifestation of malevolent forces of the Dark Snake of the North, the traditional direction from which evil dark waters and winds come from.

In order to counter the powerful and evil ***Mao Shan*** magic, the genuine Taoist Master, knowing the nature of ***Mao Shan***, would use the highly secretive but supreme **Thunder Magic**. **Thunder Magic** is based on the circular array of the ***Pakua***. In ***Mao Shan***, the eight trigrams are also used, but they are lined into a horizontal array with ***Chen*** **Arousing Thunder** as the deadly evil "serpent head"; this is a reason why the Chinese traditionally associated evil demons with a straight line.

THE THUNDER GOD

NOTE THE WINGS AND CLAWED FEET. THE THUNDER GOD IS ACTUALLY THE PHOENIX, THE ENEMY OF EVIL.

Thus, the origin of this ***Pakua*** magic is linked to "the legend about **Thunder Magic** and the slaying of a great serpent" (Saso 1978 p. 235). The **Thunder Magic** is actually the ***Pakua*** magic, which is primarily an art to combat the "serpent black magic". This is why the ***Pakua*** is invoked at the 5th Day of the 5th Moon against the **5 Poisonous Animals** which include the serpent.

In **Thunder Magic**, the formation is arranged into a powerful circle to form an impregnable barrier against the "serpent head". This circle is, of course, the popular notion of drawing a symbolic magic circle around the person to protect him. This is also the reason why the Taoist Master walks in a circular clockwise pattern when performing his magic rituals. Thus, the Chinese households too hang up the ***Pakua*** over the doors to ward off evil.

Though there seems to be countless spells and rituals in Taoist magic, the central rituals are based on the sequences of the numbers of the ***Lo-shu***. The whole ritual is a summoning of the forces of the **Four Directions**. Crucial to the success of the whole ritual is that, "the power of the thunder is first stored by meditation". (Saso 1978 p.242). The ritual also uses the yellow paper charm on which is written **"Nine phoenix symbol for the destruction of filth"** (Lagerway 1972 p.73). The **Thunder Magic** is related to the power symbolized by the **"Nine-Phoenix"**. In illustrations of the Thunder God the so-called god is a bird-like deity. Thunder God is actually the phoenix! **Thunder Magic** against **Mao Shan** is actually the fiery South-Red Phoenix pitted against the dark North-Black Serpent of the ***Pakua***!

THE *PAKUA* THUNDER MAGIC IS IN MEMORY OF LAO-CHUN THE DEMON-SERPENT SLAYER

Now, these highly regarded Taoist **Thunder Magic** rituals are actually recognized as a repetition of some ancient battles!:

As the modern high priest repeats the struggle of Chang

> **Tao-Ling, so did Chang Tao-Ling imitate that of the Human Sovereign. The Human Sovereign (Lao-Chun) was also called Lao-Kuei (Old Demon), after having won his battle with the demons of the Six Heavens** (Lagerway 1972 p.28).

This ancient battle was conducted against forces represented by the Serpent as the legend records: **"All Thunder Magic sects attribute the founding of the method to Hsu Hsun, a legendary Taoist said to have died in A.D. 374. Hsu was wafted up to heaven in broad daylight but left behind twelve disciples to spread his doctrines. The story of Hsu Hsun seems to be a Sung dynasty fabrication; his name appears in the dynastic histories, but the legend about Thunder Magic and the slaying of a great serpent do not occur in Taoist writings until the mid-Sung about 1100"** (Saso 1978 p.235).

What is this ancient battle? Who is this "Human Sovereign" "Lao-Chun" or "Lao-Kuei"? "Human Sovereign" is actually a term for third world Emperor Huang Ti. He was the third of the triad Emperors, viz. Heaven Emperor Fu Hsi, Earth Emperor Shen Nung and Human Emperor Huang Ti. Emperor Huang Ti is also the **Golden *"Lung"*** and the Dragon Boat Festival is about him!

Therefore, the use of the ***Pakua*** to counter evil influences on the 5th Day of the 5th Moon is actually in memory of Emperor Huang Ti's use of **Thunder Magic** against the Serpent! As Emperor Huang Ti is the **Golden *"Lung"***, the day is linked with the ***"Lung"*** bringing water by destroying the Serpent. As we recall earlier, the ***Pakua*** was used against the **"Five Poisonous Animals"**, one of which was the serpent. This ancient event is linked to the Serpent trying to control the water and denying it to the people. Apparently, the Serpent seeks human sacrifices. The hardship ended only when Emperor Huang Ti the **Golden *"Lung"*** marshalled up forces to destroy the Serpent and thus releasing the water to the people.

THE LEGEND OF CH'IH YU'S BATTLES AGAINST EMPEROR HUANG TI

This is the legend of Emperor Huang Ti's wars against Ch'ih Yu, the leader of the giants. Ch'ih Yu's name contains the sub-characters for **"Mountain Serpent"**. He was bare-chest and wore a two-horned headdress.

Ch'ih Yu was originally the general of Huang Ti and often led the armies of Huang Ti. Then Ch'ih Yu plotted rebellion. He defeated Huang Ti a number of times until Huang Ti was assisted by a young hero, ***Ying Lung***, and the "Dark Lady". Huang Ti had to call in forces from all over the world to defeat and capture Ch'ih Yu, who was then executed.

Other ancient nations also recorded these wars: the Ramayana of the Hindus; the clash of the Titans with the Greek Gods and the Twilight of the Gods as in the Teutonic Europeans. Among the Middle East nations, there were the wars between the Hittite "Storm God" Teshub (also "provider of rains") against Kumarbi and his offspring Ullikummi. This legend tells how Teshub fought to overcome the **"illuyanka" Serpent** in order to secure the much-needed rain for the land (Kramer 1961 pp.158-175). Teshub was at first defeated by the Dragon-Serpent but was later assisted by the Goddess Inara and a mortal man who became Inara's love. Inara is also the Assyrian Isara; a whirlpool serpent goddess and beloved of Tammuz (MacKenzie 1926 pp.73-74). Kramer (1961 p.139) identifies Inara as the daughter of the "Storm God".

Note well the similarities between this Middle East legend and that of Ch'ih Yu's battles against Huang Ti:

- o The Hittite Storm God battled against the Serpent even as Huang Ti battled against Ch'ih Yu, the "Mountain Serpent".

- o Initially, both Teshub and Huang Ti were defeated by the

"Serpent". But they received help from a young man and a lady who also appeared to love the young man.

- o The Hittite Storm God's victory over the Dragon-Serpent to secure water for the land is also the same as that of the Chinese Dragon Boat Festival to secure rains for the land. Thus this event is also remembered by the Chinese as the legend of the Dragon Boat Festival of the 5th Day of the 5th Moon. This date, the Summer Solstice, is traditionally the most evil and dangerous time of the year.

The killing of the Serpent by the Hittite Storm God is the same legend as the use of the ***Pakua*** **Thunder Magic** by the "Human Sovereign" Huang Ti alias "Lao-Chun" against the Six Demons. It is "the legend about **Thunder Magic** and the slaying of a great serpent" (Saso 1978 p.235). The Westerners remember this as the legend of St. George killing the "large worm-dragon".

The ancient Middle East reeled with mighty wars related to the need to secure water or rains. There was a Middle East food crisis which was linked to shortages of water for crops. The ancient nations went to wars against each other to secure their food supplies, including water supplies for food crops. The Serpent was trying to monopolise the water. The **Golden *"Lung"*** Huang Ti, was forced to kill the "Serpent" to release the water for the people and bring peace to the world. This is the actual basis of the powerful Taoist ***Pakua*** **Thunder Magic** and the real significance of the 5th Day of the 5th Moon when the **5-Poisonous Animals** version of the ***Pakua*** is used against evil. Hence, the Dragon Boat Festival.

CHAPTER 8

THE *I CHING'S* VIEW OF THE *"LUNG"*

Continuing the Dragon Boat Festival's Significance of *"Lung"*

INTRODUCTION

The ancient semi-divination classic ***I Ching*** (or Book of Changes) is one of the texts of the ***Pakua***, or **"Eight Diagrams"**. As this text dates back to 1120 B.C. and before, its contents about the ***"Lung"*** is very fundamental and original.

Due to the many hidden meanings, it is difficult to determine what the ***I Ching*** has to say about the ***"Lung"***. The ***"Lung"*** could be signified by the ruler or a great man and even thunder and Heaven. However, it is worthwhile to look at what the ***I Ching*** in its more clearly understood passages and commentaries say. Several symbolisms associated with the ***"Lung"*** are indicated in the ***I Ching*** which may reflect its original significance.

CH'IEN, CREATIVE HEAVEN AS THE *"LUNG"*

The first of the 64 hexagrams of the ***I Ching***, ***"Ch'ien"*** (Creative Heaven), is associated with the 4th Month (about May to June) when light-giving power is at its zenith and must decrease thereafter. The six lines representing the six steps of the hexagram are related to ***"Lung"*** (Wilhelm 1951 pp.3-5, 369). ***"Lung"*** is the symbol of Heaven's power.

The association of the 4th Month with the "power of Heaven" is significant, for the 4th Month would be followed by the 5th Month,

THE □*I CHING*□ SYMBOLS FOR □*LUNG*□

乾

"CH'IEN", CREATIVE HEAVEN. **THE FIRST OF 64 HEXAGRAMS OF THE *I CHING*. IT TELLS OF THE EMERGENCE OF *"LUNG"*.**

雷

"CHEN", AROUSING THUNDER. **ONE OF 8 TRIGRAMS OF THE *PAKUA*. THE SYMBOL FOR SPRING AND *"LUNG"* IN THE EAST.**

which signals the waning power of ***"Ch'ien"*** and the beginning of evil influences. The Dragon Boat Festival of the inauspicious 5th Day of the 5th Moon is thus related to this link between the ***I Ching***'s ***"Ch'ien"*** and the 4th Moon, which indicates the ancient origin of the Dragon Boat Festival. Thus, on the inauspicious 5th Day of the 5th Moon, special rituals have to be carried out to ward off the rising evil influences.

Thus, the ***I Ching*** too, links the ***"Lung"*** with the Dragon Boat Festival.

THE CONDITIONS THAT AFFECT *"LUNG"*

The ***I Ching*** saying in each of the six lines of the hexagram ***"Ch'ien"***, shows that though the power of ***"Lung"*** of Heaven is great, this power could be restricted by various conditions (**"Nine"** denotes a solid line, in contrast to **"Six"** which denotes a broken line):

1. Nine at the beginning means:
   Hidden ***"Lung"***. Do not act.

   The lowest place is far down deep below the earth.

   The **Great Man** who is true to himself is stlll unrecognised. But he bides his time, wisely consults the oracle and does not prematurely expose himself nor act too soon.

   That is, the rising ***"Lung"*** needs to prepare himself and harness the resources before he acts.

2. Nine in the second place means:

"Lung" appearing in the field.
It furthers one to see the great man.

The second line often represents the surface of the earth. It is also the central line of the lower trigram denoting its regulating influence over the lower trigram.

The **Great Man** has declared his intention, he is surfacing. He is with peers but is different in his disposition. Destiny is with him. Those who could recognise him should associate themselves with him.

3. Nine in the third place means:
   All day long the superior man is creatively active.
   At nightfall his mind is still beset with cares.
   Danger. No blame

   Third line is the position of the transition from the lower to the higher trigrams. It thus always denotes unsettled conditions.

   His fame increases and the masses flock to him. There are many things to do. But danger lurks in the transition from lowliness to greatness. Ambition can destroy integrity.

   How well this observation fits so many who rose to greatness in today's world!

4. Nine in the fourth place means:
   Wavering flight over the depths.
   No blame

No longer is the man on square ground. Any further action must be equal to the elements of Heaven.

A cross-road is reached. The great man could either become the hero or withdraw to be the holy hermit sage.

Confucius, recognising the auguries of the times, retired to become a sage.

5. Nine in the fifth place means:

   Flying ***"Lung"*** in the heavens.

   It furthers one to see the **Great Man**.

Like the central line of the lower trigram, this fifth line is the central; and hence influencing line of the upper trigram.

Water flows to what is wet and fire to what is dry. Clouds follow the ***"Lung"*** and wind, the tiger. The **Great Man** now in his venture automatically attract those he needs to him.

6. Nine at the top means:

   Arrogant ***"Lung"*** will have cause to repent.

Whatever reaches the top must now turn back. Do not be extreme.

The **Great Man** is isolated in the heights and failure will follow. Such a great man stands high but have no real following. Advisors abound but their advice are not heeded.

7. When all the lines are nines, it means:
   There appears a flight of ***"Lungs"*** without heads.
   Good fortune.

   This always signifies the harmonious merging of the meanings of the hexagram with its opposite.

   The hexagram changes to ***"K'un"***, the Receptive, which represents devotion. The great power is in devotion and peace will follow.

Correct behaviour, appropriate to the changing circumstances, is paramount in the development of righteous power. With success, this would be said of the person:

> **"In his own time he mounts toward heaven on six Lungs. The clouds pass and the rain falls" All this means peace coming to the world in the ordering of the empire** (Wilhelm 1951 p.379).

One change in the hexagram ***"K'un"*** concerns the ***"Lung"***:

> Six at the top means:
> ***"Lungs"*** fight in the meadow.
> Their blood is black and yellow.

This represents a dark power which has managed to rise to a top powerful position — it is the ***"false Lung"***. The true ***"Lung"***, symbolising Heaven, has to come to fight it. But the powers are strong and hence both forces would be injured in the fight.

This change is said to represent Lucifer's rebellion against God and forms a parallel to the Greek legend of Icarus. It also resembles the battle between darkness and the gods of Valhalla that ended with the twilight of the Gods (Wilhelm 1951 p.15).

These lines of the ***I Ching*** directly call ***"Lung"*** the **"Great Man"** or **"Superior Man"**. These interpretations of the conditions affecting ***"Lung"*** shows that as far as the ***I Ching*** is concerned, ***"Lung"*** is primarily the **Great Man.** This ***"Lung*-Great Man"** is seen as a man of destiny having the "Mandate of Heaven". ***"Lung"*** may be the **Great Man** but he is not infallible. ***"Lung"*** is something very close to Heaven, but is not Heaven itself. ***"Lung"*** may be said to be the representative of Heaven or the One with the "Mandate of Heaven". This **Great Man** is often the next Emperor and founder of a new dynasty.

"*LUNG*" AS THE "AROUSING THUNDER" IN THE EAST

The ancient tradition of associating ***"Lung"*** with the East is reflected in these comments of the ***I Ching***:

> **The Arousing thunder is the *Lung*. It is dark yellow, it is a spreading out, a great road, the eldest son. It is decisive and vehement; it is bamboo that is green and young, it is reed and rush. Among horses it signifies those which can neigh well, those with white hind legs those which gallop, those with a star on the forehead. Among useful plants it is the pod-bearing ones. Finally, it is the strong, that which grows luxuriously** (Wilhelm 1951 p.276).

The passage above portrays the symbolic powers of ***"Lung"*** as the influence of Spring. "Spreading out" denotes blossoming and "Luxuriant growth" being the characteristic feature of Spring. "Neigh" denotes thunder and the "horse gallops" the gait at which the rejuvenating power of the ***"Lung"*** works.

In King Wen's Later Heaven arrangement of the trigrams of the ***Pakua***, the power of the **"Arousing Thunder"** is the ***"Lung"*** (Wilhelm 1951 p.273). This is represented by the East, the symbolic position of Spring. But East was the original location of ***"Li"***, the Fire, in the Fu Hsi Earlier Heaven's arrangement of the trigrams. Previously the position of **"Arousing Thunder"** in the Fu Hsi arrangement is in the North-East, while ***"Li"*** the Fire's position in King Wen's arrangement is now in the South. It may seem difficult to account for the reasons why King Wen changed the arrays from those of the earlier Fu Hsi arrangement. Some possible reasons would be:

- The change in position of ***"Li"*** the Fire is not too difficult to guess. Originally the Chinese were located in a place where the sun (as represented by ***"Li"*** the Fire) usually shines in from the East. But by King Wen's time, the Chinese people had migrated, to a new region further to the north, where the sun's rays now shine in from the south. The change in the positions of ***"Li"*** is thus a memory of the Chinese migration from Mesopotamia to China!

- This power of ***"Lung"*** the **"Arousing Thunder"** located to the North-East in the earlier Heaven array is interesting to note. It is the position where the Taoist Master, in the important ritual of the Star Dance of the 8 Constellations, would lead his summoned forces against the great evil. The Six Taoist Masters would harness this ***"Lung"*** power to destroy evil in this location. It must have been some significant ancient event of a very grand scale.

- It is not clear why the position of ***"Lung"*** the **"Arousing Thunder"** was shifted to the East — unless it was a prophecy that the same punishing power would come from the East? Or, as a later chapter on the **"Tli"** dragon may indicate, the change is part of some ancient attempt to change the significance of ***"Lung"***.

"*LUNG*" AS THE SACRED GUARDIAN OF DIVINE KNOWLEDGE

The ancient Chinese ***I Ching*** commentators also describe:

> **it is straight, it is the *Lung*, the upper garment, the word** (Wilhelm 1951 p.275).

This strange association of the ***"Lung"*** with the "word" may be clarified better by another comment on the ***I Ching***:

> **..*"Lung"* and snakes hibernate in order to preserve life. Thus, the penetration of a germinal thought into the mind promotes the working of the mind. When this working furthers and brings peace to life, it elevates a man's nature. Whatever goes beyond this indeed transcend all knowledge. When a man comprehends the divine and understand the transformations, he lifts his nature to the level of the miraculous** (Wilhelm 1951 p.338).

The essence of knowledge is also symbolised by the ***"Lung"***. There is a moral lesson imbued, as the comments show that the **Great Man** must take time to think and meditate — only then would his knowledge grow and eventually he would surpass that very knowledge to enter into a mysterious divine realm.

So, what does the ***I Ching*** say about ***"Lung"***? ***"Lung"*** is the **Great Man** who is deemed as the one having not only the authority given by Heaven but also one who possess the wisdom or knowledge to carry out the divine task. There is certainly no easy path to greatness!

CHAPTER 9

THE "*LUNG*-PHOENIX" PAIR

Marriage Symbol associated with 8th Moon

INTRODUCTION

There are certain pairs of animals which form auspicious symbols in the Chinese culture:

- Two ***"Lungs"*** with the "dragon pearl" between them, commonly seen on roofs of temples. A pair of ***"Lungs"*** could also be used as decorations, one on each of the two pillars facing or by the sides of the front door. The significance of the **"Double *Lungs*"** has been discussed earlier.

- Two lions depicted with or without playing with an embroidered ball, the latter common on doors of buildings.

- A ***"Lung"*** and a tiger. This symbol is used to represent the two animals guarding the inner door of the temple of the **Nine Emperor Gods**. It also features in Taoist ***Mao Shan*** magic.

- The most significant of all is the pairing of the ***"Lung"*** and the phoenix with the "pearl" between them. It is often seen in wedding cards. The saying is ***"Good fortune of the Lung-Phoenix"***.

What is the significance of this **"*Lung*-Phoenix"** symbol, so popular in wedding ceremonies? The ***"Lung"*** is supposed to be the symbol of the male force while the phoenix that of the female, representing respectively the bridegroom and the bride. So blessings are wished for the happy couple. However, there are other reasons why this symbol is associated with the marriage ceremony!

"PHOENIX-*LUNG*" ALSO IN HEBREW KABALIC PHILOSOPHY

The paired ***"Lung*-Phoenix"** symbol is also found in the Hebrew Kabalic philosophy. The phoenix is known as the **Hermes Bird** in Hebrew Kabalic philosophy where it is also paired with the dragon (Shumaker 1972 p.195). This is illustrated as follows, in a similar parallel to the Chinese pairing of the **"Phoenix-*Lung*"**.

> A double headed dragon is shown, the heads facing away from each other. The mouth of one head opens to a golden sun and the other mouth to a silver moon. This has obvious parallels to the Chinese **Dragon-Pearl** which could be the moon or sun. The dragon's body is that of a fish and the animal seems to be a mer-animal, which again has parallels to the half-man, half-fish form of the Chinese ***"Lung"***, which is primarily a water creature. Above the doubled headed dragon is the Hermes Bird coming down through the clouds. This **Hermes Bird** is regarded as the symbol of the Holy Spirit descending from the Father hidden by the clouds.

This Kabalic pairing of the phoenix and ***"Lung"*** is not associated with marriages but instead imbued with these ten philosophical qualities:

Left: Cunning or Knowledge
Experience
Practice
Prudence
Patience

THE PHOENIX - □*LUNG*□

MARRIAGE SYMBOL

"GOOD FORTUNE IN THE PHOENIX-LUNG ".

THE "HERMES" BIRD

SIMILAR TO THE CHINESE "3 REALMS" ARRAY. THE HERMES BIRD IS AT THE TOP, WITH TWO DRAGON HEADS BELOW AND 8 MEN ON THE LOWEST LEVEL. HERMES IS ALSO THE GOD OF MEDICINE, AND HENCE EQUIVALENT TO THE CHINESE GOD OF LONGEVITY.

□3 REALMS□ SYMBOL FOR PHOENIX-□*LUNG*□

AT THE TOP IS THE PHOENIX MOUNTED BY THE GOD OF LONGEVITY FOLLOWED BELOW BY THE DOUBLE "*LUNG*s" AND BY 8 MEN ON THE LOWEST LEVEL.

Right: Grace
Nature
Reason
Speculative Faculty
Holy Living

The Kabala has a warning attached to the two animals, which is — the Philosopher Stone is best not searched for: "Cover not thing that may not be." It indicates that the status or power symbolised by this ***"Lung*-Phoenix"** pair is a very difficult and dangerous thing to look for. In the Chinese mystic culture, there are also things that are dangerous to look at. The Chinese Taoist warns that highly sacred things are not to be ill-treated; **"Some who borrowed the books did not care for them with proper respect and dignity and soon died. When he attempted to read one of the books, a certain Wang Ch'ing saw fire come down from heaven and destroyed it."** (Saso 1978 pp.48-49).

There is also a more complicated Chinese arrangement of the ***"Lung*-Phoenix"** in the **Three Realms** concept (Huang 1986 p.71). This Chinese version, from the Ching dynasty, is rather alike to the **Hermes Bird** version noted by Saso (1978):

> The **Three Realms** are Heaven, Earth and Man. Right at the top is a single god riding the phoenix representing Heaven. Note the two ***"Lungs"*** below the phoenix — thc two ***"Lungs"*** hang over five persons symbolising the **Five Emperors**, representing Earth. Below these **Five Emperors** are eight persons representing Man — these eight persons also correspond to the eight persons beside the two-headed dragon in the Hebrew Kabalic version. The similarities between the Chinese ***"Lung*-Phoenix"** pair and the Hebrew Hermes Bird-two headed dragon are very striking.

Also, Hermes, besides being the messenger of the gods, is

> also the god of medicine. A close parallel to the Chinese god of Longevity, depicted riding the phoenix!

Both the Chinese and Hebrew cultures have such striking similarities in the ***"Lung*-Phoenix"** pairing! Again, they do not refer to marriages, but have something to do with the philosophical interrelations between Heaven, Earth and Man.

THE STATUS OF THE PHOENIX

To understand the ***"Lung*-Phoenix"** pairing, it is necessary to examine the significance of the "phoenix".

In the ***"Lung*-Phoenix"** pairing, the phoenix is regarded as a higher creature than the ***"Lung"***. In the Hebrew Kabalic philosophy, the phoenix is the symbol of the Holy Spirit, indicating its supreme status as a symbol of God's power. The Chinese is also not ignorant of this "fire power" of the phoenix:

> In Taoist mysticism, the high priest would write onto a yellow slip of paper: **"Nine-Phoenix symbol for the destruction of filth"** (Lagerway 1967 p.73). He would light it allowing it to burn almost to his fingers and then blows it into the air. The symbol is regarded in Taoism as the purifying role of fire — this is paralleled by western symbolism of the phoenix as the bird rising, resurrected, from the flames — the resurrection part being a clue to the significance of the ***"Lung*-Phoenix"** pairing.

The phoenix is the heraldic animal of the south whose Taoist number is nine, hence the term **"Nine-Phoenix"**. This **"Nine-Phoenix"** significance appears to be appropriated by the **"Nine-*Lungs*"** symbol. The number "Nine" is rightfully the number of the phoenix and not the ***"Lung"***. That is, the **"Nine-*Lungs*"** symbol is the Taoist secret knowledge that **"Nine *Lungs*"** combined are still

THE PHOENIX

ENEMY OF THE SERPENT

AUSPICIOUS SYMBOL OF THE SUN AND WARMTH SHINING IN FROM THE SOUTH. IT APPEARS ONLY IN REIGNS OF VIRTUOUS RULERS.

inferior to the phoenix. The ***"Lung"*** is the symbol of the priest-king that is, the Chinese Emperor and hence symbol of nature's high power, while the phoenix is really the symbol of God's supreme power.

The phoenix used to be "seen" during the reigns of legendary emperors and Emperor Huang Ti-Shun's times were the last when it was most frequently seen. Since then the phoenix is no longer available to mankind. Its power could only be symbolised vaguely by **"Nine-*Lungs*"**. The Taoist knew so and preserved this indication of the unavailability of the phoenix in the modern character for ***"Feng Huang"***. The oracle bone character shows a free bird. But the modern character symbolises the bird being hidden under a shell, denoting its existence but that it is no longer free. It is an ancient prophecy that such a power would one day become available again.

THE SCORPIO LINK

An ancient hint about the Phoenix is found in the astrological significance of the southern constellation of **Scorpio.** The Chinese Red Phoenix is the heraldic animal of the south and is associated with the planet **Mars.** The southern constellation in Hebrew astrology is **Scorpio** which is chiefly marked by is brightest star, the huge red star **Antares**, well known in Chinese astronomy as the "Fire Star" (Needham 1959). **Scorpio** is also associated with **Mars**. In its "eagle" form **Scorpio** is thus analogous to the Red Phoenix.

The **Scorpio** in Hebrew astrology has two aspects, one being the generous, refined, reliable and astute being of the good "eagle" **Scorpio**; while the bad "snake" **Scorpio** will be destructive, unreliable, deceitful, irascible, calumniators and prevaricators (Joel 1977 p.71). In western astrology, the **Scorpio** also has its scorpion form or its eagle form (Lutin 1988). Hence, the **Scorpio** is either an eagle or a snake.

Western astrology recognises the southern constellation of **Scorpio** to be either the biting scorpion dying from its own poison in its struggle for survival or as the noble eagle; healer and magician who battle the forces of evil and darkness and triumph (Lutin 1988 p.11). The eagle unafraid, is the embodiment of truth and lives to heal the wounds of his fellow-beings. Fear and evil flees from the noble eagle which wings into heaven in joyous celebration of victory. Scorpio is thus the representation of conflict and has three decans all symbolising conflict (Seiss 1972 p.18):

1. The Serpent (**Serpens**) with which **Ophiuchus** struggled.

2. **Ophiuchus**, struggling with **Serpens** and being stung by the **Scorpion**, also crushing the **Scorpion**.

3. **Hercules** holding the three-headed snake or dog of hell.

The full significance of **Scorpio** cannot be understood unless we realise that the conflicts represented by the three decans of **Scorpio** are actually the tasks of **Ophiuchus** and **Hercules** in preventing the seizure of the **Crown** (in nearby **Libra**) which is located just above the **Serpens**' mouth.

The Christian writers Seiss (1972) and Flemings (1981) picture **Scorpio** as the suffering Christ in His mortal struggles against the forces of evil. The Christians represent Christ as rising from the dead; like the Phoenix-like resurrection from the purifying fire! The Taoist knows it as the **"Nine-Phoenix symbol for the destruction of filth"** (Lagerway 1967 p.73).

The southern Chinese Red Phoenix and **Scorpio** are therefore the symbol of eternal conflict between good and evil, and of the ages-old work of God's supreme power in overcoming evil opposition. There is a secret cost to God as is evident by the suffering this symbol represents. The goal is the eternal Crown; but this Crown is forbidden to the wicked, implying only the good and courageous could ever hope to achieve it. The Devil sought it but failed, being thwarted by God.

THE PHOENIX IS THE SYMBOL OF THE SUPREME MYSTIC FORBIDDEN ART REQUIRED TO REACH THE CROWN. The supreme art requires the supreme power of the Holy Spirit which is represented by the eagle **Scorpio-Phoenix-Hermes Bird**. It contains the secret of the sacrificial attitude required to master this supreme art; it is no journey for the faint-hearted nor the wicked, for only the courageous and pure could make it through.

THE MARRIAGE FEAST OF GOD

This **Scorpio**-related symbol of the final outcome of the battles between good and evil is not unknown to the Christian mystics. The Bible indicates it in this mystic passage of the book of Revelation:

> ***Let us be glad and rejoice, and give honour to Him for the marriage of the Lamb is come and His wife hath made herself ready ...Blessed are they which are called unto the marriage supper of the Lamb.....And I saw an angel standing in the sun; and he cried out with a loud voice, saying to all the fowl that fly in the midst of heaven. Come and gather yourselves together unto the supper of the great God; that ye may eat the flesh of kings, and the flesh of captains, and the flesh of mighty men and the flesh of horses, and of them that sit on them, and the flesh of all men, both free and bond, both small and great*** (Revelation 19:7-9, 17-18).

Note who fights the battle. The battle is seen as the fight of God against the enemies of His people:

> ***"As birds flying so will the Lord of hosts defend Jerusalem; defending also He will deliver it; and passing over He will preserve it"*** (Isaiah 31:5).

As the Bible states, these final battles are symbolised as a **"Marriage Supper of the Lord"**, to which the fowl and birds are gathered. The **"fowl, the birds flying"** are the symbol of God's power. In Hebrew Kabalic philosophy, this is symbolised by — **The Hermes Bird, the astrological eagle-Scorpio, the Chinese Phoenix!**

The Chinese Phoenix is therefore a marriage symbol, where God God fights for His people! This is the real significance underlying the paired **Phoenix-*Lung*"** of marriage. The heroic bridegroom fights for his bride. The ancient Chinese may have known about the prophecy of the coming marriage of God with His people, where the **"fowl and flying birds"** will destroy all the enemy and filth. Several times in the Gospels, the Lord Jesus Christ foretold this coming mystic marriage feast — q.v. Matthew 22:1-14, Luke 14:15-33. It always pertains to the time when evil and wickedness will come to an end and only goodness will prevail. Then God's people would enter into a symbolic marriage feast to celebrate the final victory.

One other important point to note — the enemy and his filth is always symbolised in the Bible as the "generation of vipers" — the "serpent". So, is it not significant that the southern constellation **Scorpio** represent the struggle against the snake which tried to seize the supreme **Crown** of **Libra**! And the mortal enemy of the snake is the noble Eagle — that Red Phoenix.

SIGNIFICANCE OF THE "*LUNG*-PHOENIX" PAIR

The **"Three Realms"** illustration of the phoenix coming down, the two ***"Lungs"*** waiting, and of the eight men denote a philosophical condition. This could now receive an appropriate interpretation:

- The **Red Phoenix-Hermes Bird** is the symbol of God's direct power. It is a prophecy of the coming of the Day when God Himself would directly step in and destroy all evil, thereby

PHOENIX - □*LUNG*□

AS ILLUSTRATED IN SHANG DYNASTY STONE CHIME.

THE BIRD IS EQUIVALENT TO THE PHOENIX, WHILE THE "KNEELING ANIMAL" IS THE *"LUNG"*. NOTE THE OTHER SHANG RELICS, AT THE BOTTOM, OF THE "KNEELING *LUNG*".

reconciling Man (the eight men) to Him, forever, like in a marriage.

- Until the Phoenix comes to destroy all evil, ***"Lung"*** is the interim mediator between God (the Phoenix) and Man (the eight men) Hence, ***"Lung"*** is the "Great Man with the Mandate of Heaven".

  This interim mediation is in the form of the **"Double *Lungs*"** or the **Two Door Gods**! This is another illustration of the meaning of **"Double *Lungs*" *as*** the sacred guardians of Heaven's Will.

The **"Three Realms"** illustration thus shows ***"Lung"*** as the interim mediator of God's divine power; the ambassador of God.

Just how old is this ***"Lung*-phoenix"** symbol? Several relics of the Shang dynasty have been uncovered. One of them is that of a stone chime, shaped in the form of a door or gate frame. Usually, the door or gate would be flanked by the **"Double *Lungs*"** or double lions. But, in this stone chime, the two animals which flanked the door or gate frame are a bird and a "kneeling animal." The bird is obviously equivalent to the phoenix. The "kneeling animal" resembles a number of Shang jade carvings of the ***"Lung"***. The "kneeling animal" is the ***"Lung"***! The ***"Lung*-phoenix"** symbolism was thus known during the Shang dynasty (1700-1200 B.C.) and possibly much earlier.

Part B:

CLEARING MISCONCEPTIONS ABOUT THE *"LUNG"*

CHAPTER 10

THE WESTERN DRAGON

MODERN WESTERN CONCEPT OF THE DRAGON AS "EVIL"

With the ***"Lung"*** so auspicious, why and how is the western concept different and considered to be one of dark evil? Note again the western view of the "dragon", as written by Seiss (1972 p.58):

> **One of the most famous mythological creations in the history of human thought is the horrid serpentine monster called the dragon. Together with the serpent and other things of the same repulsive and dangerous class, this is the universal symbol of evil — of some living power inimical to God and all good and the just terror of all men. The Serpent stands for that form of the Evil One in which cunning, artifice, deceit and malignant subtlety are the characteristics. The Dragon represents the same power armed, defiant, and putting forth in imperial forms and devastating by force. The Serpent is the sly and creeping deceiver, smoothly gliding in to betray, insinuating his poison and destroying by stealth. The Dragon is the terrific oppressor, assailing with teeth and claws, armed all over with spikes, lifting speary wings and tail, spouting fire and fury, and rushing upon its prey with every vehemence of malignant energy. The Serpent and the Dragon are one and the same, only in different modes of manifestation. Hence the Devil is called "the Dragon, that old Serpent". Whenever the power of evil is clothed in political sovereignty, persecuting, tyrannising, and oppressing, it is**

always the Dragon, or some rampant figure of destruction answering to it.

ORIGINAL WESTERN VERSION OF DRAGON AS "GOOD"

It may surprise some to discover that originally the western dragon is not an evil creature!:

> **As the beneficent life-giving element of water, the dragon is the national symbol of imperial China and the emblem of the Japanese Emperor. The Romans adopt it as their standard (along with the eagle) and it also appeared as the emblem of English-Welsh kings like Henry VII, Henry VIII, James I. The dragon was also the emblem of the West Saxons. The dragon is further represented as a guardian of treasure. The golden apples of Hesperides Garden were guarded by Ladon, the hundred-headed dragon. It appears that it was only in the Bible that the dragon was associated with the evil serpent** (Whittick 1960 pp.177-178).

In the Greek legends about heroes fighting "dragons", the "dragons" were guarding the scared treasures. The so-called Greek "heroes" were nothing more than thieves! What we have is an ironical twist of story. The good "dragon" trying to protect the sacred treasures is made into an evil fearsome animal, while the thieves become "good men"! In these Greek legends, the roles of ***"Lung"*** as "the guardian of sacred things" stand out.

THE ORIGINAL EVIL "DRAGON" WAS A LARGE SNAKE

The most remarkable thing is that the evil "dragon" St. George fought against is not the type of "dragon" the Greeks depict as guarding the sacred treasures:

Our popular story of St. George and the Dragon has numerous parallels in Western folklore. The stories of the laird who slew the "worme of Linton", of the knight who killed the Lambton worm, of the Chamion Conyers who delivered Sockburn in Durham from a "worm, dragon or fiery flying serpent"... (Dennys 1968 p.110).

The "evil dragon" of St. George is nothing more than a "large worm"; that is, a limbless snake!

The earliest traces of European civilisation not only belong to Greece, but the oldest traces of the European "dragon" are also found in Greek legends, as preserved by such writers like Homer and Hesoid (Ingersoll 1928 pp.118-124). In those earliest times, the earth was possessed by the Titans, whose bodies were supported, not by two legs, but by a serpent's tail. The chief god of that time was Ophion, the "Great Snake". Saturn, Neptune (himself half-man, half-fish) and Zeus struggled against Ophion and his serpent horde for mastery of the world.

In the Greek legends, Cecrops, the mythical founder of Athens, was a being whose body terminated in a fat and scaly serpent. The companions of Cadamus, sent to a fountain pool, were killed by a huge serpent, which later, was slain by Cadamus with the help of Athene. It was the teeth of this serpent that Cadamus sown and from which sprang the armed men from the "Dragon Teeth". The sun-gods incessantly battled against serpent deities. There was Python, half-man, half-snake, slain by Apollo with his first arrows shot from his infant bow. Python was one of the offsprings of the serpent monster Typhon and his wife Echidna, the wife being half-woman, half-snake. There is Hydra, a water fiend, with nine heads, one of which is immortal. Hercules killed Hydra by cutting off the eight heads and burying the ninth under a stone. The Hydra seems to reflect the Indian many headed Naga. There is the hundred headed serpent monster Ladon, last of the progeny of Typhon and Echidna.

ST. GEORGE KILLING THE DRAGON

MANY OF THE ANCIENT WESTERN LEGENDS SHOW THE "DRAGON" AS A "WORM-LIKE" SNAKE .

The Roman writer, Pliny, also showed in his writing that the evil Western "dragon" was a snake (Gould 1882 p.166): **"The dragon is a serpent destitute of venom; its head placed beneath the threshold of a door,the gods being duly propitiated by prayers, will ensure good fortune to the house, it is said."**

Aristotle wrote, also indicating the Western "dragon" is a snake (Gould 1882 p.165): **"The eagle and dragons are enemies, for the eagle feeds on serpents."**

Gould (1882 pp.171-172) notes that what many voyagers called "dragons" were large snakes without venom. He concluded that these snakes were likely boas or pythons.

It is interesting to note that the Biblical Greek term for "dragon" is **"draco"**. In Greek, **"draco"** means "snake"! Ingersoll (1928 p.146) notes that the terms dragon, drake, serpent, worm, were more or less interchangeable in the traditions of northern Europe. The fabulous **"wurm-bett"**, the serpent's bed, was the term used to convey the place of gold with a dragon-guardian.

VARIATIONS IN CHRISTIAN VIEWS ABOUT THE DRAGON

Whittick (1960) notes **"It appears that it was only in the Bible that the dragon was associated with the evil serpent."** Among some Christian groups any piece of material with illustrations of ***"Lung"*** is deemed "evil" and should be discarded; some even insist that new converts with the surname ***"Lung"*** should change their surname!

Christians also have ambivalent views about the ***"Lung"***. The Chinese Christian community, aware of the Biblical connection of the "dragon" with the serpent and Satan, has problems with the ambivalent views about ***"Lung"***:

a. Mandarin Bible Dictionary, p.714: In "Revelation the dragon [***"Lung"***] signifies Satan".

b. A New Complete Chinese-English Dictionary: The dragon is one of the four supernatural creatures..These four are: unicorn, phoenix, tortoise and dragon.

c. Chinese Hasting's Bible Dictionary: ***"Lung"*** (dragon). According to the Hebrew language there are several meanings for "dragon": dragon, snake, whale, crocodile, jackal, etc.

d. Reverend John E. Su, a popular Chinese writer, editor and pastor in Hongkong in his book "Difficult Issues in the Bible, Volume 9, p.44 have this to say (original in Chinese, English translation by Wayne Siao's 1990): Dragon, originated from the Greek word DRAKON and in the New Testament (NT) has been used in Revelation only 13 times. In the Old Testament (OT) the word translated "dragon" means great snake, great fish, or wild dog, etc. So in the Chinese version of the OT there is no ***"Lung"*** mentioned. We do not know why in Revelation in the NT the word is translated as ***"Lung"*** for 13 times. (Actually the ***"Lung"*** here is entirely different in meaning from the ***"Lung"*** in Chinese concept. The ***"Lung"*** in the Chinese mind represents the Emperor and is a blessed creature. From the saying "Good fortune of the Dragon-Phoenix", it is clear both the dragon and the phoenix are good creatures with nothing to be afraid of). Actually, except for the extinct...***"Lung"*** there is no such thing as dragon in history. So in the OT it is considered only as a kind of monster or fearful beast. In the NT, because of the Greek language various versions do inherit the Greek impression of the dragon and called it dragon. In fact, what John saw in his Vision was only a great monster. It without having a name, was called dragon, the dragon of the Greeks.

e. Reverend Eu's interpretation is in line with Harper's Bible Dictionary, p.141: "Dragon. A mystical monster depicted in the literature of ancient Middle East. It is akin to the subtle serpent of Genesis 3, and is openly called in Revelation 12:9 "the great dragon..that old serpent called the Devil and Satan which deceived the whole world...The iconography of the Far East, however, depicts the dragon as a symbol of strength and virtue, denoting the coming of spring and rain — a once worshipped river beast."

So, why is the western and eastern concept of the "dragon" so different? The truth is that there has been some significant confusion. The difference in thinking should have warned that the benevolent Chinese ***"Lung"*** could not be the same as the evil "Biblical Dragon"! Examination of the reasons for the confusion will reveal the cause why the Chinese ***"Lung"*** is such a unique animal symbol of China!

THE BIBLE ASSOCIATES THE DRAGON WITH THE SERPENT

Westerners confusingly link ***"Lung"*** to the "Dragon" mentioned in the Bible to be the same as the Old Serpent, the Devil. If close attention have been paid to the meanings of both the Hebrew-Greek and Chinese words or characters for ***"Lung"***, "Dragon" and "Serpent" it would have been found that the ***"Lung"*** is not the "Dragon". The Bible calls the Devil, Satan, the Old Serpent:

> ***And the great dragon [1404] was cast out, that old serpent [3789], called the Devil and Satan which deceiveth the whole world: he was cast out into the earth and his angels were cast out with him*** (Revelation 12:10).

> ***And he laid hold on the dragon [1404] that old serpent [3789] which is the Devil and Satan and bound him a***

> ***thousand years*** (Revelation 20:2).
>
> ***But I fear lest by any means as the serpent [3789] beguiled Eve through his subtility..*** (2 Corinthians 11:3).
>
> ***Now the serpent [5175] was more subtil than any beast o*** ***the field which the Lord God had made*** (Genesis 3:1).

The Lord Jesus Christ called Satan's followers:

> ***Ye serpents [3789], ye generation of vipers, how can ye escape the damnation of hell?*** (Matthew 23:33 — also 3:7, 12:34 and Luke 3:7)

There is no doubt that the Holy Scriptures associate the "Serpent" with aspects of evil. How about the "Biblical Dragon"? It is obviously associated with the "Serpent" and the Devil as quoted above.

THE BIBLICAL DRAGON IS A NATURAL WILD ANIMAL!

Besides mentioning of the "Biblical Dragon" [1404] as Satanic in Revelation 12 and 13, the Bible also mentions the "Biblical Dragon" in other places:

> ***In that day the Lord with his sore and great and strong sword shall punish leviathan the piercing serpent [5175] even leviathan the crooked serpent [5175]; and he shall slay the dragon [8577] that is in the sea*** (Isaiah 27:1).
>
> ***And I will make Jerusalem heaps and a den of dragons [8577] and I will make the cities of Judah desolate without an inhabitant*** (Jeremiah 9:11).

Behold the noise of the bruit is come and a great commotion out of the north country to make the cities of Judah desolate and a den of dragons [8577] (Jeremiah 10:22).

The passages of the Biblical Book of Jeremiah indicate that the "Biblical Dragon" is not a mythological creature but an animal commonly seen in the Middle East! The Biblical "Dragon" — a natural wild animal found in the Middle East! Really, what kind of natural wild animal is this "Biblical Dragon"?

THE REAL MEANINGS OF ORIGINAL BIBLE WORDS FOR DRAGON

Note that numbers are attached to the words "Serpent or Dragon" — these numbers indicate the original Hebrew and Greek words as follows (Strong, 1890; Thayer, 1901):

SERPENT:

5175	**nachash**	a snake from its hiss, a serpent. From the root word nachash [5172] which also means divine or enchantment.
3789	**ophis**	a snake, malicious sly person, Satan — serpent.

BIBLICAL DRAGON:

8577	**tanniym**	a marine or land monster, i.e. sea-serpent or jackal — dragon, sea-monster, serpent, whale.
1404	**drakon**	a fabulous kind of serpent — dragon. (Thayer 1977 also defines "drakon" as a "great serpent, a fabulous animal".)

The scriptural usages of "Dragon" indicate that the "Biblical Dragon" is an animal very much like the "Serpent"! Although in Jeremiah, the "dragons" inhabiting the ruins of the cities could be "jackals", it is likely they were used in reference to "venomous snakes". The primary symbolisation of the "Biblical Dragon" is the **"limbless snake"**! After-all, did not the Book of Revelation define the "Dragon" as the "Serpent"?:

> ***And he laid hold on the dragon [1404] that old serpent [3789] which is the Devil and Satan and bound him a thousand years*** (Revelation 20:2).

Ingersoll (1928 pp.133-134) notes that the Jewish Cyclopedia put the word for "Dragon" as signifying a dangerous monster whose bite is poisonous. The arid and hot areas of the Middle East are favourable to serpent life. The Bible allude to several venomous species as lurking in the thickets, hedges, rocks and also houses where they searched for mice, insects, etc.

The lexicon meaning of the Greek word **"drakon"** is "Serpent". Ingersoll (1928 pp.125-126) notes:

> **The third class of genii is terrestrial, inhabiting mountains, rocks, caves and other grim and desolate places. These genii are the most frequent of all, and are known as dragons. Not, of course, that all dragons are terrestrial; the dragon form has already been mentioned as among the forms proper to the genii of springs and wells... The term *drakos* or *drakontas* indicates to the Greek peasant a monster of no more determinate shape than does 'dragon' among ourselves. The Greek word, however,...is often employed in a strict and narrow sense to denote a 'serpent' as distinguished from a small snake (*phodi*). On the other hand a Greek 'dragon' in the wider sense of the word is sometimes distinctly anthropomorphic in popular stories,**

and is made to boil kettles and drink coffee without any sense of impropriety. It is in fact only from the context of the story that it is possible to tell in what shape the dragon is imagined....

Hence, it is true that the "Biblical Dragon" is actually the "Serpent", a limbless animal. But **"drakon"** is not the proper term for limbed animals like the ***"Lung"***.

THE CHARACTER FOR THE CHINESE *"LUNG"*

We should look at the forms of the Chinese character for ***"Lung"*** Weiger (1965 p.309, Lesson 140) writes:

> *LUNG*. **The dragon. When it ascend to heaven and flies, it rains; when it hides in the wells, there is a drought. Vapours and clouds personified. The ancient form is a representation sufficiently recognisable. The modern form is explained thus: on the right, "Fei" (to fly) contracted, the wings; on the left, at the bottom "Ju" or "Jou" (pieces of dry meat) the body; on the top, "li" is thought to be "Tung" contracted and used as a phonetic...**

Vaccari and Vaccari (1950 p.58) write:

> **..dragon — The last symbol on the right is a fanciful sketch of the fabulous animal. As to the middle symbol which is near in shape to the modern one, its right component is supposed to be a contraction of "Fei" to fly (in this case symbolising the dragon's wings), the lower part ("Jou") of the left component represents the body and its upper part ("Li") is thought to be a contraction of "Tung" heavy..**

FUNDAMENTAL SUBCHARACTERS OF *LUNG* AND *SHE*

A. *LUNG*, "DRAGON".
Vapour and clouds personified, giving rise to rains when it flies in heaven and causing drought when it hides in wells. The ancient word is pictorial. The modern word: *"Fei" on right means "contracted wings". "Li" on right, top, is the contraction of "Tung" for "heavy", used as phonetic with "Ju" on the right, bottom, meaning "body".*

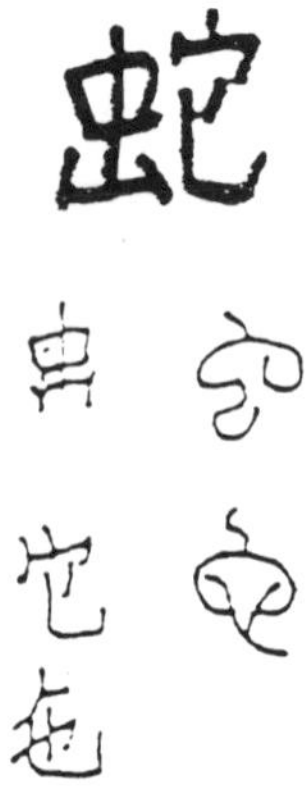

B. *SHE*, "SERPENT".
Made up of *"Hui"* and *"T'o"* as below. It especially refers to the Serpent or Cobra.
***"Hui"* refers to crawling creatures such as snakes, worms.**
***"T'o"* refers to the snake upright on its tail with its tongue darting out.**

THE *"LUNG"*, IN THE EAST, IS A FOUR-LIMBE BEING; IN CONTRAST, THE *"SHE"*, IN THE NORTH, IS THE POISONOUS COBRA OR NAGA A LIMBLESS BEING, VIZ. THE SNAKE.

Both Weiger (1965) and Vaccari and Vaccari (1950) point out the winged nature of the Chinese ***"Lung"***. Besides showing the presumed "wings", the pictorial form of Chinese ***"Lung"*** has:

1. four protrusions on the top of the head — likely representing the horns.

2. four limbs.

On Shang oracle bone and early bronze vessels, the graphs are of a creature with short legs (Hsu and Ward 1984 p.459). Therefore, from very ancient times, the ***"Lung"*** is known to be a limbed creature.

To emphasise further the difference between the ***"Lung"*** and the "Serpent" we should study the Chinese character for "Serpent". The Chinese character forms for ***"She"*** the "Serpent" (Weiger 1965 pp. 259, lesson 108 and p.261, lesson 110A). ***"She"*** for "Serpent" is formed from ***"Hui"*** for "crawling" and ***"To"*** for "Snake". The pictorial representation for ***"To"*** shows the typical hissing tongue of the snake while ***"Hui"*** shows its crawling form. There are no limbs, wings and horns to the ***"She"*** "Serpent". The Chinese characters thus show that the Chinese ***"Lung"*** is limbed, winged and horned, unlike the limbless **"*She*-Serpent"**! The Chinese ***"She*-Serpent"** is definitely not the Chinese ***"Lung"***!

Although most modern Chinese illustrations often do not show wings on the ***"Lung"***, the Chinese ***"Lung"*** is by implication a winged creature: **"There are several varieties; some are horned and others hornless, some are scaleless, and one kind has no wings... Celestial Dragon... Spiritual Dragon ... Winged Dragon.. Horned Dragon ..Coiling Dragon ...Yellow Dragon..."** (Williams 1931 pp.110-111). Actually, the Winged ***"Lung"*** is the highest of the order of ***"Lung"***.

The "Biblical Dragon" is not the same creature as the mythological

"Lung" of China! The "Biblical Dragon" is like the Chinese "Serpent" an animal symbolising evil while the Chinese ***"Lung"*** symbolises goodness. The "Biblical Dragon" is not only limbless, unlike the limbed Chinese ***"Lung"***; but the "Biblical Dragon" is actually a commonly known animal in the Middle East; it is the wild serpent! This is why the term "Dragon" is often associated with "Serpent" in the Bible.

Ingersoll (1928 p.126) notes:

> **Now, a striking feature of this whole race of prehistoric Greek 'dragons' is that they have no lizard-like, four-footed body, no kindliness of disposition, and nothing to do with rainfall or productivity of the soil. The exception to complete dissimilarity with the Chinese variety is that some of them have the office of guardians of women and treasures. On the other hand these fierce and horrid 'Pelasgian' creatures of a lively imagination portray, far more evidently than do the Oriental 'dragons', the fears and emotions of a people half-savage, it is true, yet possessed of an alertness of mind very different from the rather bovine and 'single-track' mentality of the Hindoos and Chinese.**

Hence, the Western "Dragon" is recognisably serpentine and limbless in nature, while the Oriental one is bovine and possessing limbs in nature.

Actually, the Chinese word ***"She"*** is the one which should have been translated as "Dragon". ***"Lung"*** should never have been translated as "Dragon". If the Chinese ***"Lung"*** is not the "Biblical Dragon" then what is the Chinese ***"Lung"***? Is it ever mentioned in the Holy Scriptures? Yes, it is indeed! The Holy Scriptures do describe the Chinese ***"Lung"*** not as "Dragon" but by a different term! Find out what this Biblical term for ***"Lung"*** is in the chapter after next!

CHAPTER 11

THE INDIAN "NAGA"

MISTRANSLATION OF THE INDIAN "NAGA" AS "*LUNG*"

The Hindu **"Naga"** (cobra) has been confused with the Chinese ***"Lung"***:

> **"Modern superstition has further originated the idea of four Dragon Kings — identified with the "Nagas" or Serpent Spirits of the Hindoos — each bearing rule over one of the four seas which form the border of the habitable earth; and the subterranean palaces which form their respective abodes are named as follows: in the east sea; in the south sea; in the west sea; in the north sea."** (Williams 1931 p.111).

Among the nature gods worshipped by the Indians is serpent veneration. The particular object of worship is the deadly cobra, called **"Naga"**. Every one of these hooded reptiles was regarded as the reincarnation of a great and fearful company of mythological nagas, uncertain of temper and fearful. Less civilised tribes, known as Naga men, particularly worshipped the cobra and they were despised by the higher Brahmanic caste. It is said that the early Buddhists found it hard to combat the serpent worship; hence, the Buddhists tried to improve its features to absorb the worship into Buddhism. One of the problems faced by the early Buddhists is that the Naga king foretold the ascension of Guatama to Buddhahood and sheltered Lord Buddha for seven days with its coils and spreading hoods. The **"Nagas"**, like the Chinese ***"Lungs"***, were also able to raise rains and thunder in their temper.

As the Indian **"Naga"** is the venomous cobra, logically, the Chinese should have associated **"Naga"** with the Chinese word ***"She"*** which, after-all, is the "cobra". However, in the Chinese culture, ***"She"***, the venomous serpent, has always been an evil symbol. So, the Lamas and Chinese Buddhists, not daring to call the mythical Indian "dragons-serpents" (**"Naga"**) ***"She"***, termed these **"Nagas"** as ***"Lung"*** in their translations of the Sankrit Buddhist scriptures (Williams 1931 p.109).

The Indian **"Naga"** and the Chinese ***"She"*** for "Serpent" are the same Biblical "Dragon". But ***"Lung"*** was never the Biblical "Dragon" nor was it the Indian **"Naga"**.

THE INDIAN NAGA AS THE BASIS OF ECLIPSE THEORY

When the sun, earth and moon are in conjunction solar or lunar eclipses would occur. The ancients associated eclipses with an ecliptic dragon; the apparent results of a dragon-like monster eating the sun or moon.

> **This dragon becomes the "black and darkling star called *head and tail*"** (Sharf 1976 p.39).

Thiswise, the ***"Lung"*** has been closely linked to the lunar movements. However, Needham (1959 p.252) regards the theory of the role of the dragon in eclipses as an Indian theory imported into Chinese astrology and wrote:

> **"It is important to note that the dragon here is the symbol of a palace, i.e. a whole quarter of the heavens. The limits of this region happen to correspond approximately with those of the occidental constellation Draco, but this can**

"*SHE*" for COBRA

alias the INDIAN NAGA-DRAGON

THE CHINESE CALL THE COBRA *"SHE"*, THE SYMBOL OF EVIL. IT IS ALSO THE CHINESE *CHIAO* DRAGON OF THE MARSHES AND IS EVIL.

> **hardly be more than coincidence. In any case the Chinese sky-dragon had originally nothing whatever to do with the idea of a dragon whose head and tail represented the moon's nodes and which accordingly "ate the sun" at eclipses. From this no doubt, we derive our term "draconitic months" to designate the time between the moon's successive passages through these points...Noteworthy in this connection is the fact that the value of the period 27.2122 days was obtained by Tsu Chhung-Chih already in the +5th century...but since the nodes are of course not fixed, rotating round the ecliptic once in 18.6 years approximately, the original symbolism cannot have applied to them... and if it was transferred to them later on this can only have been due to the importation of the Indian idea of the monster (or monsters) Rahu and Ketu...The ball was then no longer the 'moon pearl' but the sun, and is indeed represented as red in colour, with issuing flames. In a case like this multiple layers of symbolism are naturally to be expected.."**

The Indian describes this dragon's head and tail as **Rahu** and **Ketu** as also involved in the solar and lunar eclipses; **Rahu** and **Ketu** being two additional bodies to the existing seven planets (Sharf 1976 p.42). In the Indian Buddhism theory, the two imaginary planets **Rahu (Lo-Hou)** and **Ketu** (***Chi-Tu***) are the head and tail of the **"Naga"** and personify the ascending and descending nodes of the path of the moon and therefore also account for the eclipses (Needham 1959 p.228).

It should be instructive to note here that as **"Naga"** is really the "Serpent", evil influences attributed to such a creature as the "Serpent" would be logical. But as ***"Lung"*** is not the "Serpent" and never the **"Naga"**, the malevolent eclipses should not be linked to the auspicious ***"Lung"***.

AN ANCIENT CHANGE IN DIRECTION OF THE DRAGON

The false association of the ***"Lung"*** with eclipses could be linked to an ancient purposeful attempt to change an original North-South axis of the being called **"Tli"** to an East-West one and therefore lunar orientation. Sharf (1976) shows that:

> **Originally, the Hebrew Tli dragon has an "axis mundi" which is a north-south direction. However, the Byzantines with the Arabs and West has a dragon which is the name given to the imaginary line joining the lunar nodes, the points where the monthly orbit of the moon crosses the ecliptic, the zodiacal belt which is of course the apparent annual orbit of the sun. The ascending node where the moon passes from south to north of the ecliptic is called the dragon's head or "caput draconis" (Western) or "ra's al-jawzahr" (Arab). The reverse where the moon moves from north to south is the dragon's tail "cauda draconis, dhanab al-jawzahr"** (Sharf 1976 pp. 38-39).

Note this admission: **"And the Tli has obviously turned here (in the Kabalic Donnolo concept) into the lunar dragon, just as it has in the Baraita. The 'axis mundi' cannot darken the sun and the moon, nor can it be oriented east to west."** (Sharf 1976 pp. 40-41).

It is the animation of the "head and tail" of the **"Tli"** as the "exaltation and dejection" (strongest or weakest zodiacal powers) of the dragon that leads to the seven planets becoming nine (Sharf 1976 p.42). This newness of the two additional planets is recognised as "two new planets were taken into account of by Hellenistic and Byzantine astrologers" (Sharf 1976 p.42).

The myth of the fearful dragon is the result of an ancient change in the direction of the so-called "astrological dragon". When the Kabalic **"Tli"** dragon is in the south-north alignment it could not possibly be associated with eclipses. It is only when the ancients falsely turned the direction along an east-west alignment of the ecliptic that the "dragon" could assume its false fearful reputation of causing eclipses.

The "dragon", as represented by **"Tli"**, was never originally a black and darkling star! Remember, it was stated earlier:

> **"The false association of the dragon with eclipses could be attributed to the spread of Indian theory with Buddhism that two imaginary planets Rahu (Lo-Hou) and Ketu (Chi-Tu) which personified the ascending and descending nodes of the path of the moon also account for the eclipses"** (Needham 1959 p.228).

It was the **"Naga"** which caused later misleading changes to the original Chinese picture of the ***"Lung"*** into a more but still not totally serpentine creature. For ***"Lung"***, before the advent of Indian Buddhism into China around the second century B.C., was originally a more humanoid creature. The Shang ***"Lung"*** was a Doubled-Horned, Two-Limbed, half-man, half-fish. It was only during the Han dynasty, when Indian theories reached China, that the ***"Lung"*** assumed the traditional Doubled Horned, Bearded, Four-Limbed, Serpentine form.

"LUNG" AND SERPENT HAVE DIFFERENT POSITIONS

The Chinese ***Lung*** has been persistently confused with the western dragon. As the western dragon is the serpent, the Chinese ***"Lung"*** has been taken to be a form of serpent. But these considerations further show that the Chinese ***"Lung"*** is very different from the serpent:

THE DIFFERENCE IN THE POSITIONS OF THE FOUR HERALDIC ANIMALS

In the **Four Animals-Four Cardinal Directions** symbolism, the position and status of ***"Lung"*** are different from those of the "serpent". We should not confuse the ***"Lung"*** with the "snake":

- **"According to the I Ching, the symbol "Chen" corresponding to the third of the four primary developments of the creative influences, is synonymous with *"Lung"*, the dragon; and in conformity with his dictum, the powers and functions of nature governed by the forces thus indicated, such as the East, Spring, etc. are ranked under the symbol the Azure Dragon, which also designates the eastern quadrant of the uranosphere."** (Williams 1931 p.113).

- On the other hand, the position of the "serpent" in the North is often ominously associated with the evil influences of cold winter and the cold water and wind.

The Chinese associate the blue-green **Azure *"Lung"*** as the creature of the East symbolising the First World Emperor Fu Hsi. The **Golden *"Lung"*** is also the animal in the centre and of the Third World Emperor Huang Ti. Through two ways, the eastern **Azure *"Lung"*** — and the central **Golden *"Lung"***, the Chinese ***"Lung"*** therefore has auspicious and good symbolism in ancient Chinese culture.

Among the **Four Cardinal Directions**, the Chinese associate the North with evil; and the animal of the North is the "snake". The Chinese, like many races, associate the "snake" with evil, in contrast to ***"Lung"*** which is a creature of good.

Note the Chinese animals of the **Four Cardinal Direction** points and their similarities to the Jewish Kabala representation of four animals. In Chinese symbolism, the ***"Lung"*** is a different animal from the "snake". There are obvious parallels between the Chinese animals associated with the **"Four Cardinal Direction"** points and that of the Kabala as indicated. The connection between the Chinese "Black Snake of the North" with the Jewish Kabalic "Typhon-double snakes" is quite clear.

The Chinese ***"Lung"*** is the Kabalic **"kerub"**; a bull-horned bearded man with limbed forefront and the backbody and tail of a fish. It is really the Greek god of the sea, Poseidon better known as Neptune — the bearded crowned god having a man's upper torso and fish tail pictured holding a trident. This bull-headed sphinx is featured in Assyrian, Egyptian and Indian hieroglyphs and according to Kabalic tradition, is also the angel placed to prevent Adam and Eve from re-entering the Garden of Eden to partake of the Tree of Life (Whittick 1960, p.137). The Bible indicates that this gate to the Garden was located to the East; the Chinese ***"Lung"*** is to the East.

In the Kabala system, this **"kerub"**, a bearded, horned, fish-tailed being, is a different angelic creature from the limbless Typhon snakes. It is again obvious that the Chinese ***"Lung"***, which is the bearded ,horned, fish-tailed being; is not the "serpent" or "snake"

DIFFERENCE IN THE HORARY TWELVE ANIMALS POSITIONS

Gould (1882 pp.220-221) also wrote that the ancient Chinese differentiated between ***"Lung"*** and the serpent: **"Similarly, we find the twelve symbolical animals, representing the twelve branches of the Horary characters to be the rat, the ox, tiger, hare, dragon, serpent, horse, sheep, monkey, cock, dog, boar, where the dragon is the only one about whose existence a question can be raised. From this latter we learn that there was no confusion of meaning then between dragons and serpents; the distinction of the two creatures was clearly recognised, just as it was many centuries afterwards by Mencius, who, in writing of these early periods, says, 'In the**

time of Yaou, the waters flowing out of their channels, inundated the Middle Kingdom. Snakes and dragons occupied it, and the people had no place where they could settle themselves'; and again, 'Yu dug open their obstructed channels and conducted them to the seas. He drive away the snakes and dragons, and forced them into the grassy marshes.' "

THE "PHOENIX-*LUNG*" PAIR

The ***"Lung"*** is associated with the phoenix as the best of auspicious pairs. The equivalent of the phoenix could be birds like the eagle, falcon and even peacock. Yet, the ancients knew "The eagle and the dragon are enemies, for the eagle feeds on serpents". (Gould 1882 p.165). The peacock is also the enemy of the serpent. The Chinese also regard the phoenix as the enemy of the serpent. The "dragon" could not be the ***"Lung"***.

Furthermore, as discussed earlier in Chapter 9, there is a Shang dynasty stone chime which is shaped in a door or gate frame flanked by a bird and a "kneeling animal", obviously a rather old form of the **"*Lung*-phoenix"** pair. This indicates that the **"*Lung*-phoenix"** pair were as old as the Shang dynasty. But at this time, the ***"Lung"*** was pictured, in the stone chime, not as a limbless serpent but as a kneeling figure with hands on top of the kneeling legs. This ***"Lung"***, the "kneeling animal", was actually a kneeling man!

BIRTH OF THE "DRAGON"

The dragon is as old as the sensitiveness and imagination of man. It assumed definite shapes as soon as man begin to paint or carve in wood and on stones.

Early in human history the dragon was linked to the land where water is the most important thing in nature to human existence, the essential requisite for life and happiness. It is linked to the early rise of irrigation in agriculture, when the control of the water supplies for the fields was important. It is also linked to the attempts to fight floods which have always been the bane of mankind.

BIRTH OF THE DRAGON IN BABYLON: THE ORIGINAL "DRAGON" WAS HALF-MAN, HALF-FISH

Sumer was the oldest civilisation. Among the earliest pictures of the Sumerian-Babylonian legends is that of Quranos, a human figure whose body from the middle downwards is that of a fish. Also, high among the gods was Ea, another a human with the body and tail of a fish.

Then emerged chaos personified, in the form of Tiamat, the great she serpent and a water devil. She was a thick-bodied snake wih one third of her front portion upreared with two little arm-like appendages, extended tongue and a single goat-like horn on the head. This Babylonian Tiamat is the Greek Typhon, that great serpent monster. Tiamat was eventually slain by Marduk, the son of Ea (the Babylonian Marduk is equivalent to Jupiter, King of Gods, who eventually slew Typhon):

> **Chaos bred monsters, and then the divine Heaven and Earth, as Anshar and Kishar, ancestors of Anu, Enlil, and Ea, prepared for conflicts, to maintain order... The eleven opposing monsters of Chaos are created by Tiamat and headed by Kingu, to whom Tiamat gives the tablets of destiny and whom she made her consort. The peace-loving gods seem to fear; they sent a messenger to Tiamat, "May her liver be pacified, her heart softened"... At any rate, we next see Bel-Marduk, at the command of his father, going joyfully into battle after preparing for the conflict by making weapons, bow, lance, club, lightning-bolt, storm-winds and a net wherewith to catch Tiamat. The gods got drunk with joy, anticipating victory and hailing Marduk as already lord**

of the universe. On Storm (his chariot) he rushes forth, haloed with light, from which Kingu shrinks. Him follow the seven winds. Tiamat, however, fears him not, but when Marduk challenges her, she fights, "raging and shaking with fury," yet all in vain. For Marduk stifles her with a poisonous gas, and then transfixes her, also taking the tablets from Kingu and netting the other monsters. But Tiamat he cuts into two, making one half of her the sky. (Ingersoll 1928 pp.20-21).

Anshar and Kishar sent Anshar's son Anu and the god Ea to appease Tiamat. But Tiamat could not be reconciled to the orderly and ethical ways of the gods. Much time passed before the gods could find a champion to slay the serpent monster.

Many Sumerian-Babylonian reliefs show the half-man, half-fish Ea and the snake-like Tiamat. Ingersoll (1928 p.23) notes that often there is a third smaller dragon, running on all fours like a dog and whose significance is unexplained.

The composite animal-form of the benevolent rain-god of Sumerian-Babylonian legends is that of the horned sea-goat Marduk, usually shown with only two front legs, and always with a fish-tail. This is also the Zodiac star constellation of Capriconus, the symbol of Jupiter. This form is also that of the Indian Varuna (equivalent to the Sumerian-Babylonian Quranos).

Marduk is also said to be a bull god (Coyajee 1929 p.252). He is also identified with the god Asshur. On one banner pole, the god Asshur stood on a disc as an archer between two bulls, and the top of the pole had a large bull's head with horns.

BIRTH OF THE "DRAGON" IN INDO-ARYAN: THE EVIL SERPENT

The Indo-Aryan traditions have among the oldest gods, Ormuzd, the "Wise Spirit". In opposition to Ormuzd was a host led by the Lie-Demon, the "Hostile or Harmful Spirit", Angra Mainyu, Ahriman. In this evil host is that being Azhi Dahaka, a serpent **druj**, half-human, half-beast with three heads and six eyes, and which created drought and disease. He was at times pictured as with two snakes or dragons, one on each shoulder.

According to Coyajee (1929 pp.240-241), the evidence indicates that Azhi Dahaka was the first king of the Medes. Azhi Dahaka started the kingship in Persia and was impious and wicked. He had a dazzling palace set in the mountain, so tall that it threatened to "seize the stars". This fortress palace had seven concentric walls. Azhi Dahaka and his people were of the ten varieties of men and fifteen semi-human monsters with common ancestors. The Persian legends assigned a long reign to Azhi Dahaka.

The legends indicate that Azhi Dahaka was driven into excesses, like the building of his magnificent city-fortress-palace. Azhi Dahaka was said to be very fond of choice beauties, whom he took captives to his seraglio. The people suffered. In his arrogance he also made enemies of neighbouring rulers.

Azhi had carried away certain benevolent goddesses, described as "milch cows" and kept captives among the clouds. This indicates that eventually Azhi Dahaka attempted to seize control of the precious life giving waters of the land. Revolts against Azhi Dahaka started.

Finally, Indra (in Indian mythology) or Feridun (in Persian mythology) killed this Azhi (or Azi), the "monster which kept back the waters". In the Indian Vedas, Azhi is called Vritra, the leader of the demons. Vritra was called the serpent lying in the mountain.

Like the Babylonian Ea and Marduk, Feridun is said to be a "bull hero" bearing a bull-headed mace, with which he smashed the head of Azhi Dahaka. Feridun also had as foster mother a cow, and his brother was a male ox (Coyajee 1929 p.251).

BIRTH OF THE DRAGON IN EGYPT: TWO SETS OF ORIGINAL "DRAGONS" — THE SERPENT AND THE GRIFFINS

Coyajee (1929 p.249) noted **"after 2500 B.C., the Asiatic myth of the combat between the god of heaven and light (Bel-Marduk) and the abysmal dragon of the ocean (Tiamat) penetrated into Egypt, where it gave rise to the story of the gigantic serpent 'Apop' the enemy of the sun-god."**

Egypt was among the oldest of the civilisations. Among the earliest deities of Egypt, the supreme one was Ra, with whom was associated Hathor, the "Great Mother", the origin of all earth life, including human beings. But Set, the water snake-like reptile devil, instigated mankind into rebellion. Hathor punished mankind but eventually gained the reputation of a malignant "seven headed" spirit. Hathor became Isis, the consort of Osiris. They had a son, Horus, whose symbol is the falcon, sometimes depicted with two serpents in its claws. Horus rode into battle on a chariot drawn by **griffins**, the most primitive form of dragons.

Set is the same as the Greek serpent monster Typhon, gigantic leader of the enemies of the Greek gods. Sometimes, Set is depicted as the crocodile.

TWO SETS OF ORIGINAL "DRAGONS": THE HALF-MAN, HALF-FISH AND THE SERPENT

The ancient traditions indicate that there were, in the earliest memories of the ancient cultures, at least two major opposing forms

EGYPTIAN DRAGON-SERPENTS

CHANUPHIS
or BAIT

GODDESS
MERSOKAR

GODDESS
EILEITHYA

THE "WINGED" SERPENTS ARE THE COBRA WITH ITS HOOD EXTENDED. WHEN THE COBRA STRIKES, IT GIVES THE IMPRESSION OF FLYING.

of "dragons":

- o The first, and earliest form which is also benevolent, is always that of the half-man, half-fish. This form is the enemy of the second form of "dragons" below.

- o The second form is that of a monster serpent and is evil. The legends show that this serpent-dragon kept back the waters, thereby causing drought and eventually diseases linked to lack of water and sanitation.

The half-man, half-fish "dragon" was very often the leader of the peace loving gods. He was Ea or the son Marduk in Sumeria-Babylon, Horus in Eygpt, Indra in India, Jupiter-Neptune-Thor in Europe. He is often depicted as the Storm God with the thunder bolts as his characteristic weapon.

The serpent monster was Tiamat in Sumeria-Babylon, Set or Apop in Eygpt, Azhi-Vritra in Indo-Aryan areas and Typhon in Greece. He grew in arrogance and excesses, causing widespread sufferings. This monster serpent became the leader of the gigantic enemies of the gods and was often depicted as holding back the waters.

The half-man, half-fish "dragon" fought the serpent "dragon" and defeated the serpent "dragon" with his thunderbolts. When the former destroyed the latter, the former was said to have released the life-giving waters for the crops and people.

The Chinese ***"Lung"*** is another variant of the half-man, half-fish "dragon". Which is why the oldest Chinese relics, those of the Shang dynasty, show ***"Lung"*** as a half-man, half-fish and not as a serpent. The Chinese ***"Lung"*** is the enemy of the serpent "dragon"!

CHAPTER 12

"*LUNG*" AS THE "SERAPHIM"

"*LUNG*" AS ONE OF THE CHERUBIM

The Chinese ***"Lung"*** is associated with one of the angelic creatures of Heaven. As discussed earlier, the ***"Lung"*** (heraldic being of the East) is equivalent, not to the serpent (heraldic animal of the North), but to the ox (also heraldic animal of the East), one of the four main cherubim in the Bible:

> ***And before the throne..were four beasts full of eyes before and behind. And the first beast was like a lion and the second beast like a calf, and the third beast had a face as a man and the fourth beast was like a flying eagle. And the four beasts had each of them six wings about him and they were full of eyes within and they rest not day and night saying Holy, holy, holy, Lord God Almighty which was, and is, and is to come*** (Revelation 4:6-8).

> ***Now the cherubim stood on the right side of the house when the man went in and the cloud filled the inner court ...And when I looked behold the four wheels by the cherubim, one wheel by one cherub and another wheel by another cherub: and the appearance of the wheels was as the colour of a beryl stone..And every one had four faces: the first face was the face of a cherub, and the second face was the face of a man, and the third the face of a lion and the fourth the face of an eagle...And the cherubim..stood at the door of the east gate of the Lord's house...*** (Ezekiel 10:3,9, 14, 19 - verse 9 indicates there were four cherubim).

These are winged angelic creatures resembling man, the ox (or calf), lion, and the eagle. Not to mention the snake, which is the symbol of Satan and is described in the Biblical Book of Genesis as a magnificent animal in the Garden of Eden. ***"Lung"*** is one of the cherubim:

> **Cherub, Cherubim. The symbolical figure so called was a composite creature-form which finds a parallel in the religious insignia of Assyria, Egypt and Persia, e.g. the sphinx, the winged bulls and lions of Nineveh, etc. A cherub guarded paradise. Gen 3:24. Figures of cherubim were placed on the mercy seat of the ark. Ex. 25:18. A pair of colossal size overshadowed it in Solomon's temple with the canopy of their contiguously extended wings. 1 Kings 6:27...It is remarkable that with such precise directions as to their position, attitude and material, nothing, save they were winged, is said concerning their shape. On the whole it seems likely that the word "cherub" meant not only the composite creature-form, of which the man, lion, ox and eagle were the elements, but, further, some peculiar and mystical form. Ezekiel 1:6....** (Peloubet 1947).

The term "cherubim" is that referring to a certain class, category or group of angels. The term is not restricted to any particular form, as it could cover those like man, the ox, eagle, lion, and possibly fabulous forms like the ***"Lung"*** and phoenix. The Biblical prophecies of Daniel and Revelation contain vivid descriptions of these angelic beasts, including the seemingly terrible composite forms.

"*LUNG*" AS ONE OF THE "SERAPHIMS" — HIGHEST OF ANGELS

However, the ***"Lung"*** is more than a cherubim. The Bible also refer to those unique creatures called **"seraphims"**:

> ***Above it stood the seraphims [8314]: each one has six wings; with twain he covered his face and with twain he covered his feet and with twain he did fly. And one cried unto another and said, Holy, holy, holy is the Lord of hosts; the whole earth is full of his glory...*** (Isaiah 6:2-3).

> ***Then flew one of the seraphims [8314] unto me, having a live coal in his hand which he had taken with the tongs from the altar...*** (Isaiah 6:6).

The Isaiah's **"seraphim"** has "hands" to enable it to handle a tong to collect the coal. Note too that the Isaiah's **"seraphims"** are similar to the **Four Beasts or Heraldic Animals** of Revelation 4 in:

- o having six wings
- o having limbs
- o praising God "Holy, holy, holy" all the time.

The **Four Heraldic Animals**, which surround the throne of God, are **"seraphims"**. It is quite clear that each of the **Four Heraldic Animals** (man, ox, lion and eagle) is synonymous with the **"seraphim"** of Isaiah! That is, the **Four Heraldic Animals** are of **"seraphim"** level — the highest among angels. The **"seraphims"** are, therefore, of the world of God's angelic beings and they are the special class of cherubim closely associated with God.

In fact, the Jewish Kabalic system regards **"seraphims"** as the highest of the angels, with the "cherubim" ranking just below. Although the term "cherubim" already represents a very high class of angels, the term **"seraphim"** represents the highest category within that special class of cherubim.

As the Chinese Phoenix, Tiger, Snake-Tortoise-***"Lung"*** are also **Four Heraldic Animals** equivalent to the **Four Beasts** of the Bible, they

THE SERAPHIM HIGHEST OF THE ANGELS

WINGED AND LIMBED LIKE THE *"LUNG"*.

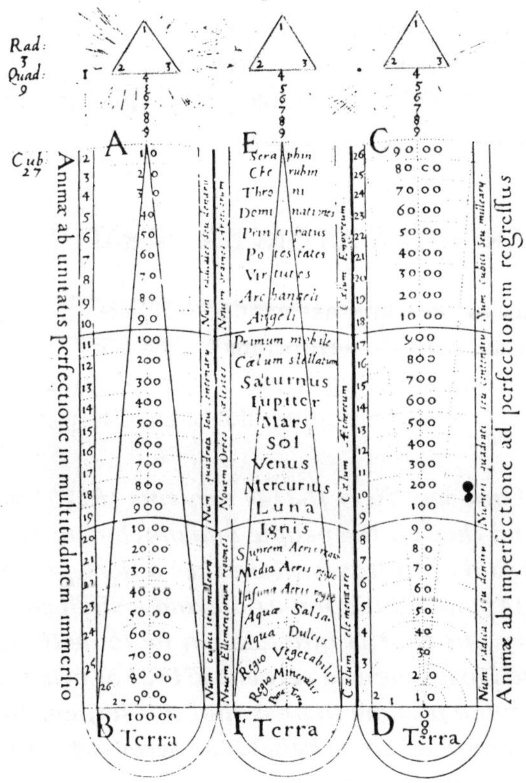

IT IS INTERESTING TO NOTE THAT THE NEXT LEVEL OF ANGELS BELOW THE CHERUBIM HAVE ANIMAL FORMS.

too are **"seraphims"**.

These Chinese **Four Heraldic Animals** are also represented by four ***"Lungs"***. Hence, the term ***"Lung"***, like the term **"seraphim"** or even "cherubim", denotes a class, rank or category, rather than a definite physical form. So, the Chinese ***"Lung"***, as a **"seraphim"**, is the title or rank of the highest angelic beings!

The word **"seraphim"** is from the Hebrew ***"saraph"***, which is from another ***"saraph"*** (coded 8314), which in turn, is from another ***"saraph"*** (coded 8313 — primary root meaning being to "set on fire", to burn or kindle). Hence, ***"saraph"*** came to denote the fiery nature of a creature — the angelic **"seraphims"** of Isaiah 6:2-3,6.

"SERPENT" WAS ONCE A "SERAPHIM"

There appears to be some association between the ***"nachash"*** serpent and the ***"saraph*, seraphims"**. The term ***"saraph"*** was associated with the fiery serpent [8314] of Numbers 21:8, which Moses placed on a pole to counter the bites of serpents [5175]:

> ***And the Lord sent fiery [8314] serpents [5175] among the people and they bit the people and much people died ..And the Lord said unto Moses, Make thee a fiery [8314] serpent [also 8314] and set it upon a pole and it shall come to pass that every one that is bitten when he looketh upon it he lived. And Moses made a serpent [5175] of brass and put it on a pole and it came to pass that if a serpent [5175] had bitten any man when he beheld the serpent [5175] of brass he lived...*** (Numbers 21:6-9).

The term ***"saraph"***, denoting "fiery", was applied to the serpent to denote its fiery nature and quality. But the term ***"saraph"*** is not unique to the ***"nachash"*** serpent, but would have been applied to any other creature to denote a "fiery nature".

Of the term ***"nachash"*** for serpent, Bullinger (1964 - Appendix 19) wrote:

> **The Hebrew for "serpent" (Gen 3:1) is "nachash" from "nachash" to hiss, mutter, whisper, as do enchanters. Secondary senses are to divine, enchant, whence the frequent use of noun as "serpent". The allied Chaldean word means brass, copper, from "an assumed root" meaning to be bright. Various passages tell us that Satan possess a glorious appearance and the Hebrew term probably includes the sense of fascinate, enchant (see Deut 18:10 et al). This element of fascination connects with the later use of "nachash" as "serpent". The term "saraph" (Pl seraphim) is derived from "saraph" a Homonym meaning (1) to burn, (2) to be elevated. In Num 21:8 "a fiery serpent" = saraph; in the following v. "a serpent" = nachash; while in v.6 both words are given for "fiery serpents". The same "saraph" (seraphim) is used of the heavenly ones of Is. 6:2,6. Thus "saraph" is used of a fiery serpent and of an exalted celestial being; "nachash" being similarly used to designated a serpent and a glorious spirit-being.**

Hence, unlike the term **"seraphim"** or "cherubim", which refers to a class, rank, group or category rather than a form, the term ***"nachash"*** refers to a definite physical form denoting a hissing limbless snake.

The Bible indicates that the ***"nachash"*** serpent was once of the different forms of **"seraphims"**. The Bible shows that Satan the "Dragon-Serpent" was once a cherub of **"seraphims"** rank. Thus, the evidence shows that the ***"nachash"*** serpent had lost its position among the **"seraphims"**.

The ***"nachash"*** serpent in the Bible is an animal associated with evil — and, similarly, the Chinese, while associating ***"Lung"*** with good auspicious things, do associate the snake with evil. The Biblical "Dragon-Serpent" was one of the cherubim and **"seraphims"**, while the Chinese ***"Lung"*** not to be mistaken with the former, was another different cherubim and **"seraphims"**! While the "Biblical Dragon-Serpent" is a fallen angel (namely Satan), the Chinese ***"Lung"*** remains a faithful angel of God.

The Bible brands the snake evil and many cultures similar to that of the Chinese do likewise. The Bible calls the **"seraphim"** holy of God — the Chinese similarly do the same thing for ***"Lung"***. All the while, the Chinese are correct to maintain ***"Lung"*** as a Godly symbol.

THE CHINESE EMPEROR TAKING THE STATUS OF *"LUNG"*

The **"seraphims"** have various forms, such as ox, lion, man and snake. This indicates that the term **"seraphim"**, like the term **"cherubim"**, is not distinguished by any particular physical form but is more a title reflecting a status. In contrast, ***"nachash"*** denotes a physical form, that of the serpent.

In fact, the Bible shows that the title "cherubim" was appropriated by the king of Tyrus:

> ***take up a lamentation against the king of Tyrus, and say unto him... Thou art the anointed cherub that covereth; and I have set thee so; that thou wast upon the holy mountain of God...*** (Ezekiel 28:11-19).

The term "cherub" is a title for the upper echelon of beings "anointed" to stand before the throne of God. It is a title which could be appropriated by any man, creature or spirit who qualifies.

Of these "anointed" beings, the **"seraphims"** are the highest, being closest to God.

Knowing that the ***"Lung"***, like the **"seraphim"**, reflects the rank of the highest of angels standing around the throne of God, we may begin to understand why the Chinese Emperor appropriated the ***"Lung"*** as his symbol. Just like the Bible describing the "cherub" as the title of the king of Tyrus. The term ***"Lung"*** is befitting the status of the Chinese Emperor as the highest of his people.

The **"seraphims"** are **"an order of celestial being... act[ing] as the medium of communication between heaven and earth"** (Peloubet 1947 "seraphims"). Likewise, the Chinese Emperor is said to mediate between God in Heaven and the people.

CHAPTER 13

"*LUNG*" AS THE EMBLEM OF THE EMPEROR

DIFFERENT "*LUNGS*" SIGNIFYING DIFFERENT IMPERIAL LEVELS

Why is the Chinese Emperor represented by ***"Lung"*** — that **"seraphim"** or highest angel?

The Chinese Emperor is symbolically the ***"Lung"*** seating on the ***"Lung"*** throne and wearing the ***"Lung"*** robes of gold embroidered with **"nine *Lungs*"** (or eight ***"Lungs"***, as the Emperor himself is the ninth ***"Lung"***). His bedstead is the ***"Lung's"*** bedstead. The emperor's face is the ***"Lung's"*** face and his eyes the ***"Lung's"*** eyes. Proclamations coming from the emperor would be written on yellow paper, of the colour of the **Golden *"Lung"***, and on which was sometimes drawn the **Double *"Lungs"*** with the pearl in between.

In Chinese philosophy, the ***"Lung"*** is the symbol of the **Great Man**. ***"Lung"*** has been appropriated by the Imperial family of China as its family emblem. Since the reign of Kao Tsu of the Han dynasty, 206 B.C., variations of ***"Lung"*** symbolise the different levels of the Imperial family:

- The five-clawed ***"Lung"*** was the emblem of imperial power; the Emperor's throne, his robes, and articles of household use, etc. all bore the device of this scaly monster. It was also assigned to the use of the Emperor's sons, and princes of the first and second rank.

- o Princes of the third and fourth rank were allowed the use of the four-clawed ***"Lung"***.

- o Princes of the fifth rank and certain officials were only entitled to employ the use of a serpent-like creature with five claws as their emblem.

In parallel, the unicorn is the emblem of first rank military officials while the lion is for military officials of second rank and the leopard for officials of third rank.

The following description of court ceremonial, as practiced early in the seventeenth century, will serve as an illustration of the vanished splendour of the past:

> **"When the Emperor of China takes his seat on the dragon throne, flags, chowries, and satin umbrellas are arranged on his right and left hand, and a band of music plays in a large building to the southward. On his right are the military officers, and on his left the civil officers; and they all, at a given signal, bow their heads nine times. The Emperor comes out of his palace in the following manner:- He is seated in a sedan chair covered with yellow satin, with three rows of fringes, twelve chowries and twelve flags, upwards of twenty spears having the points sheathed, and ten horses with saddles and bridles complete, and upwards of twenty horses with the brothers and sons of the Emperor dressed in yellow stain jackets, and armed with bows and swords. Immediately in front of the Emperor is carried an umbrella of yellow satin with three rows of fringe and having the figure of a dragon worked upon it in gold thread and upwards of a hundred men in charge of the women (eunuchs) surround the Emperor's chair. The band of music which plays when the Emperor comes out or enters the palace, consists of a pipe with six stops, two trumpets,**

a fiddle, a lyre, and an alligator harp." (Williams 1931 pp.113-114 — later part quoted 8.).

THE ASSOCIATION OF *"LUNGS"* WITH SAGACIOUS CHINESE EMPERORS

Chinese Emperors regard the ***"Lung"*** as the symbol of themselves the Emperor. Why is it so? There are a number of ways the Chinese Emperors have been associated with the ***"Lung"***.

THE FIVE EMPERORS SYMBOL:

When the **Five Emperors**, Fu Hsi, Shen Nung, Huang Ti, Shao Hao and Chuan Hsu were canonised as the **Five Emperor Gods**, they were associated with certain animals:

> **In The Five Elements according to the Former Heaven Sequence, the five elements of wood, fire, earth, metal, water correspond respectively to east, south, centre, west and north. They are also connected respectively to the five animals azure dragon, red phoenix, yellow dragon, white tiger and black snake-tortoise and the five emperors Fu Hsi, Shen Nung, Huang Ti, Shao Hao and Chuan Hsu.** (Skinner 1982, Table 5 pp.58-59).

In the worship of the **Nine Emperor Gods**, the East, West, South, North and Centre are guarded by the Green, White, Red, Black and Yellow Dragon-Generals (Cheu 1988). Animals of the **Four Cardinal Points**, viz. **Azure *"Lung"***, Red Phoenix, White Tiger and Black Snake-Tortoise, are inter-represented by the ***"Lung"***; so, the **Five Emperors** are symbolically **Five *"Lungs"***.

While the **Five Emperors** were all Chinese Emperors, the Chinese race particularly claim descent from at least three of them; Fu Hsi the first world Emperor, Shen Nung the second world Emperor and Huang Ti the third world Emperor. As these Emperors are regarded as ***"Lungs"***, the Chinese race, therefore, refer to themselves as descendants of the ***"Lung"***. (Hsu and Ward 1984).

THE NINE EMPERORS SYMBOL:

The ***"Lung"*** and moon motif is common in Chinese art. Needham (1959 p.242) writes:

> **"It is important to note that the dragon here is the symbol of a palace, i.e. a whole quarter of the heavens. The limits of this region happen to correspond approximately with those of the occidental constellation Draco, but this can hardly be more than coincidence. In any case the Chinese sky-dragon had originally nothing whatever to do with the idea of a dragon whose head and tail represented the moon's nodes and which accordingly "ate the sun" at eclipses. From this no doubt we derive our term "draconitic months" to designate the time between the moon's successive passages through these points."**

Needham (1959 p.253) notes a symbolism of the ***"Lung"*** and the moon as a portion of the Nine Dragons Screen wall in the Imperial Palace at Peking. **"Nine *Lungs" is*** a well known Imperial motif. Why **"Nine *Lungs"***, not ten or five etc.?

Nine is the number of several auspicious things in ancient China. Is this number ever associated with the Emperor? Yes, in the **Nine Emperor Gods**! The **Nine Emperor Gods** are believed to be the nine human sovereigns who lived in antediluvian times and came after non-human rulers (Cheu 1988; Hirth 1908). These **Nine Emperor Gods** are really the nine patriarchs of the Bible from Adam to Lamech the father of Noah. Therefore, **"Nine *Lungs"*** are the symbol of the **Nine Emperor Gods** or the Chinese memory of the

Biblical nine patriarchs! Again, as these **Nine Emperor Gods** would obviously be the ancestors of all mankind after the Noachian Flood, these **"Nine *Lungs*"** would be the ancestors of the Chinese race!

Not every Chinese Emperor is canonised into an "Emperor God" and thus associated with a ***"Lung"*** of the Heraldic or **Nine Emperor Gods** stature. Such a ***"Lung"*** or "Emperor God" is properly applied only to certain sagacious Chinese Emperors whose feats strike the Chinese memory and hence form the basis of the legend of the ***"Lung"***.

"*LUNG*" OR "SERAPHIM" IS A TITLE MEANING "GOD'S PRIEST-KING"

The Chinese word for "king" is ***"Wang"***, which is an ancient pictorial illustration of the fire (Hsu and Ward 1984 ; also Wu 1982).

Hsu and Ward associate the word ***"Wang"*** with the word ***"Huang"*** for yellow. Despite the attempt of Hsu and Ward (1984) to associate ***"Huang"*** and hence ***"Wang"*** with a "cap", it should be noted that the ancient graph for ***"Huang"*** indicate a light halo, not a cap at the top! Note the graphs for terms associated with light; the small round circles with the central dots really are "lights". Hence, the round circle with a central dot in ***"Huang"*** is not a "cap" but a "light"! The association of ***"Wang"*** and also ***"Huang"*** with the sacrificial fire and light is more correct. Is this not the ancient precedent for the tendency to draw halos around the heads of saints and deities?!

"Wang", being the sacrificial fire, originally means **"priest"** standing in front of the sacrificial fire; so the fire would be seen as "glowing from and above the head". Which is why the ancient priests and sages are shown with halos around their head. But in those ancient days, the priest was also the chief of the people. Or rather, the king usually was the one who performed the sacred ceremony and therefore was the priest of the people. In ancient times, ***"Wang"***, the king, is the chief priest!

Until 500 B.C., ancient China worshipped only one God, the imageless ***Shang Ti*** (Supreme God) (Bilsky 1965). The other religious ceremonies were ancestral memorials which later corrupted into ancestor worships. Only the Chinese Emperor was allowed to offer the annual sacrifices to ***Shang Ti***. The people could not do this on pains of death. The Emperor offered the sacrifices for the people alike the high priest of Israel offering the final annual sacrifice to purge the sins of Israel! The Chinese Emperor is a Emperor-High Priest or Emperor-God!

How is this connected to ***"Lung"***?

In the previous chapter it has been discussed that ***"Lung"*** is not the ***"nachash-draco"*** limbless Serpent of Satan the Devil but the ***"saraph"*** winged-with-hands **"seraphim"** of God. The ***"nachash-draco"*** Snake being is recognised as a wise animal:

> **But I fear lest by any means as the serpent [3789] beguiled Eve through his subtility..** (2 Corinthians 11:3).

> **Now the serpent [5175] was more subtil than any beast of the field which the Lord God had made** (Genesis 3:1).

The **"seraphim"**, while embodying the same wisdom as the ***"nachash-draco"*** serpent, also has another function:

> ***Above it stood the seraphims [8314]: each one has six wings; with twain he covered his face and with twain he covered his feet and with twain he did fly. And one cried unto another and said, Holy, holy, holy is the Lord of hosts; the whole earth is full of his glory...*** (Isaiah 6:2-3).

> ***Then flew one of the seraphims [8314] unto me, having a live coal in his hand which he had taken with the tongs from the altar... Lo, this hath touched thy lips and thine iniquity is taken away and thy sin purged*** (Isaiah 6:6-7).

The **"seraphim"**, highest of angels, carries out the functions of a priest in the purging of sins. Likewise, the Chinese Emperor has his role as a **"King-Priest"**, who dealt and took away the sins of his people through the Imperial worship of ***Shang Ti,*** the Supreme God. The Chinese **"seraphim-*Lung*"** is therefore the title of the Chinese Emperor as God's **"King-Priest"**.

Huang Ti, the Yellow Emperor, is also associated with the central **Golden "*Lung*"**. Fu Hsi (the Biblical Adam), another Emperor-Priest-God, is called **Azure "*Lung*"** of the East. ***"Lung"*** represents the Emperor as the **"King-Priest"** of ancient China. ***"Lung"***, the **seraphim**, is not only the symbol of the highest of angels; it also symbolises the highest human being, the **"King-Priest"**. Hence, the Chinese Emperor appropriated the ***"Lung"*** as his Imperial symbol.

In very ancient times, ***"Lung"*** is a title meaning **"King-Priest"**

CHAPTER 14

ETYMOLOGY OF "*LUNG*"

PART I. THE LEFT SIDE OF THE IDEOGRAM FOR "*LUNG*"

INTRODUCTION

Through etymology, the origin and development of a word or the scientific study of word origins, we can determine the original nature of ***"Lung"***. Both Weiger (1965 p.309) and Vaccari and Vaccari (1950 p.58) interpret the word ***"Lung"*** as an animal with a heavy set body and wings (q.v. Chapter 10). Various theories have been given about the origins of ***"Lung"***:

- o From some lost, ancient flying reptile resembling the alligator or crocodile.
- o From the sinuous form of the Hwang Ho.
- o From the whirling shape of whirlwinds and storms.

But, the evidence so far discussed is that *"Lung"* is a universal heraldic animal of the East in the Four Heraldic Animals representing the Four Cardinal Directions in many cultures.

Thus, the evidence does not support the "Hwang Ho river" or "crocodile" theories, which reflect rather localised significance.

Some more common wider meanings form the real original significance of ***"Lung"***.

The kind of significance found in several cultures which could be connected with a wider significance for the ***"Lung"*** would be:

- o A primary significance as a class of the highest angels, such that its rank was appropriated by the ruler. This significance as an "exalted class" is linked with roles described below.

- o Sacred guardians against evil.

- o A connection with the significance of the East, the direction of the rising sun. This significance could be a mixture of related things like "light", "spring", rains, crop productivity.

In the **Four Heraldic Animals** array, the ***"Lung"*** is interchangeable with the Red Phoenix, White Tiger and Black Serpent. The ***"Lung"*** could be of various forms, though the ancient Chinese relics indicate that it was originally a half-man, half-fish image, evolving into the present popular serpentine form.

Also, only in some cultures like the Chinese is there a secondary additional role of "water regulation". For Hsu and Ward (1984 p. 462) noted a significant historical fact which indicates the "water roles" ***"Lung"*** are additional and came later:

> **..the Shang seldom prayed to the *Lung* for rain ..**

This important clue means that the "*Lung*" originally has nothing to do with water!

CHARACTERS FOR □*LUNG*□

HE VARIOUS DIFFERENT WAYS OF WRITING

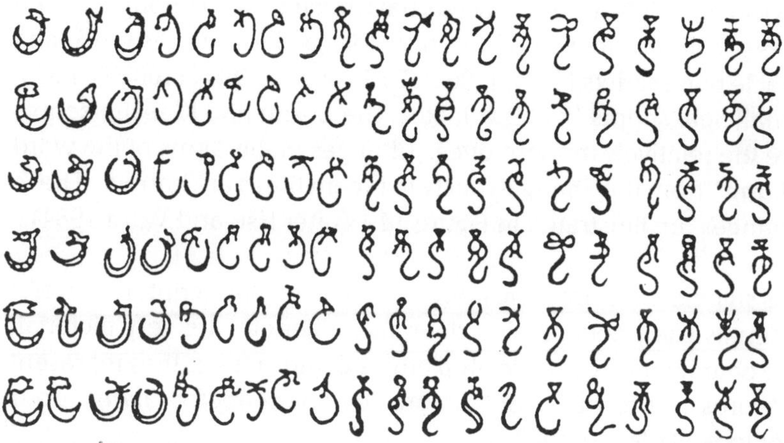

BOVE: ***Oracle bone script*** **BOTTOM:** ***Bronze script***

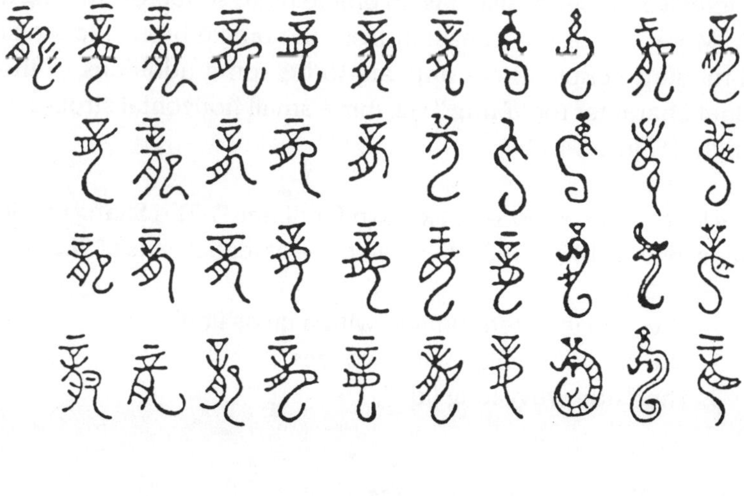

This later addition of the "water roles" is surprisingly indicated by the etymology of the Chinese word for ***"Lung"***. Bearing in mind the several significance of ***"Lung"*** in cultures all over the world, it is possible through etymology to elucidate the origins of the Chinese word for ***"Lung"***.

VARIOUS FORMS OF THE WORD *"LUNG"*

Etymology of Chinese characters have been studied through several sets of scripts uncovered in archaeological digs, such as the Shang oracle bone scripts (1400-1100 B.C.), Bronze scripts (1100-300 B.C.), Small Seal scripts (300 B.C.), etc. The Li-shu and K'ai-shu scripts are the relatively modern ones. Changes in the forms of the word ***"Lung"*** from the Shang dynasty to recent times are known. These changes are illustrated in Figure 14.1 (after Hsu and Ward 1984).

It is significant to note one thing. The oracle bone scripts for several animals like phoenix, bird, deer, fish, tiger etc. are very pictorial; the characters are practically pictures of the animals they represent (Figures 14.1 to 14.7). But the oracle bone script for ***"Lung"*** does not look like an animal!

This is not because the ***"Lung"*** is a mythological creature, for the mythological phoenix also has an oracle bone script resembling a bird. Moreover, in the transition from the oracle-bronze to small seal-modern scripts, there appears to be some additions to the original character for ***"Lung"*** viz. three small horizontal strokes at the right (Figure 14.1).

Let us look at the oldest script known for ***"Lung"***. The Shang oracle bones scripts of 1400-1100 B.C. show three essential parts of ***"Lung"***:

1. The "top inverted triangle with a cross line".
2. The "lower triangle with two legs".
3. The "side wavy long line".

FIGURE 14.1

LUNG IDEOGRAM FOR DRAGON

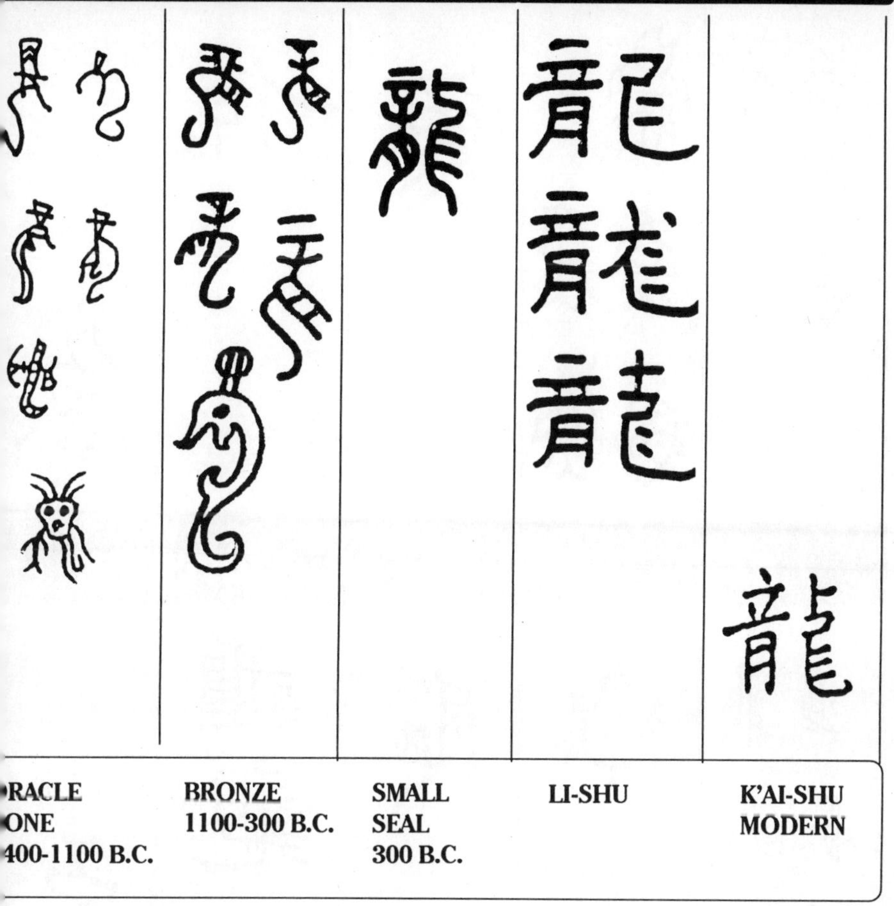

FIGURE 14.2

YU IDEOGRAM FOR FISH
KUEI IDEOGRAM FOR TORTOISE
ORACLE BONE 1400-1100 B.C.
BRONZE 1100-300 B.C.
SMALL SEAL 300 B.C.
LI-SHU
K'AI-SHU MODERN

FIGURE 14.3

FENG IDEOGRAM FOR PHOENIX
NIAO IDEOGRAM FOR BIRD
RACLE
ONE
00-1100 B.C.
BRONZE
1100-300 B.C.
SMALL
SEAL
300 B.C.
LI-SHU
K'AI-SHU
MODERN

FIGURE 14.4

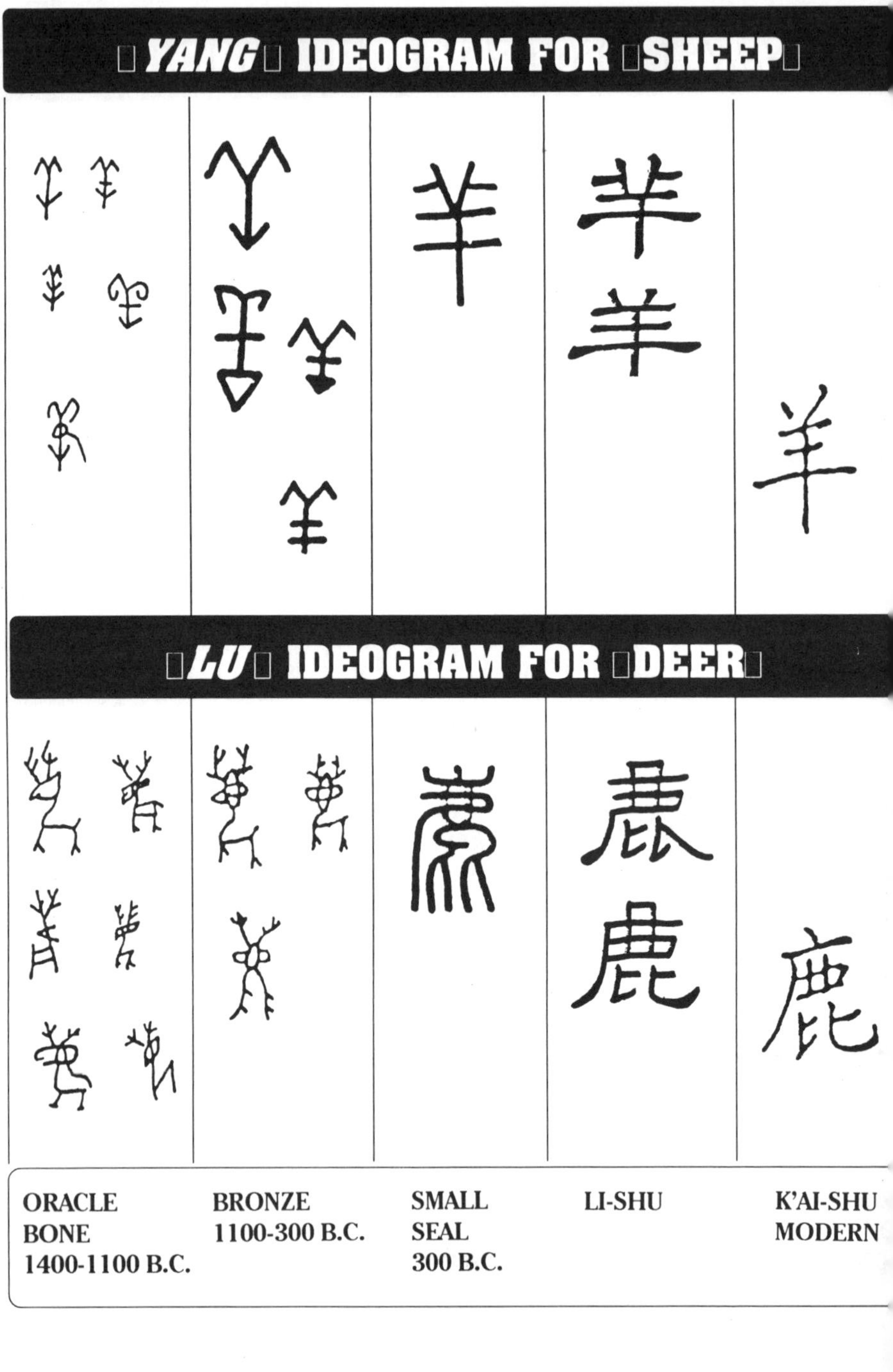
YANG IDEOGRAM FOR SHEEP
LU IDEOGRAM FOR DEER
ORACLE BONE 1400-1100 B.C.
BRONZE 1100-300 B.C.
SMALL SEAL 300 B.C.
LI-SHU
K'AI-SHU MODERN

FIGURE 14.5

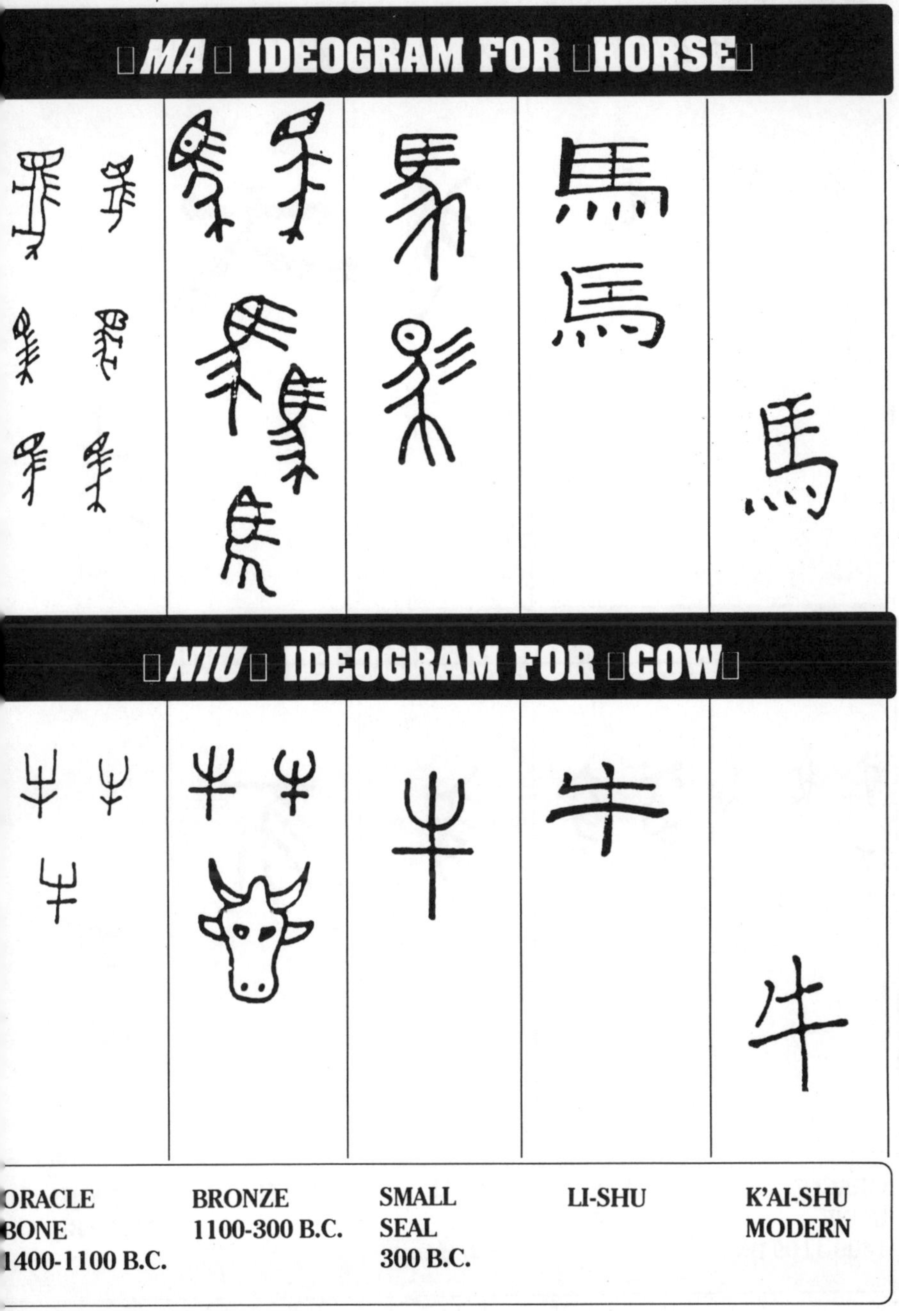
MA IDEOGRAM FOR HORSE
NIU IDEOGRAM FOR COW
ORACLE BONE 1400-1100 B.C.
BRONZE 1100-300 B.C.
SMALL SEAL 300 B.C.
LI-SHU
K'AI-SHU MODERN

FIGURE 14.6

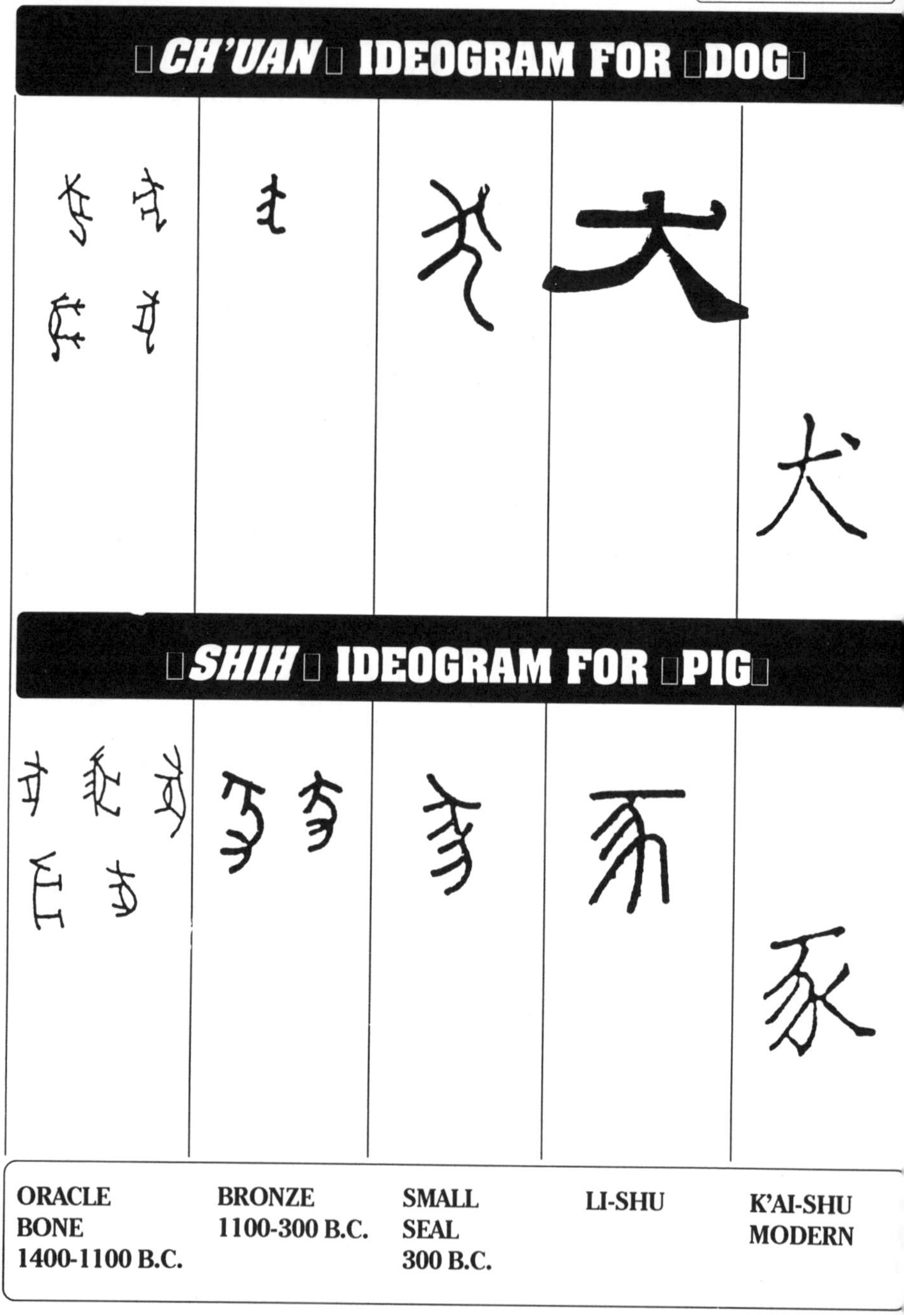
"CH'UAN" IDEOGRAM FOR "DOG"
"SHIH" IDEOGRAM FOR "PIG"
ORACLE BONE 1400-1100 B.C.
BRONZE 1100-300 B.C.
SMALL SEAL 300 B.C.
LI-SHU
K'AI-SHU MODERN

FIGURE 14.7

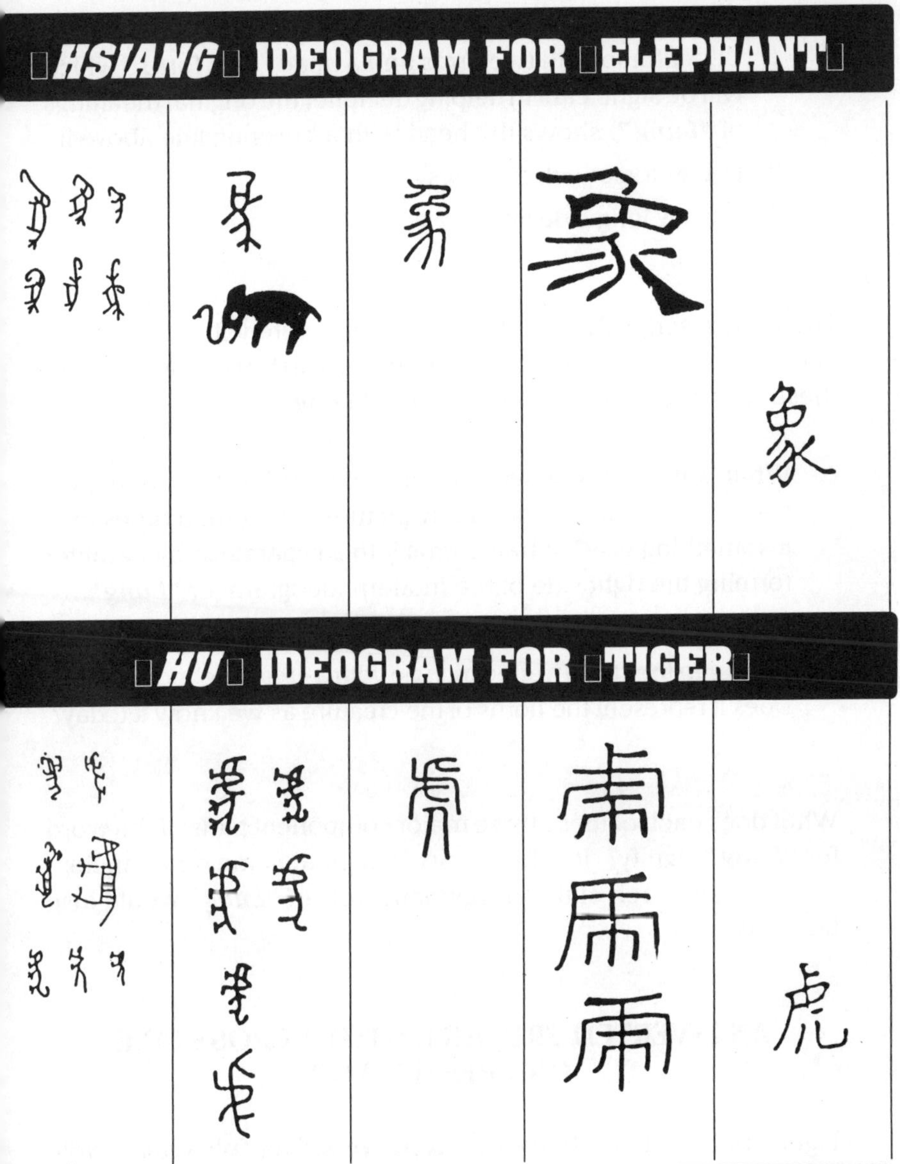
HSIANG IDEOGRAM FOR ELEPHANT
HU IDEOGRAM FOR TIGER
ORACLE BONE 1400-1100 B.C.
BRONZE 1100-300 B.C.
SMALL SEAL 300 B.C.
LI-SHU
K'AI-SHU MODERN

The Bronze script of 1100-300 B.C. also has the three parts:

1. Upper torso with two arms and a head. One form, (which will be significant in helping decipher the original meanings of ***"Lung"***) shows the head with a hovering line above it.
2. Lower torso with two legs.
3. A wavy long side line.

The Bronze script shows a four limbed creature with a long wavy line attached at the waist. There are at least two mysteries to these Shang and Bronze scripts about ***"Lung"***:

- o What is this "long wavy line" at the waist level? Is it really a "tail" as in the image popularly pictured in modern times or is it something else? It transforms into a separate sub-character forming the right side of the modern ideogram for ***"Lung"***.

- o What can the "top inverted triangle with a cross line" possibly be? Does it represent the horns of the creature as we know it today?

What does each of these three major component parts of the word for ***"Lung"*** signify? It is necessary to look at some other ancient words where each of the component parts of ***"Lung"*** would also be shown.

AN INVERTED TRIANGLE WITH A CROSS LINE OR CRESTED TOP

Figure 14.8, middle, shows the word ***"Feng"*** for "phoenix". Note the "inverted triangle at the top with a cross line" found in both ***"Lung"*** and ***"Feng"***. This "inverted triangle" is alike to the "head crest" of the "phoenix" bird. Hsu and Ward (1984) would interpret this as a "horn" for ***"Lung"***. The evidence indicates otherwise:

- o A "Horn" would be as what is seen in the word ***"lu"*** or "deer" (Figure 14.8, bottom). Hence, the "inverted triangle with the cross line" could not be "horn".

- o Should not this "inverted triangle" be a form of "head crest" for ***"Lung"***? As the phoenix obviously does not have a horn, the "head crest" therefore could not be a horn.

Now, look at the "wings" of the phoenix in the oracle bone scripts. The ***"Lung"*** does not have these "wings" strokes. Weiger (1965) and Vaccari and Vaccari (1950) were incorrect to maintain that the modern character of ***"Lung"*** contain "wings".

This "inverted triangle with a cross line" is also found in the word ***"Ti"*** for "Supreme God" (Figure 14.9, middle — which also means "Emperor"). In the Small Seal script, the top is alike to an upper human torso with a head with a line hovering above it in both ***"Lung"*** and ***"Ti"***. The line hovering above the head is associated with something sacred and holy!

The "crested top" of both ***"Lung"*** and the phoenix is this "line hovering above the head" and it is a symbol of the "sacred and holy"! It is not a "horn". But there is something around or on top of the head which is indicative of the "sacred and holy" and hence shows the divine nature of ***"Ti"*** for God, ***"Feng"*** for phoenix and ***"Lung"***.

The word for ***"shang"*** "to deliberate or discuss" (Figure 14.9, bottom) also has an "inverted triangle with cross line". The Small Seal Script has some similarities at the top. This "line hovering above the head" relates to a human head.

Some, following Hsu and Ward's (1984 pp.29-33) interpretation of

FIGURE 14.8

INVERTED TOP TRIANGLE of "*LUNG*"

FOUND IN BOTH *"LUNG"* AND PHOENIX

HORNS IN *"LU"* FOR "DEER" NOT FOUND IN *"LUNG"*.
THE TOP OF "LUNG" IS NOT HORN

ORACLE BONE 1400-1100 B.C.	BRONZE 1100-300 B.C.	SMALL SEAL 300 B.C.	LI-SHU	K'AI-SHU MODERN

the words for "king", may attempt to interpret this "top head crest" as a "feathered cap", on various reasons such as that in battle those in higher authority needed to be identified by their soldiers and tall feathered caps seemed useful this-wise. However, in ***"Feng"*** for phoenix the "top head crest" is obviously not a tall feathered cap! Also, for the words ***"Ti"*** for God or Emperor, ***"shang"*** for "discuss", the similarities at the top indicates this "top head crest" is not a "feathered cap" but is instead associated with **"something hovering above the head"**.

THE TOP OF THE WORD *"LUNG"* IS A HALO

The top of the left sub-character of the word ***"Lung"*** has close resemblance to the word ***"Wang"*** and ***"Huang"*** also meaning "Emperor" (Figure 14.10, middle). According to archaeological evidence the title ***"Wang"*** was first used by the Shang people, though it is likely that term was inherited from the Hsia dynasty (Hsu and Ward 1984 p.29).

Hsu and Ward (1984 p.29) postulate that the two words ***"Wang"*** and ***"Huang"*** are related. They claim that the top, especially in ***"Huang"*** is a feathered ceremonial cap though they noted that other scholars think ***"Wang"*** represents "fire, male organ, axe, a king sitting upright, royal crown".

What does the image of the "top round circle with a central dot and three or four lines" really mean? Look at the word for ***Hsing*** for stars and lights objects (Figure 14.10, bottom). The round circles with or without central dots always signify things related to "lights" and also glorious bright things. They are really shining things! Not caps!

That is, the "top round circle with a central dot and three or four lines" is actually a "light" symbol at the head of the Emperor! It is important to realise this — for this "light" symbol is also seen in one form of the word for ***"Lung"***! (Figure 14.1). The "head with two eyes and four lines" of ***"Lung"*** alike to the "top round circle with a central dot and three or four lines" of ***"Huang"*** — they mean "lighted head".

Both the forms of the words for Emperor and ***"Lung"*** actually have heads which depict something shining or bright there. Something like a "halo" around the head! Which is why that "top round circle with a central dot and three or four lines" actually denotes the "sacred holy" nature of both the Emperor and ***"Lung"***.

How did the "halo" arise? The Emperor is the Priest-King standing in front of the sacrificial fire! So the Emperor's figure would be silhouetted against the fire which would make it seem to radiate from the Emperor's head. The fire could not be drawn in front of the Emperor as this would obscure the image of the Emperor. So what is drawn is the sacrificial fire behind the Emperor. The standing form of the Emperor is obvious. The sacrificial fire would be burning behind the Emperor and would look like fires emitting from the Emperor especially from above his head; hence the "halo" around the head!

Remember earlier we have analysed the words ***"Ti"*** for God or Emperor, ***"shang"*** for "discuss" where the similarities at the top indicates this "top head crest" is associated with "something hovering above the head? This "something" is actually the light of the sacrificial fire — that "halo"! The "halo" as represented by the "top head crest" naturally symbolises something sacred and holy.

The "line above the head" is a "hovering thing", it is the **"halo formed by the sacrificial fire behind the emperor"**!

As for further confirmation that the top hovering line is really the light of the sacrificial fire, we have to look at the word ***"shih"*** for "omen". The word is a radical for many names and things associated with sacrifices and spiritual things, including ***"Ti"*** for "God" or "Emperor" (Hsu and Ward 1984 p.406). It is believed to denote the flat top of the high sacrificial altar. Now what would normally be found at the top of the sacrificial altar? A **"fire"** of course!

FIGURE 14.9

TOP OF "LUNG"

FOUND IN *"TI"* FOR "SUPREME RULER" AND *"SHANG"* FOR "DISCUSS"

TOP OF "LUNG" REFLECTS "HUMAN HEAD" IN "DISCUSSION"

ORACLE BONE 1400-1100 B.C.	BRONZE 1100-300 B.C.	SMALL SEAL 300 B.C.	LI-SHU	K'AI-SHU MODERN

FIGURE 14.10

TOP OF □LUNG□

FOUND IN *"HUANG"* FOR "SUPREME" AND RELATED TO *"HSING"* FOR "STARS AND LIGHT POINTS"

THE TOP OF "LUNG" SIGNIFIES "BRIGHT LIGHT" IN REFERENCE TO "EXALTED POSITION"

ORACLE BONE 1400-1100 B.C.	BRONZE 1100-300 B.C.	SMALL SEAL 300 B.C.	LI-SHU	K'AI-SHU MODERN

So the hovering line really represents the fire and its light and the "halo" it would give out. This is, of course, the real meaning of the "top crest or inverted triangle with the cross line" of ***"Lung"***.

> **The ancient Emperor stood in front of the sacrificial altar. His head would be "bathed" in the glow of the burning fire. Thus, a "halo" surrounded the head, giving rise to the stroke in the ideogram representing something "hovering over the head."**

THE GOLDEN *"LUNG"*

As the Emperor is really the ***"Lung"***, it is not surprising that, in the **Five Emperors** motif, the Emperors were associated with **Four *"Lungs"*** of the **Four Cardinal Directions** plus the **Golden *"Lung"*** at the centre. They represent the major king-priests standing around ***Shang Ti*** the Supreme God. Also, in the **Nine Emperor Gods** motif, they are the nine major king-priests, one after another from Fu Hsi to before Shen Nung. Hence the **Nine *"Lungs"*** as the symbol of the Imperial family. These ***"Lungs"*** are all Priest-Kings! It is not a wonder that ***"Lung"*** symbolises the "divine power" and the "Mandate of Heaven". As king-priests they are also custodians of sacred things!

In the heraldic **Four Cardinal Directions**, Emperor Huang Ti is at the centre symbolised by the **Golden *"Lung"***. Culture historians have wondered why Emperor Huang Ti's colour was "yellow". "Yellow" is also the colour of the Imperial robes. Hsu and Ward (1984) argue that "red" is a more auspicious colour and wondered how "yellow" the so-called colour of earth could be appropriated by the Emperor. Well, the answer is that the Emperor is the king-priest offering the annual sacrifices to ***Shang Ti*** the Supreme God. **"Yellow" is the colour of fire, not red!**

The colour "yellow" therefore signifies the role of the Emperor, as king-priest, standing in front of the roaring golden sacrificial fire! "Red" the colour of blood, while truly symbolising auspicious blessings, is commonly used by the ordinary people. However, "yellow" is usually forbidden to them. Only the Imperial family and those favoured by the Imperial family could use the colour "yellow" to reflect their sole right to act as the king-priest to ***Shang Ti*** the Supreme God. Thus, the colour is connected with something only the Emperor is involved in — the annual sacrificial fire ceremony.

Therefore, it is no wonder why "yellow" is adopted as the Imperial colour.

Emperor Huang Ti was the one who performed this annual sacrifice to ***Shang Ti*** the Supreme God. Hence the memory of Huang Ti as the **Golden *"Lung"***. This is why the ancient Chinese always called the Emperor ***"Lung"***. It is not because the so-called animal ***"Lung"*** is symbolically the Emperor, but rather that the word ***"Lung"*** is the title of the Emperor as the Priest.

This king-priest role is the basis of the several significances of the ***"Lung"*** as the symbol of "divine power" and of its roles as "guardian of sacred things".

Before Huang Ti, the most prominent ***"Lung"*** was Fu Hsi to the East, the **Azure *"Lung"***. Then came Huang Ti, an equally great man, hence a second ***"Lung"*** or the **Golden *"Lung"***. The **"seraphims"** were their angelic spirit counterparts and mediators in their worships of ***Shang Ti*** the Supreme God. All those legends about how Emperors and royal princes appeared imbued with so-called supernatural powers and protections must be due to their association with the **"seraphims"**.

FIGURE 14.11

BOTTOM TRIANGLE OF "*LUNG*"

FOUND IN *"P'U"* FOR "SLAVE" AND *"K'U"* FOR "WORK IN FIELD"

BOTTOM OF "LUNG" REFLECTS LOWER TORSO WITH TWO LEGS

ORACLE BONE 1400-1100 B.C.	BRONZE 1100-300 B.C.	SMALL SEAL 300 B.C.	LI-SHU	K'AI-SHU MODERN

LOWER TRIANGLE WITH TWO LEGS

How about the "lower triangle" which seems to have two legs from the lower edge? Look at the word ***"p'u"*** for "slave" in Figure 14.11, middle. The cross line across one side is the act of cutting off one leg (Hsu and Ward, 1984). This "lower triangle" for the "slave" is indeed the lower part of the human body, i.e. the lower torso and the two legs.

Also see word for ***"k'u"*** "to work in the field" (Figure 14.11, bottom), which shows the "lower triangle with two legs" of the farmer in the field.

For the ***"Lung"***, the "lower triangle" is also the "lower torso with two legs." They are the lower torso of a human being, dressed possibly in a robe, hence the short legs.

CHAPTER 15

ETYMOLOGY OF "*LUNG*"

PART II. THE RIGHT SIDE OF THE IDEOGRAM FOR "*LUNG*"

THE "LONG WAVY LINE" ALONG THE SIDE

Upon the basis of what has been discussed, the image of ***"Lung"*** is that of a standing dressed being standing on two legs, having two hands and with something "sacred or holy" hovering over the head. This is what the left part of the word ***"Lung"*** signifies.

It is the "long wavy line along the side on" the right part of the ideogram for ***"Lung"*** which poses a more difficult mystery. What is it?

- o Firstly, the ***"Lung"*** is not an animal but man! As shown earlier, the oracle bones characters for many animals and birds are pictorial, the character resembling very much the animal it portrays. But the oracle bone script for ***"Lung"*** is very unlike the animal it depicts today!

  A first glance at the oracle bone script for ***"Lung"*** would have drawn a guess that it resembles a standing man. Indeed, that is what it originally is! The Emperor standing in front of the sacrificial fire, the fire roaring above his head, forming what seems a **"halo"** above his head.

- o It would be easier to guess the significance of this right part of the word ***"Lung"*** if we realise that the left part, based on the above image of a standing being with something hovering are the head, is connected to the ancient relationship of ***"Lung"*** with the Emperor. ***"Lung"*** and ***"Ti"*** for God have similar tops in the Small Seal script; perhaps it would be significant to realise ***"Ti"*** also means "Emperor"! In ancient times, the "Emperor" is actually a "God-figure"! It denotes that the "Emperor" is fundamentally a "King-Priest"! The left side of ***"Lung"*** is the sacred "Emperor" in representation of "God"!

"Lung" is really the multiple symbolism of the ancient Emperor as the King-Priest! The left part of the word ***"Lung"*** is the first and primary significance and actually represents the standing Emperor with the sacred thing near his head.

THE "LONG WAVY LINE" SIGNIFIES ADDED ROLES OF WATER REGULATION

The "long wavy line" along the side on the right part of the ideogram for ***"Lung"*** has some characteristic not seen in the earliest ideograms for ***"Lung"***: "three strokes". These "three strokes" appeared only in writings of the Small Seal script of 300 B.C. onwards, but not in earlier scripts! Thus, these "three strokes" were not found in the older oracle bone and bronze scripts.

In Weiger (1965 p.308) and Vaccari and Vaccari (1950 p.58), the "long wavy line" has three lines attached to it. These three lines represent the word ***"shui"*** for "water". The "three strokes" on the right part in later scripts looks like "water" and signifies some later secondary role of the Emperor in water regulation.

IDEOGRAMS WITH LONG SIDE LINES

There are a few ideograms with long side lines.

The word ***"sheng"*** for "holy, sacred" also has a long side line (Figure 15.1, middle). This "holy or sacred" is probably the original root significance of the "long wavy line" in the word for ***"Lung"***.

Probably closest to the long line in the ideogram ***"Lung"*** is the ideogram ***"yang"*** for "sheep" (Figure 15.1, top). In the oracle bone scripts one of the forms has a long line attached to the middle, also on the right. It is quite obvious what such a long line means in the word for "sheep": obviously it represents the string or rope tied to the sheep! In fact, as we shall soon see, the long wavy line in ***"Lung"*** is actually the same string or rope-like thing.

This long line in the ideogram for sheep may also be linked to "holiness or sacredness". This is because the sheep was a very common sacrificial animal.

In the word ***"shui"*** for "water" — some of the forms also have this long curved line (Figure 15.1, bottom). The "sacred, holy" identity could be connected with "water", as water is often considered the symbol of cleansing and therefore holy.

It appears that the "long wavy line" found in ***"Lung"*** was originally associated with something "holy or sacred". Later, it was merged with the "three strokes" to signify "water", apparently in connection with some holy ritual concerning water. They argue that the significance of the "top triangle" of the word for ***"Lung"*** also reflects something holy.

The line along the side on the right part of the ideogram for *"Lung"* denotes "holiness". This "holiness" originally had nothing to do with water. But, later, it was merged with the three strokes denoting water, for water also has auspicious significance.

FIGURE 15.1

IDEOGRAMS WITH SIDE "LINES"

FOUND IN *"YANG"* FOR "SHEEP", *"SHENG"* FOR "HOLY" AND *"SHUI"* FOR "WATER".

THE LINE ALONG THE SIDE SIGNIFIES SOMETHING RELATED TO "HOLINESS".

ORACLE BONE 1400-1100 B.C.	BRONZE 1100-300 B.C.	SMALL SEAL 300 B.C.	LI-SHU	K'AI-SHU MODERN

In later writings from the Small Seal scripts onwards, the right side has an added secondary role of the Emperor — the role as the regulator of water for his people. That is, the right side has the characteristic for "water" as the ancient scripts really show. This right side is not "wings" as Weiger (1965) and Vaccari and Vaccari (1950) postulated. However, this "three lines" for ***"shui"*** is not seen in the original oracle bone scripts and is not the original meaning of this "long wavy line".

It is not only in the word "water" where early ideograms contain the long line associated with "three strokes". This is also clearly and closely seen in the ideogram ***"li"*** for "ploughing" (Figure 15.2, top). The ancient sacredness of "water" could be linked to water supply and irrigation for agriculture!

THE ORIGINAL, TRUE SIGNIFICANCE OF THE LONG SIDE LINE

Now, for that final unravelling of the mysterious " long wavy line".

The answer lies in understanding the ancient Imperial ceremony of the annual sacrifices to ***Shang Ti*** the Supreme God. The Emperor is the only person allowed to worship ***Shang Ti*** while other officials may assist. However, only the Emperor is allowed to step onto **Tien-An-Mien** main altar to ***Shang Ti***. It is similar to the High Priest of Israel who alone, could enter once a year into the holiest Temple to offer the final sacrifice.

What would happen if God struck down the King-Priest or High Priest? No one is allowed into the most holy place. The others could only get the dead body away if one thing is done as the ancient Jews did. The High Priest always wears at his side a long rope or sash! This rope or sash is for the others to use to pull away his dead body!

The Emperor-Priest has to wear a long sash!

FIGURE 15.2

LONG LINES

FOUND IN *"LI"* FOR "PLOUGHING" AND *"CH'OU"* FOR "ARABLE LAND".

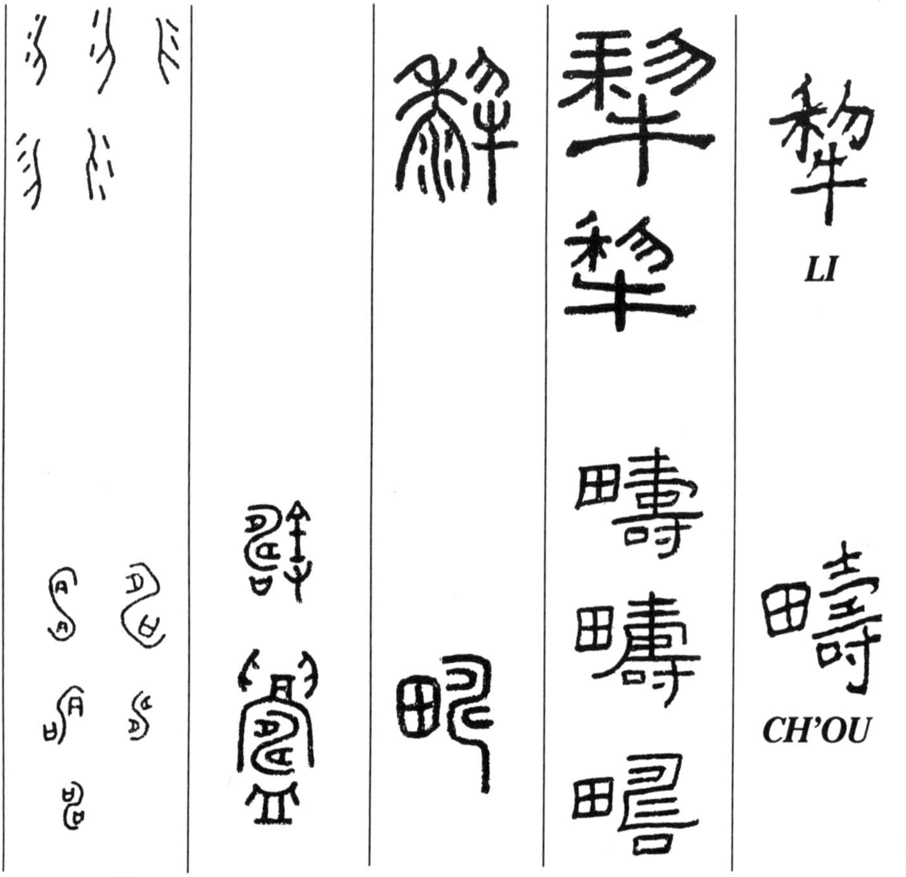

THE LONG WAVY LINE IS ASSOCIATED WITH IRRIGATED AGRICULTURE.

ORACLE BONE 1400-1100 B.C.	BRONZE 1100-300 B.C.	SMALL SEAL 300 B.C.	LI-SHU	K'AI-SHU MODERN

FIGURE 15.3

LINE AT THE SIDE OF "*LUNG*"

A LONG LINE AT THE SIDE MUST BE ALIKE TO THE SASH, *"TAI"*; ALSO SEEN IN *"TI"* FOR "SUPREME RULER".

A LINE AT THE SIDE OF "LUNG" REFLECTS A SASH-LIKE OBJECT DENOTING "EXALTED POSITION".

ORACLE BONE 1400-1100 B.C.	BRONZE 1100-300 B.C.	SMALL SEAL 300 B.C.	LI-SHU	K'AI-SHU MODERN

THE TAIL OF THE "LUNG"
THE PRIEST'S SASH

SHANG JADE CARVINGS

NOTE THE LONG SASH FROM THE WAIST OF THE KNEELING PRIEST. THIS IS THE LONG LINE FROM THE "WAIST" IN THE IDEOGRAM FOR *"LUNG"*.

Hence, the Emperor-Priest originally wore a long sash at his waist! The "long wavy line" is that sash on his side! It is not really "water" or "wings"! This is also why ***"Huang"*** the jade pendant, to hold the sash; is worn at the waist. "***Huang***" thus evolved into a symbol of royalty because it was originally worn to hold the sash when the Emperor acted as the King-Priest!

Some ancient pictures show figures with rather long extended sashes from the waists. Such long sashes have no practical use in normal dress wear. Why were they so long? They were the sashes of the sacred priests! Also, in some words for ***"tai"*** (belt or sash or scarf — Figure 15.3, middle) and ***"chih"*** (towel) and ***"pei"*** (to wear at waist), the lower U-like line clearly indicates the waist apparel. This is the significance of the lower U-like line in ***"Ti"*** for "God or Emperor". The waist apparel, the **sash**, signifies the Emperor as the Priest.

The sash was anciently associated with "holiness" or "sacred office". The long wavy line along the side is the symbol of sacred position.

The whole word ***"Lung"*** really is the ancient memory of the Emperor in his role as the sacred King-Priest of ***Shang Ti*** the Supreme God.

The original Shang oracle bones reveal this true original meaning (Figure 15.4). The Bronze script still preserves this meaning. By the time of the Small Seal script of 300 B.C., the original meanings have been obscured. Later, the "water role" was added and this obscures the significance of the "long wavy line". The "long wavy line" is still there — with the three strokes representing the "water". What we need to realise is that in the Small Seal script period, the "water" identity was added to the word ***"Lung"*** to signify the "water roles". Hsu and Ward (1984 p.462) noted a significant historical fact:

> **..the Shang seldom prayed to the *"Lung"* for rain..**

Of course! For, originally the ***"Lung"*** was not seen as a water creature but was the sacred Priest-King standing in front of the sacrificial fire to ***"Shang Ti"***, the Supreme God and wearing a long sash at his waist.

The line on the right side of the ideogram for "*Lung*" is the "sash". In ancient times, the "sash" was the symbol of "exaltedness" and truly signifies "holiness". Later, it was merged with the three strokes for water, for a key feature of the exalted holiness is the regulation of water.

The various parts of the ideogram ***"Lung"*** emphasise the "holiness" aspects:

- The top stroke on the left side of the ideogram signifies the halo formed by the fire, in front of which the Emperor stood.

- The long wavy line on the right side is the string, rope or sash connected to the holy office of the priest.

  The top stroke on the left side of the ideogram and the long wavy line on the right denote the original sacred status of the Emperor, as the sacred guardian.

- It was later, that the "three strokes" of water were also added. Water has holy significance and further augments the "holiness" of ***"Lung"***.

Keightley (1983 p.346) reported the discovery of ancient Chinese pottery at Kansu dating from a "Hsin-tien Age" of 1300-1000 B.C.

FIGURE 15.4

LINE AT THE SIDE OF □LUNG□

A LINE FROM THE SIDE OF *"LUNG"* IN THE ORACLE BONE SCRIPT HAS BECOME SEPARATED AND, IN LATER SCRIPTS, ADDED WITH 3 MORE LINES.

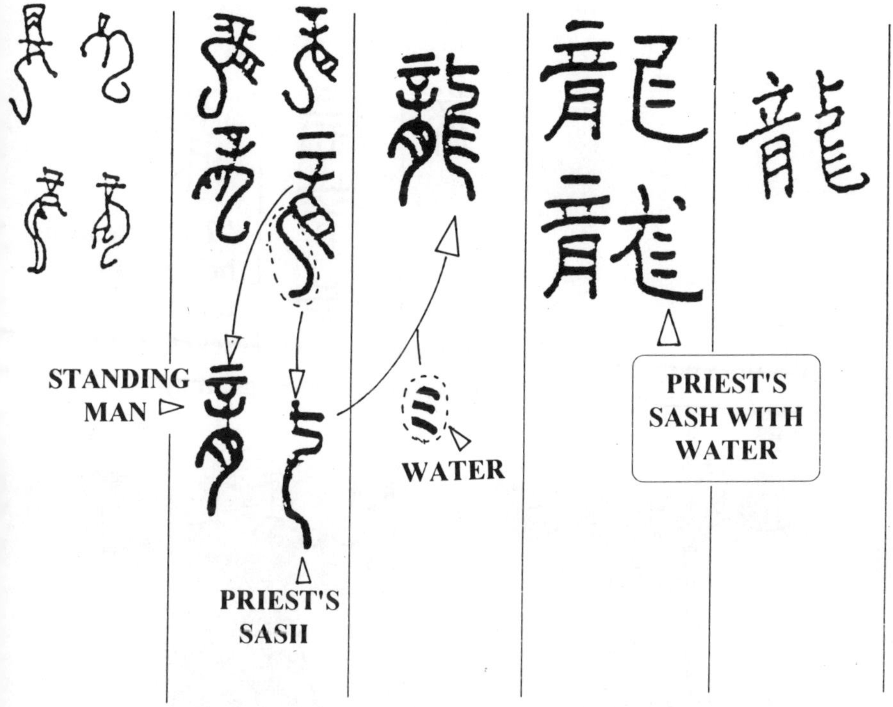

THE 3 ADDITIONAL LINES ARE THE SYMBOL FOR "WATER". THIS REFLECTS A RAIN MAKING ROLE, PERFORMED IN ANCIENT TIMES ONLY BY THE PRIEST.

A LONG LINE WITH 3 STROKES ON THE RIGHT SIDE OF "LUNG" REFLECTS EXALTED PRIEST STATUS.

ORACLE BONE 1400-1100 B.C.	BRONZE 1100-300 B.C.	SMALL SEAL 300 B.C.	LI-SHU	K'AI-SHU MODERN

THE TAIL OF THE □*LUNG*□ THE PRIEST'S SASH

SPRING & AUTUMN POTTERY

"*TAI*" meaning belt, girdle, tape, sash, scarf, bear, carry.

Spring and Autumn pottery figures showing the shape of the sash depicted in the graph *tai*.

SASH AT THE WAIST OF THE PRIEST BECAME A SYMBO OF HIGH OFFICE. AS THE PRIEST WAS THE RAIN-MAKE THE SASH WAS ASSOCIATED WITH WATER, AS REFLECTED BY THE "3 STROKES" ADDED INTO THE SID LINE OF THE IDEOGRAM FOR *"LUNG"*.

INSCRIPTIONS FROM HSIN TIEN POTTERY

1300-1000 B.C.

SOLAR DISC

URENUS SERPENT

BIRD

4-LEGS ANIMAL

2-LEGS MAN (*"LUNG"*)

□LUNG□

THE PRIEST AS RAIN-MAKER

THE ANCIENT EMPERORS, LIKE YAO, SHUN AND YU, HAD DUTIES TO REGULATE THE WATER FOR THE PEOPLE. *"LUNG"*, THEREFORE, BECAME THE EXALTED TITLE OF THE "KING-PRIEST".

Among the selected characters found were five which appear to show the **Four Heraldic Beings** with the fifth as a radiating disc. Three of the four beings were recognisably the limbless snake, the two-legged bird, the four legged tiger. However, the fourth is a standing man with raised hands — the ***"Lung"***! This fourth standing man image is alike to the Shang oracle bone script for ***"Lung"***!

This is why the oracle bone script for ***"Lung"*** does not resemble any animal. For ***"Lung"*** is initially the image of a standing human being, not an animal, and primarily acts as the symbol of "sacred guardian against evil". The modern image of the serpentine animal-like ***"Lung"*** is a contamination made by the introduction of the Indian "Naga-Serpent" into Chinese culture around 200 B.C.

Thus, ***"Lung"*** gets its multiple symbolism from that ancient Emperor the King-Priest, and it is not the other way round. ***"Lung"*** means "King-Priest", the Emperor.

Part C:

DEEPER MEANINGS OF "*LUNG*"

CHAPTER 16

THE DRAGON-PEARL

PART 1: THE ENIGMA

THE DRAGON-PEARL CHASE

The ***"Lung"*** is commonly associated with a red flaming ball called the "dragon-pearl", in front of its mouth. Two ***"Lungs"*** with this "dragon-pearl" between them form a common emblem decorating the roofs of temples. During the Han to the Ch'ing dynasties, the Imperial coat of arms is a pair of ***"Lungs"*** with a pearl in between (Williams 1931 p.112). Two lions playing with an embroidered ball are a common design on cloths and porcelains, which may have the same significance as two ***"Lungs"*** and the pearl of supremacy (Williams 1931 p.218). In a more significant symbol, the pairing of the ***"Lung"*** and the phoenix with the "pearl" between them is another auspicious emblem, often seen in wedding cards. The saying is **"Good fortune of the *Lung*-Phoenix"**.

This **"*Lung*-pearl"** has been represented as a perfect spherical object or ball and is often never depicted by itself. It is white or bluish with a reddish or golden halo and may have antler-shaped flames rising from its surface.

The "dragon-pearl" has been interpreted as the moon, the sun, the symbol of thunder rolling, the egg symbol of the dual influences of nature (***Yin Yang***), the pearl of potentiality (the loss of which betokens deficient power — or the "night-shining pearl", which could be a carbuncle). The "dragon-pearl" is said to be primarily the moon, but for some reasons, may also symbolise other things like the sun.

But, what really is this ***"Lung*-pearl"**?

AUSPICIOUSNESS OF THE "*LUNG*-PEARL"

The ***"Lung"*** is supposed to carry a pearl on its forehead or under its chin, like what the Indians envisaged of their naga-cobra carrying a "serpent stone" in its mouth. In this, the ***"Lung"*** displays a penchant for gems characteristic of celestial beings.

The ***"Lung*-pearl"** has several shades of significance in the various cultures:

- In Taoist and Buddhist religions, it is the jewel in the lotus — "the jewel that grants all desires".
- The Koreans believe the ***"Lung*-pearl"** has supernatural and healing powers.
- The Japanese ***"Lung*-pearl"**, the ***tama***, is a symbol of purity.
- The Indian Vedas calls it "the jewel of good luck".
- The pearl is a valuable item and is one of the Taoist **Eight Ordinary Symbols**. By itself, the pearl is the emblem of good and precious augury, genius in obscurity and also feminine beauty. The offspring of aged parents is called a "pearl".
- In Chinese ***Feng Shui*** or geomancy, a location at the "dragon-pearl" position is considered a very blessed location and good fortune would come to all staying or working at that location.

In some drawings, the ***"Lung*-pearl"** may be delineated as a spiral. The spiral is the symbol of the rolling action of thunder from which issues the flash of lightning. The Japanese dragon may be

THE DRAGON-PEARL

THE CARP LEAPS *"LUNG-MENG"* TO BECOME A *"LUNG"*; SO, THE *"LUNG"* MUST IN TURN SOAR TO THE SKY TO REACH TO THE "DRAGON-PEARL".

THE DRAGON-PEARL IS THE SYMBOL OF THE SEARCH FOR "ETERNITY".

frequently accompanied by a huge spiral to indicate the thunderstorm caused by him. Perhaps, the antler-like flames rising above the pearl are intended to represent the lightning flames.

Two ***"Lungs"*** playing with the ***"Lung*-pearl"** are often depicted with clouds. This play is said to cause the beneficial rains to fall.

Such pearls are especially regarded as the special possessions of sea-gods and water-spirits. Thus, several stories about the ***"Lung*-pearl"** are often connected with the ocean. In these stories, the resemblance to the oyster pearl is obvious. Oyster pearls are anciently regarded as "little moons", being drops of moon-substance which fell from heaven into the gaping oyster. Hence, pearls acquired the reputation of shining at night, like the moon which they were supposed to have come from. Hence, too, the theory that the ***"Lung*-pearl"** is the moon.

THE LINK WITH THE GOLDEN CARP LEAPING "*LUNG-MENG*"

All the Chinese motifs show that the ***"Lung*-pearl"** represents something very sacred and supreme. In fact, the arrangements in the motifs indicate that the ***"Lung*-pearl"** is even more sacred than either the ***"Lung"*** or the phoenix.

The significance of the ***"Lung*-pearl"** can be better understood if we look at the theme of the **"Golden Carp leaping over the *Lung-meng*"**. We have noted earlier that among the various creatures which could develop into a ***"Lung"*** is the carp.

The golden carp is a symbol of good luck and wealth. The theme **"Golden Carp leaping over the *Lung-meng*"** is a common blessing symbol during the Chinese New Year and is also supposed to be specifically the symbol of the Dragon Boat Festival of the 5th day of the 5th Moon. The constant activity of the carp in swimming against the current denotes persistence. The theme also reflects success in the Imperial examinations. The moral is that industrious knowledge is the basis of wealth and prosperity. Hence, **"Golden Carp leaping over the *Lung-meng*"** really symbolises the persistence required to excel in the quest for knowledge.

When the person excels in the quest for knowledge, he becomes, like the successful carp, a ***"Lung"***!

It is when the person becomes a ***"Lung"***, that his quest for the ***"Lung*-pearl"** starts! The ***"Lung*-pearl"** is meaningless to a person unless he is that "carp" which succeeded in **"leaping *Lung-meng*"**.

QUEST FOR "*LUNG*-PEARL" AS ON IMPERIAL ROBE

The theme of **"Golden Carp leaping over the *Lung-meng*"** forms part of the design on the richly embroidered imperial robe of the Chinese emperor. The design on this imperial robe is not created by chance, but purposefully drawn to illustrate the sequence of certain principles the emperor must have in mind. There are three tiers to the design:

- **Quest for Knowledge**. At the lowest parts of the robe, at the feet of the emperor, are designs of water waves with the three-sections ***"Lung-meng"***. This reflects the theme of **"Golden Carp leaping over the *Lung-meng*"**. The first initial step is, therefore, to excel in the quest for knowledge.

  This first step is for the emperor to prepare himself through the quest for knowledge. This quest must include self-realisation.

- **Cooperation.** Then rising above the water waves and the three-sections ***"Lung-meng"*** are two ***"Lungs"***, each on one side of the emperor. This signifies the emperor himself as one of the ***"Lungs"***. The other ***"Lung"*** signifies his assistants like the ministers and generals, with whom the emperor must cooperate with.

The second step concerns inter-human relationships. Cooperation and mutual respect are the keys at this level.

- o **Benevolence**. The third tier is the **"*Lung*-pearl"**, located directly in the middle of the chest of the emperor. A ***"Shen-Lung"*** is coiled around this **"*Lung*-pearl"**.

Thus, the theme **"Golden Carp leaping over the *Lung-meng*"** merely forms the initial part of the story. The third tier of the design, the **"*Lung*-pearl"**, signifies the final and most sacred objective, which the emperor must further reach out for. In ruling the kingdom the emperor must accept his people and the differences therein, strong and weak. To reconcile his people, the emperor must exercise benevolence, especially in leading the strong to help the weak.

Thus, the commentator would be right if he visualises the **"*Lung*-pearl"** as one of the significances noted earlier — **"the egg emblem of the dual influences of nature (*Yin Yang*)"**.

This three-tiered design is also seen in the roofs of some of the Chinese temples. It has been noticed that the lower parts of the roofs may have fishes. These fishes have been taken as talismans against the roof being struck by lightning and fire. However, its real parallel to the three-tiers imperial robe design should be noted. For, above the fishes are the two ***"Lungs"*** on the roof top. Between these two ***"Lungs"***, right at the very topmost height of the temple, is the **"*Lung*-pearl"**!

The **"*Lung*-pearl"** must therefore represent something not only sacred but rather "supreme"!

□*LUNG*□ EMERGING FROM THE □*LUNG-MENG*□

AS EMBROIDERED ON THE EMPEROR'S ROBE.

⇦ **PEARL**

⇦ **DOUBLE □*LUNGs*□**

⇦ **□*LUNG-MENG*□**

THE "GREAT MAN", OFTEN THE NEXT EMPEROR, IS CALLED *"LUNG"*.

THE SIGNIFICANCE OF THE "*LUNG*-PEARL"

As Ong (1994 pp.143-148) shows, the most consistent meaning of this ***"Lung*-pearl"** is that of unity and harmony rooted in benevolence. That the ***"Lung*-pearl"** is but a variant of the mystic round symbol of the ***Yin-Yang Pakua.***

The symbol of the ***Yin-Yang Pakua*** represents the family of eight in harmony; the father and mother with their three sons and three daughters-in-law. The symbol recognises that people are different. Thus, it is the sacred duty of the leader to be able to accept these differences and make use of them in a harmonious way as one big **"family"**. This is not necessarily the same as "unity", as tyrants could impose "unity" with the sword. Rather, the ***"Lung*-pearl"**, or ***Yin-Yang Pakua,*** urges the emperor to lead, in harmony, his people by example and with benevolence.

It is only through benevolence that the leader can hope to create a lasting relationship, be it the family, organisation or the kingdom. The kingdom forced to unite under a tyrant must eventually collapse and break up.

To further impress on the significance of the ***"Lung*-pearl"**, the emperor also wore on his crown a round jade piece. The jade is the sacred stone of the royal family. But the roundness of the jade is to signify the qualities of unity and harmony with which the emperor must rule his kingdom.

The ***"Lung*-pearl"** is thus associated with enduring survival and longevity, for such a benevolence will lead to sustaining of all things. In the **"Three Realms"** concept, this ***"Lung*-pearl"** is rode by ***Shou Hsing***, the God of Longevity.

The ***"Lung*-pearl"** also encompasses several other related qualities, like filial piety, the annual cycle of reunion festivals.

The ***"Lung*-pearl"** thus represents that most important and sacred of all qualities a person, whether an emperor or not, must possess: **"benevolence"**. The ***"Lung*-pearl"** rightly takes its place as being more auspicious than ***"Lung"***, phoenix, emperor or even temple, for the quality of **"benevolence"** of a ***"Lung*-pearl"** is a divine thing.

CHAPTER 17

THE DRAGON-PEARL

PART 2: MYTH OF THE DRAGON "CAUSING" ECLIPSES

FEARFUL DRAGON CAUSING ECLIPSES

When one talks of the "dragon-pearl", one quickly brings to mind the myth that eclipses are caused by monster beasts trying to swallow the sun or moon. We now know that when the sun, earth and moon are in conjunction, solar or lunar eclipses would occur. However, some ancients associated eclipses with that of a fearsome ecliptic dragon — the apparent result of a dragon-like monster moving along the lunar ecliptic and swallowing the sun or moon:

> **This dragon becomes the "black and darkling star called *'head and tail'* "** (Sharf 1976 p.39).

There are evidence that the dark aspects attributed to the astrological dragon came from the Greeks and sources giving rise to Greek mythology:

> **When the seven illuminaries saw the great and fearful dragon with its swift and contrary movement in the company of the twelve distinct and different signs of the zodiac, they suddenly took fright and lost their proper courses, straying from their path: one stood still and another went backwards, one fled to the north, another to the south. And for this reason they have been named "strayers" (the Greek meaning of planets)** (Sharf 1976 p.38, quoting F. Cumont, CCAG Vol. 5 part 2 p.134).

Needham (1959) regards that Chinese astrology originally did not have the "dragon eclipse" theory:

> **"It is important to note that the dragon here is the symbol of a palace, i.e. a whole quarter of the heavens. The limits of this region happen to correspond approximately with those of the occidental constellation Draco, but this can hardly be more than coincidence. In any case, the Chinese sky-dragon had originally nothing whatever to do with the idea of a dragon whose head and tail represented the moon's nodes and which accordingly 'ate the sun' at eclipses. From this no doubt we derive our term 'draconitic months' to designate the time between the moon's successive passages through these points...Noteworthy in this connection is the fact that the value of the period 27.2122 days was obtained by Tsu Chhung-Chih already in the +5th century...but since the nodes are of course not fixed, rotating round the ecliptic once in 18.6 years approximately, the original symbolism cannot have applied to them... and if it was transferred to them later on this can only have been due to the importation of the Indian idea of the monster (or monsters) Rahu and Ketu...The ball was then no longer the 'moon pearl' but the sun, and is indeed represented as red in colour, with issuing flames. In a case like this multiple layers of symbolism are naturally to be expected.."** (p.252).
>
> **The false association of the dragon with eclipses could be attributed to the spread of Indian theory with Buddhism that two imaginary planets Rahu (Lo-Hou) and Ketu (Chi-Tu) which personified the ascending and descending nodes of the path of the moon also account for the eclipses.** (p.228)

There is a later development of a close connection between the ***"Lung"*** and the lunar movements; hence the dragon becoming a creature responsible for eclipses. The later association of the ***"Lung"*** with eclipses could be attributed to the spread of Indian Buddhist theory that two imaginary planets ***Rahu*** (***Lo-Hou***) and ***Ketu*** (***Chi-Tu***), which personify the ascending and descending nodes of the path of the moon also account for the eclipses (Needham 1959 p.228).

"TLI" DRAGON AS FIRST OF SACRED TRIADS

The controversy about the "pearl" being the moon is elaborated in the Jewish Kabalic treatment of the **"Tli"**, a creature which is the equivalent of ***"Lung"***. Remarkably, the Jewish Kabalic tradition shows that, like the Chinese ***"Lung"***, this **"Tli"** also suffered a transformation from an original auspicious entity into something malevolent; in both cases, into the evil serpent.

The Hebrew Kabalic book **Sefer Yetsirah** (Book of Creation) mentions the **"Tli"**, a mystical entity with very great but vague powers and calls it a form of dragon (Sharf 1976 p. 6). The Kabalic writer Donnolo, attempted to connect this mystical dragon with other Jewish and non-Jewish celestial dragon of astrological and astronomical functions. By examining Donnolo's views we can detect how changes through centuries actually clouded the original meanings of the dragon.

"Here is the cycle of the planets, the dragon and the constellations for the year 4706 from the creation of the world, by which we can know in which constellations, and in which degree of those constellations will be found the seven planets and the dragon." (Sharf 1976 p. 11).

Sefer Yetsirah tells of the final triad of triads to which all creative acts of the foundation numbers and letters are tied to. This final triad rule over all the results of creation (Sharf 1976 p.33). The **Sefer** associates the Hebrew letters as a triad, the "mothers", the "heptad" and the "doubles" and these correspond to three primordial elements (air, water, fire), as well as the creation forms of universe, time and man and finally to the dragon, the sphere and the heart (Sharf 1976 pp.26-27). The dragon is regarded as the "mother" or progenitor of all that was, is and ever will be. The sphere is the universe turning around the north-south poles while the heart rules over what is fundamental for the moral order. The dragon is more difficult to define and is compared to the king ruling over the universe (just like the Chinese ***"Lung"*** is the symbol of the emperor).

The three components of dragon, sphere and heart appears to be paralleled by the Chinese representation of the **"Three Realms"** concept of Heaven, Earth and Man, with Heaven as the source of all things. This Jewish Kabalic **"Tli dragon"** is connected to the very forces of Heaven, indicating that **"Tli"**, like the Chinese ***"Lung"***, is a power at the level of Heaven. However, this parallel is not perfect.

THE "TLI" DRAGON IS NOT THE SAME AS THE "NACHASH" OR "TANNIM" DRAGONS

While the Bible translates **"tannim"** as dragon and associates it with the **"nachash"** serpent, the Kabalic dragon is not **"nachash"** but comes from a rarer word **"Tli"**. **"Tli"** is a word of doubtful etymology and has several interpretations. It is comparably rare; there are less than a dozen sources where it occurs instead of, or in addition to, the common words for a dragon, **"nachash"** or **"tannim."** (Sharf 1976 p.34).

The evidence is that **"Tli"** is the Jewish Kabalic equivalent of the Chinese ***"Lung"***:

- o Sharf (1976 p.34) writes: **"He created the Tli from water and fire in the shape of a great dragon, like the great twisted serpent, and made for it a head and a tail and put it in the fourth heaven, which is the middle heaven, the abode of**

the sun." In Chinese astrology, the abode of the sun is in the eastern quarter of heaven and is the place of the Chinese **Azure** ***"Lung"***.

- The **"Tli"** is a creature supposed to support the world on its "fins" (Sharf 1976 p.36). "Fins" are found in creatures like fishes. Thus, **"Tli"** has fish-like components like the Chinese ***"Lung"***. In fact, the world is often pictured by the Chinese as supported by four ***"Lungs"***.

- As noted earlier, this **"Tli"** dragon is compared to the king ruling over the universe. Just like the Chinese ***"Lung"*** is the symbol of the emperor.

"TLI" IS LINKED IN A SOUTH-NORTH DIRECTION, TO "WAIN"

The **Sefer Yetsirah** does mention the supreme status of the **"Tli"** dragon in regulating the heavenly bodies (Sharf 1976):

- **..two Tlis like two dragons or two twisted serpents with their twists like two rings, one against the other. One Tli is stretched out to the north of the other. The head of one touches the tail of the other and vice versa, while in their movement they change over from south to north and from north to south. They are in the fourth heaven, the abode of the sun. Six of the constellations are joined to one of them and six to the other...The two luminaries and the five planets are also joined to them ..all of them by the spirit of God...This is the Tli: it rules all the planets and the constellations** (p.35).

- **The sphere turns the constellations, the planets and luminaries..The Tli is stretched out inside the sphere...The Wain is set to the north of the Tli and close to it. Its end**

CELESTIAL GLOBE

**MADE BY FERDINAND VERBIEST
IN 1673 FOR THE PEKING OBSERVATORY**

**THE CHINESE BELIEVE THE STARRY HEAVENS
ARE CONTROLLED BY
FOUR "*LUNG*s".**

touch the ring of Tli..The Wain turns the Tli and its ends are moved by the power of the Tli's turning.... (p.35).

- **..the whole world depends on the Tli, the sphere and the heart. For just as the world with all that is in it is ruled by the Tli and the sphere, so is man ruled by the heart..The Tli is in the world like a king on his throne..** (pp.35-36).

- **..the constellations are like servants, the Tli is like a king, the Wain is like a directing agent..** (p.36).

The powers of the **"Tli"**, oriented along a north-south axis, appears to be purely physical, ruling the universe by moving and controlling the heavenly bodies. Therefore, as eclipses can only be caused by celestial movements along the ecliptic, the north-south oriented **"Tli"** cannot "eat" any heavenly body to cause eclipses.

It is supposed to be the permanent force regulating the whole universe, without which none of the heavenly bodies could move in their orbits. But, note that the **"Tli"** appears to be controlled to a certain extent by another body, the **"Wain"**. This **"Wain"** is the Great Bear, which the Chinese deem as the seat of the throne of ***Shang Ti*** the Supreme God.

Remember, earlier that it was stated the triad of **"Tli"**, sphere and heart appear alike to the Chinese **"Three Realms"** concept of Heaven, Earth and Man. Actually, Heaven is represented in the Chinese culture by ***Shang Ti*** in His seat — the Great Bear or **"Wain"**. If the heart symbolises Man at the lowest level, then the Middle Realm of Earth is really the combined **"Tli"** and sphere. The Hebrew illustration of the double **"Tli"** is illustrated by the **Hermes Bird** concept. The Chinese illustration of the two ***"Lungs"*** is shown in the **"Three Realms"** concept. The **Hermes Bird** in the Hebrew illustration or the Phoenix in the Chinese illustration is really the **"Wain"** controlling the **"Tli"**.

THE ORIENTATION OF "*LUNG*", LIKE "TLI", IS ALSO NORTH-SOUTH

Hopkins (Needham 1959 pp.249-250) suggests that the ancient forms (going back 2000 B.C.) of the character for the Chinese **"Three or Twelve Chhen"** is the tail of the scorpion or dragon and should be regarded as part of the constellations of **Scorpio**. The ***Hsin Hsiu***, which is in **Scorpio**, is symbolically the **"heart of *Lung*"** of the eastern palace. **"Chhen"** appears to mean "celestial marking point". This Chinese interpretation means ***"Lung"*** is oriented with its head to the north and its tail (or "heart") in the south (where ***Hsin Hsiu*** is). This north-south orientation is also the Hebrew Kabalic viewpoint of north-south "axis mundus" of the **"Tli"** dragon.

CHANGE OF POLAR ORIENTATION TO LUNAR PATH

Originally, the Hebrew **"Tli"** dragon has an **"axis mundi"** which is a north-south direction. However, the Byzantines with the Arabs and the Westerners have a dragon which is the name given to the imaginary line joining the lunar nodes, the points where the monthly orbit of the moon crosses the ecliptic, the zodiacal belt which is of course the apparent annual orbit of the sun. The ascending node where the moon passes from south to north of the ecliptic is called the dragon's head or **"caput draconis"** (Western) or **"ra's al-jawzahr"** (Arab). The reverse, where the moon moves from north to south, is the dragon's tail **"cauda draconis, dhanab al-jawzahr."** (Sharf 1976 pp.38-39).

The lunar nodes are not static but appear to move round the ecliptic once in every eighteen and a half years (Sharf 1976 p.41). The equinoxes, the two points where the ecliptic cuts the equator also retrogress, though much slower, for they make one revolution every 25,800 years. This means the equinoxes change into a new constellation of the zodiac once every 2,150 years. In 1980, the vernal equinox is passing through **Pisces** towards **Aquarius** — the Greeks previously saw it in **Aries**.

Sharf (1976) agrees with Needham (1959) that the **"*Lung*-Tli"** could not cause eclipses:

> **"And the Tli has obviously turned here (in the Kabalic Donnolo concept) into the lunar dragon, just as it has in the Baraita. The 'axis mundi' cannot darken the sun and the moon, nor can it be oriented east to west. But does Donnolo contradict himself in this way, just as he contradicts himself over the way in which the Tli, as 'axis mundi', is joined to the constellations and the celestial sphere, merely because he must follow the Baraita."** (Sharf 1976 pp.40-41).

The animation of the "head and tail" of the **"Tli"** as the "exaltation and dejection" (strongest or weakest zodiacal powers) of the dragon leads to the seven planets becoming nine (Sharf 1976 p.42). The Indians described this dragon's head and tail (***Rahu*** and ***Ketu***) are involved in the solar and lunar eclipses; being two additional bodies to the existing seven planets. This newness of the two additional planets is recognised as **"two new planets were taken into account of by Hellenistic and Byzantine astrologers."** (Sharf 1976 p.42).

The "eclipse causing dragon" connected with two new planets is not original but an obviously later addition. The myth of the fearful dragon is the result of some ancient change in the concept of the direction of the so-called "astrological dragon". When **"Tli"** is in the south-north alignment it could not possibly be associated with eclipses. It is only when the ancients turned the direction to try to make the "astrological dragon" lying along a east-west alignment of the ecliptic that the dragon assumes its false fearful reputation. The dragon as represented by **"Tli"** is never originally a black and darkling star!

The false approach to turn the **"Tli"** dragon into a fearsome monster could be detected in Greek mythology about the dragon. The Greek dragon is the fabled animal found in the Garden with the Forbidden Fruits of Immortality or some equivalent fabulous sacred treasures. The Greek heroes trying to take these sacred treasures had to confront the dragon guarding the Garden. The brave courageous heroes slew or tricked the dragon and went off with the sacred treasures to live happily ever after. Yet, the Greek heroes were nothing but thieves bent on a wicked act while the dragon was merely being loyal to its appointed duty to guard the Garden and the sacred treasures within. So we find the evil became "good" and the loyal dragon became the "fearsome monster". What an irony!

The original ***"Lung"*** was that good angel who was appointed by God to guard the sacred treasures of Heaven. It is those who came against this ***"Lung"*** who were the evil people. The ***"Lung"*** can be "a black and darkling star" only to the evil and the wicked. The Chinese **Azure *"Lung"*** is the heraldic animal of the East. The bull-horned bearded man with the fish tail was the cherubim who stood at the east gate to prevent Adam and Eve from re-entering into the Garden of Eden to take the fruits of the Tree of Life. The **Azure *"Lung"*** is a good creature though some have reasons to try to present it as being evil.

There are ambivalent views about the nature of the **"Tli"**. Some take the head to be warm and beneficent and the tail as cold and maleficent. The Babylonians held that the dragon's head increased the effects of both beneficent and maleficent planets. According to Hindus, the sun, Saturn, Mars, and the dragon's head are generally maleficent. In Byzantine sources both nodes are maleficent. The Baraita adopts the Muslim tradition that the head brings happiness and the tail, the opposite (Sharf 1976 p.44).

Sharf (1976 p.44) notes: **"This is one reason why Donnolo, apart from his fidelity to the Baraita, needs the Tli as a lunar dragon, in spite of the contradictions that his description of it then has to suffer." "Tli"** is originally the north-south "axis mundis" physically controlling the universe, but has been turned into an east-west "lunar dragon" to suit false theories of "malignancy and goodness". In trying to do so, Donnolo was, forever, trying to equate the **"Tli"** dragon with the "serpents". The dragon eating the sun or moon and causing the eclipses is a false, twisted story.

DOES THE BIBLE MENTION THE "TLI"?

We have noted that the **"Tli"** has a "head and tail". It is said that this "head and tail" which was actually meant by the prophet Isaiah:

> ***Therefore the Lord will cut off from Israel head and tail, brush and rush, in one day*** (Isaiah 9:14).

There was an attempt by Donnolo (Sharf 1976 p.45) to then link this head and tail to what Job wrote:

> ***By his spirit he hath garnished the heavens; his hand hath formed the crooked serpent*** (Job 26:13).

Donnolo speculated that Israel lost some astrological wisdom etc. linked with a lunar dragon. But note verse 15 of the book of Isaiah:

> ***The ancient and honourable he is the head; and the prophet that teacheth lies he is the tail*** (Isaiah 9:15).

Here, **"Head and tail"** does not refer to an astrological body but refers respectively, to the honourable person and the liar. In the wars which destroyed Israel, the honourable (the 'head') and wicked (the 'tail') of Israel would be removed. The **"head and tail"** has nothing to do with Donnolo's **"Tli"** dragon! Through such a twisted application Donnolo also tried to falsely equate **"Tli"** to the serpent.

Sharf (1976 p.48) indicates that the presentation of the **"Tli's"** head and tail with beneficent and maleficent influences could be due to Gnostic heresies, where the lunar dragon was automatically evil because it was primarily the instrument the evil god controls his creation. The early Christian Church knew Gnostics **"believe a dragon, a serpent, from the heights at the North Pole encompass the East and the West looking at everything and overseeing everything, so that nothing done in the world escapes it"** (Sharf 1976 p.49). This dragon was positioned between the **Great and Little Wains.**

THE "*LUNG*-PEARL" IS SHANG TI THE SUPREME GOD!

Yehudah ha-Levi (A.D. 1075-1145) expounded that the **"Tli"** (**"jawzahr"** of the Arabs) is the embodiment of the rationale of the universe and the hidden things which cannot be perceived by the senses. Some like Ibn-Gabirol stated that the **"Tli"** is the divine providence which could act against the rule of the stars: **"The stars have a master who darken their light."**

We have traced why the majestic Chinese ***"Lung"*** came in some way to be falsely associated with the evil Serpent. Likewise, the Western treatments of the **"Tli-jawzahr"** dragon shows that originally this dragon is a benevolent entity but that new theories tried to attribute dark influences to the **"Tli"** dragon and to turn the **"Tli"** dragon, like the Chinese ***"Lung"***, into the serpent, the representation of the Devil.

But, turning back time and tearing away the false layers, we find the **"Tli"** dragon in Jewish Kabalic philosophy is what the Chinese ***"Lung"*** is to the Chinese — a very powerful but blessed influence and the good holy creature of God.

As the "eclipse dragon" is false, the **"*Lung*-pearl"** could not be the moon nor any physical object. Certainly, nothing to do with the evil serpent. It is, as the Jewish Kabalic philosophy originally knew, the representation of sacred Heaven.

The **Four Heraldic Animals** surround this central orb, the ***"Lung*-pearl"**. The ***"Lung"*** guards the way to this ***Yin Yang*** or ***Tao*** of Heaven principle. This pearl, or central orb, is the **"Wain"** controlling the "**Tli-*Lung*"**. The **"Wain"** or Great Bear, being the symbol of the throne of ***Shang Ti***, the Supreme God, is actually the symbol of God.

This ***"Lung*-pearl"** is not the moon but represents the Formless Imageless ***Shang Ti***, the Supreme God.

CHAPTER 18

THE AZURE "*LUNG*" IN THE EAST

THE EMPEROR AS "*LUNG*"

In the heraldic positions of the ***Pakua***, the ***"Lung"*** is in the East. There must be some essential links between the claim of the Chinese to be descendents of the ***"Lung"*** and the position of ***"Lung"*** in the East! Of course, the Chinese people are from the East. But the ancient secrets tell more than that!

Why is the **Azure *"Lung"*** in the East, differentiated from the **Golden *"Lung"*** at the Centre? Look again at the associations of the Chinese Emperors with the **Four Heraldic Animals**:

> **In The Five Elements according to the Former Heaven Sequence, the five elements of wood, fire, earth, metal, water correspond respectively to east, south, centre, west and north. They are also connected respectively to the five animals azure dragon, red phoenix, yellow dragon, white tiger and black snake-tortoise and the five emperors Fu Hsi, Shen Nung, Huang Ti, Shao Hao and Chuan Hsu.** (Skinner 1982, Table 5 pp.58-59).
>
> **In the worship of the Nine Emperor Gods, the East, West, South, North and Centre are guarded by the Green, White, Red, Black and Yellow Dragons or Generals** (Cheu 1988).

Note these significant points:

- o The **Four Heraldic Animals** of ***"Lung"***, phoenix, snake and tiger could also be **Four *"Lungs"***. That is, the **Five Emperors** are equivalent to **Five *"Lungs"***! As the whole Chinese race particularly claim descent from Fu Hsi, Shen Nung and Huang Ti and these emperors are regarded as ***"Lungs"***, the Chinese therefore regard themselves as descendants of the ***"Lung"***. (Hsu and Ward, 1984).

- o Similarly, the **Nine Emperor Gods** are believed to be the nine human sovereigns who lived in antediluvian times and came after non-human rulers (Cheu 1988; Hirth 1908). These **Nine Emperor Gods** are really the nine patriarchs of the Bible from Adam to Lamech the father of Noah. Therefore, the **Nine *"Lungs"*** are the symbol of the **Nine Emperor Gods** or the Chinese memory of the Biblical nine patriarchs! Again, as these nine emperors would obviously be the ancestors of all mankind after the Noachian Flood, these **Nine *"Lungs"*** would be ancestors of the Chinese race!

The symbolism of the **Five Emperors** and **Nine Emperor Gods** keeps on stressing that ***"Lung"*** is the Emperor. The ***I Ching*** emphasises ***"Lung"*** as the **"Great Man or Ruler"**. The primary significance is that the ***"Lung"*** and the Emperor are the same. Such a significance indicates that the ***"Lung"*** is the dim Chinese memory of a great ancient Master! Someone in ancient times, someone linked to the Imperial line of ancient China, whose exploits altered significantly the fabrics of the ancient Chinese culture and gave rise to the legend of the ***"Lung"***

EMPEROR FU HSI, THE AZURE *"LUNG"* IN THE EAST

Why was Fu Hsi called the **Azure *"Lung"*** and Emperor of the East? According to one of several versions of the legend, Fu Hsi and his sister Nu Hwa were the first two human beings who existed after a time of great primeval watery waste. Fu Hsi and Nu Hwa were created in the famous ***Kun Lun*** Mountains, the legendary home of Immortals. There are two very interesting aspects in the legend of Fu Hsi and Nu Hwa:

o Firstly, they were brother and sister but yet they were also husband and wife and gave rise to the rest of the human race.

  This aspect alone would have identified Fu Hsi and Nu Hwa as the Biblical Adam and Eve! That is, the Chinese (indeed the whole human race) descended from Adam and Eve or Fu Hsi and Nu Hwa!

o Surprisingly, the geographical landmarks of the ***Kun Lun*** Mountains are known to ancient Chinese for the landmarks were given in the ***Shan Hai Ching*** (Waterbury 1952). The ***Kun Lun*** Mountains are said to be located :

  2,700 miles west of China
  South of the Western Sea
  On the shores of shifting sands (desert)
  North of the Salt Lake (Dead Sea)
  North of the Red River (Red Sea)

  Such landmarks identify the place of creation of Fu Hsi and Nu Hwa as right in ancient Mesopotamia, the Biblical location of the Garden of Eden where Adam and Eve were created!

Fu Hsi and his sister-wife Nu Hwa were the Middle East and Biblical Adam and Eve! The Chinese honour Fu Hsi as the World First Emperor. Hence, it is natural for the Chinese people to claim descent from ***"Lung"*** for the **Azure *"Lung"*** is Adam! Huang Ti, the other ***"Lung"***, is also the ancestor of the Chinese people.

FU HSI THE AZURE *LUNG*

FU HSI, FIRST WORLD EMPEROR, AND HIS WIFE AND HALF-SISTER NU HWA, WERE THE FIRST MAN AND WOMAN. (WESTERN HAN STONE RELIEF)

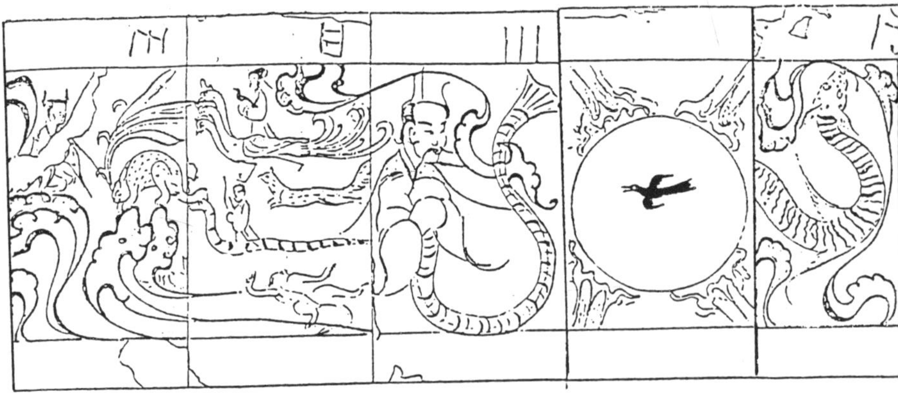

FU HSI

OTHER RELIEFS OF FU HSI AND NU HWA

Wu Liang tomb-shrine relief (second century A.D.)

TOP: WU LIANG TOMB RELIEF (A.D. 200)
BOTTOM AND RIGHT: HAN STONE RELIEFS (200 B.C. TO A.D. 220)

It is a mistake to assume that the watery waste before the creation of Fu Hsi and Nu Hwa was the Biblical Flood which drowned the whole world and through which only eight human beings of the family of Noah survived in an ark. According to the Bible the earth was also a watery waste before the creation of Adam and Eve as the first two human beings:

> ***And the earth was without form and void; and darkness was upon the face of the deep. And the Spirit of God moved upon the face of the waters. And God said, Let there be light and there was light...*** (Genesis 1:2-3).

These astonishing details show that the ancient Chinese knew the legend of the Garden of Eden. Such a remembrance should not be surprising if the human race did radiate from Mesopotamia, where the oldest civilisations were found. In the migrations, the races would carry forth versions of even more ancient tales. To determine further the secret of Fu Hsi the **Azure *"Lung"*** in the East, it is necessary to examine other versions of this tale.

The Chinese **Four Heraldic Animals** are found in other ancient cultures in the Middle East. We have noted that the Chinese ***"Lung"*** is equivalent to the ox in the Biblical-Kabalic-Jewish **Four Heraldic Animals:**

> ***And before the throne..were four beasts full of eyes before and behind. And the first beast was like a lion and the second beast like a calf, and the third beast had a face as a man and the fourth beast was like a flying eagle. And the four beasts had each of them six wings about him and they were full of eyes within and they rest not day and night saying Holy, holy, holy, Lord God Almighty which was, and is, and is to come*** (Revelation 4:6-8).

Now the cherubim stood on the right side of the house when the man went in and the cloud filled the inner court ...And when I looked behold the four wheels by the cherubim, one wheel by one cherub and another wheel by another cherub: and the appearance of the wheels was as the colour of a beryl stone..And every one had four faces: the first face was the face of a cherub, and the second face was the face of a man, and the third the face of a lion and the fourth the face of an eagle...And the cherubim..stood at the door of the east gate of the Lord's house...(Ezekiel 10:3,9, 14, 19 - verse 9 indicates there were four cherubim).

The Chinese ***"Lung"*** is the Kabalic **"kerub"** a bull-horned, bearded man with a limbed forefront and the backbody and tail of a fish. This bull-headed sphinx is featured in Assyrian, Egyptian and Indian hieroglyphs (Whittick 1960 p.137). It is also Neptune, god of the sea. That bearded crowned god having a man's upper torso and lower body that of a fish; pictured holding a trident. The fish-tailed lower part of the body is characteristic of early versions of Emperor Fu Hsi.

The Kabalic memory of the ancient animals says the bull-horned bearded man with the fish-tail (or ***"Lung"***) is the angel placed to prevent Adam and Eve from re-entering the Garden of Eden to partake of the **Tree of Life**! The Bible indicates that this gate of the Garden was in the east; the Chinese ***"Lung"*** in at the east:

So he drove out the man; and he placed at the east of the garden of Eden Cherubim and a flaming sword which turned every way to keep the way of the tree of life (Genesis 3:24).

"Lung" is this same "angel" who guarded the East gate of the Garden of Eden! Adam and Eve were driven to the East; they likely went to ancient China! Traditions indicate that Adam went to Ceylon in India and that Fu Hsi travelled to where the rising sun was, leaving Nu Hwa in the west in the ***Kun Lun*** Mountains. Thus, from ancient times, Adam was associated with the East gate and the angel who guarded East gate. The Chinese relate this to Fu Hsi, the **Azure *"Lung"*** of the East!

In the inter-relations of the **Four Heraldic Animals** of the **Four Cardinal Directions** the various cultures share a fundamental link in that the angel or being of the East is Fu Hsi who is also Adam. As the Chinese went East, the place to which Adam was once driven to, they appropriated the symbol of Adam as the angel in the East.

THE FLAMING SWORD — THE WEAPON OF THE *"LUNG"*

There is another clue to the real identity of the ***"Lung"*** viz. the Mesopotamian-Biblical memory of this angel of the East. The Chinese remember these **Four Taoist Heavenly Kings** or **Buddhist Chinkangs** (Williams 1931):

> Guardian of the East. Land Bearer. White-faced with a ferocious appearance, copper coloured beard, carries a jade ring, a spear and a magic sword .
>
> Guardian of the West. Far-Gazer. Blue-faced, carries a four-stringed guitar.
>
> Guardian of the South. Lord of Growth. Red-faced, holds an umbrella.
>
> Guardian of the North. Well-famed. Black-faced, has two whips, bag, and a snake.

Only the Guardian of the East carries a sword and also a spear. The other three Guardians do not have any actual weapons. Now, the ***"Lung"*** has always been described as a creature with a "sword"

> **So although he gives prosperity and happiness to his people, within his mouth there is also a sword ready to strike at a moment's notice. With a god of such power watching one's actions man should be most careful, so that later there will be nothing for which he can be blamed".** (Plopper 1835 pp.45-47).

> **"He is supposed to have a head like a camel, with a pearl in his forehead, with a long beard, back of which are ni-ling and with a sharp sword as a tongue"** (Plopper 1935 pp.47-49).

Is there not in the Bible any angelic creature with a sword? Of course, that very angel guarding the East gate of the Garden of Eden!:

> ***So he drove out the man and he placed at the east of the garden of Eden Cherubim and a flaming sword which turned every way to keep the way of the tree of life*** (Genesis 3:24).

This "flaming sword" is actually the so-called characteristic breath of fire depicted as coming out from the mouth of the ***"Lung"***! This is the same angel whom the renegade prophet-priest Balaam met:

> ***Then the Lord opened the eyes of Balaam and he saw the angel of the Lord standing in the way and his sword drawn in the way: and he bowed down his head and fell flat on his face*** (Numbers 22:31).

The Biblical **"Angel of the Lord"** with the flaming sword is thus ***"Lung"***! This **flaming *"Lung"*** is alluded to in other Biblical passages:

> ***And the Lord went before them by day in a pillar of cloud to lead them the way; and by night in a pillar of fire, to give them light; to go by day and night*** (Exodus 13:21).

> ***Who maketh his angels spirits; his ministers a flaming fire*** (Psalm 104:4 (also Hebrew 1:7).

This ***"Lung"*** is the **"Angel of the Lord"** and is the one who followed Israel:

> ***Behold I send an Angel before thee to keep thee in the way and to bring thee into the place which I have prepared*** (Exodus 23:20).

Remember that ***"Lung"*** or the "Double-Horned, Bearded, Fish-tailed Angel" was also the sea god Neptune with his trident. This "flaming sword" of the ***"Lung"*** is also "lightning":

> **Moving majestically among the storm clouds; it unfolds and washes its mane in the dark whirling whirlpools of heaven and earth. Its claws are like lightning forks, its scales glisten in the rains. Its voice is like thunder in the winds which scatter the withered forest leaves and renew the spring. The *"Lung"* therefore signifies the essence of flux and change, therefore of life itself.**

The "lightning" is often shown as a three or five-forked trident (Whittick 1960). The "lightning" of the ***"Lung"*** is the "trident" of Neptune! The guardian, protective and even punishing roles of the ***"Lung"*** are portrayed as such; they are the original fundamental significance of ***"Lung"***! The ***"Lung"*** brings blessings and punishments according to the moral acts of man. As the high angel **"seraphim"** the ***"Lung"*** also performs priest-like roles between God and Man.

The Bible mentions that the east gate of the Garden of Eden was guarded by "cherubim", that is, more than one angel was involved. Very likely there were two angels; hence the ancient memory of guards for doors are often in pairs. This is the real ancient origin of the **Twin Door Gods** and the **"Double *Lungs*"** as guardians of sacred things.

The **Twin Door Gods** or **"Double *Lungs*"** symbol is connected to the ***"Nien"*** Beast and the planet Jupiter:

> **The placing of these red cloths and the firing of fire-crackers during the New Year are to scare off the "Nien" Beast. The homes of those who do not perform these precautions would be entered by the "Nien" Beast and misfortune would befell the household...Now, The "Nien" Beast or "Year Beast" appeared to be related to the "Year Star" Jupiter. Jupiter, the "Year Star" (Hsu and Ward 1984 pp.434-435) is the most important planet and its movement is used to determine times of sacrifices. The Shang named Jupiter after the symbol of an execution axe. The planet Jupiter therefore appeared linked to punishments of the Shang dynasty — it is also the planet thought to be controlled by the highest god, to show the Mandate of Heaven.**

Jupiter is the Roman equivalent for the Greek God Zeus. Hence, this **"Angel of the East-*Lung*"** is linked with the ***"Nien*** **Beast-Jupiter-Zeus-Neptune"**. The ***"Lung"*** is originally a creature associated with **"guardian roles"** and is linked with Emperor Fu Hsi, the Chinese memory of Adam. The roles of ***"Lung"*** in regulating the beneficial influence of water compose a later secondary development!

THE EVOLUTION OF THE ROLES IN REGULATING WATER

When Adam and Eve were driven from the Garden of Eden, they were driven from a blissful place into a harsher world where they had to toil the grounds for their living:

> ***And unto Adam he said, Because thou hast hearken unto the voice of thy wife, and hast eaten of the tree, of which I commanded thee, saying, Thou shalt not eat of it: cursed is the ground for thy sake, in sorrow shalt thou eat of it all the days of thy life; Thorns also and thistles shall it bring froth to thee; and thou shalt eat the herb of the field; In the sweat of thy face shalt thou eat bread, till thou return unto the ground....*** (Genesis 3:17-19).

The **"Double *Lungs*"** were placed at the East gate of the Garden of Eden to prevent mankind from re-entering the sacred place to obtain the sacred treasures within. But these mighty "cherubim" were not just to guard the East gate and continue Man's misery. Why were Adam and Eve sent East?

For there is a more important reason why God sent Adam and Eve to the East. And not West, South or North. This is because mankind had been sent into a harsh world where **water** is important for the **tilling and cultivation of the grounds!** The power to regulate water appears to be in the hand of the angel of the East, **Azure *"Lung"***!

Hsu and Ward (1984) assemble evidence that agriculture originated in the East and spread from there to the rest of the world. The environmental conditions in the East were such that tilled agriculture was possible in the rich soils and fish plentiful from the rivers and seas. People would be poor but they would not starve. Such conditions have disappeared from most parts of the modern world and remained only in some isolated spots in South-East Asia.

"Lung", through its inherent powers over water, also becomes the angelic benefactor of mankind in the East.

This is why early Chinese records (e.g. ***Shu King***, Gorn 1903) show that a cardinal role of the ancient Emperors has been to regulate water and irrigation for the empire! The early Chinese Emperors were famous for their roles in regulating water supplies and control of floods. Failure in doing so could lead to being deposed from the throne. By understanding this, we may realise how the image of the ***"Lung"*** develop:

- The animal associated with the cultivation of crops in irrigated areas is the **ox**! Hence, the Double Horned head of ***"Lung"*** and the association of the **ox** with the East in other cultures.

  The oxen driven ploughing ceremony thus became a central ceremony the Emperor must observe. When the new Chou Emperor was asked to place his hands on the plough drawn by the ox, he walked 900 steps. His prophet-strategist prophesied that his Chou empire would last 900 years.

  The ox is also the animal the Emperor offered as a sacrifice before he stepped onto **Tien-An-Mien** ("Altar of Heaven") to worship ***Shang Ti*** the Supreme God. The Emperor first called on Heaven to forgive the sins of the people and then ask Heaven to bless the people.

- The rivers and lakes contain another animal associated with food — the **fish**. Hence the **"fish-tail and fish scales"** of the ***"Lung"*** and the half-man, half-fish being of the East in other cultures....and the Dragon Boat Festival....and the fish trying to leap over ***"Lung-meng"*** to become the ***"Lung"***.

  The ancients compared the art of Government with the art of fishing. The fish-turning into ***"Lung"*** became a symbol of diligence and industriousness towards success and prosperity.

- The "flaming sword" is the lightning and fiery breath of ***"Lung"***. The "pearl"? It is really the sacred object sought after — that object in the Garden of Eden — the ***Yin Yang*** principle and the real ***Tao*** of Heaven, which the ***"Lung"*** guards.

- And not forgetting the "beard". In Chinese culture the "beard" is usually a symbol of the scholar, a wise man (Eberhard 1972).

It is the Emperor who gives the ***"Lung"*** many of its significance, not the other way round.

CONCLUSION

We can now understand how the legend of ***"Lung"*** evolved from the first man, the Biblical Adam or the Chinese Fu Hsi, the first Emperor-God-Priest and first ***"Lung"***. The ***"Lung"*** was originally a bearded man with two horns and a fish-tailed lower torso carrying the "flaming sword" or trident, guardian of the "pearl". Many significance were merged into one person, the first ***"Lung"***. Despite the eventual distortion of ***"Lung"*** into a serpentine creature, some original records still show a more ancient humanoid image of the ***"Lung"***.

The ***"Lung"*** was originally linked with the **"guarding roles" of the "angel of the East"**! From time immemorial, the leader of the people offered sacrifices to Heaven, first to propitiate for the sins of the people; then, to ask Heaven to bless the people. The angelic mediator was that ***"Lung"*** — and the man who made those offerings was the Emperor, the Priest-King. The ***"Lung"*** the "Emperor" were symbolically the same single entity!

The roles of the ancient Chinese Emperor in the important cardinal task of regulation of water supplies, irrigation and floods give the ***"Lung"*** its further symbolic significance.

Other implications could be derived from the correspondence of the Chinese ***"Lung"*** of the East to the Mesopotamian-Biblical Two-Horned, Bearded, Fish-tailed Cherubim, also of the East. ***"Lung"*** is not **"Naga"** the Cobra Serpent, nor is it the western Biblical "Dragon that Old Serpent". The ***"Lung"*** stands as the **Angel of the Lord** executing the very **Will of God** in distributing blessings as well as retributions on mankind. ***"Lung"*** mediates between God and Man as the priest-like **"seraphim"**. ***"Lung"*** is therefore the highest of the angels right at the throne and hand of God in the East.

The Chinese rightly call themselves descendants of ***"Lung"*** as all are descendants of Fu Hsi the Chinese Adam, the wise sagacious **Azure *"Lung"***. It should be no more a wonder why the Chinese culture and civilisation is so appropriately and intimately linked with the glorious majestic symbol of ***"Lung"***.

CHAPTER 19

THE MAJESTIC LEGEND OF THE GOLDEN *"LUNG"*

INTRODUCTION

It is a tragedy that so many legends have been buried in the sands of time. So much so that what were once true and sacred have become tattered by doubts and cynical views. The noble great deeds of ancient heroes have become difficult to speak of, least of all believed in.

We have examined the many meanings, significance and development of the ***"Lung"*** symbolism. The primary and initial significance of ***"Lung"*** is its role as the "exalted guardian of sacred things". This significance is originally centred, in the very ancient past, in that **"Great Man"** who was that ancient Emperor, the king-priest. It is only later, still in the ancient dim past, that the Emperor was eventually responsible for the crucial ancient task of water regulation. ***"Lung"*** then got its secondary significance as a fabulous creature of water and clouds. How did ***"Lung"*** get the water roles?

It is appropriate at this point to turn back the pages of time to reach an overall perspective and reveal the real ancient reasons for the origin of the water symbolism of ***"Lung"***. These ancient reasons are linked with the association of the ***"Lung"*** with the mighty exploits of some ancient Emperor(s) which have lasting impacts through several cultures besides that of ancient China.

THE WATER LEGEND BEGINS

Out of those distant past, dim in human memory... darkened by whirling clouds and battle cries.... during the birth agonies of human civilisations... came the majestic ***"Lung"***. .....***"Lung"*** was the answer to the cries of those frightening times and Heaven's gift of mercy to that ancient world.

"Lung" was someone of international stature, that ancient Emperor, the chosen one of Heaven, who, in trying to bring harmony to a distraught Old World, had to wield the powerful sword of ***"Lung"*** under the "Mandate of Heaven". Ever since those stirring times, the legend has lived on. Let us try to understand that legend.

THE ANCIENT BATTLE OF THE GODS

Compared to the **Azure *"Lung"*** who is connected to the first world Emperor Fu Hsi the Chinese Adam, the Adamic story is more well known; being rooted in the creation tales of many cultures. It is the story of the later **Golden *"Lung"*** which was more obscure and which is connected to the water roles.

Around 2000 B.C., the ancient world was rocked by what was tantamount to an ancient international world war! The Indian legends remembered the ancient titanic battles as the wars of the demonic Rakhasas led by Vitra the Dragon-Serpent king against the devas-gods led by Indra, and in another version the Ramayana. The Teutonic legends tell of the Valhalla and the Twilight of the Gods under Odin and the Greeks remembered that ancient battle of the Titans led by Typhon the monster Dragon-Serpent against whom Zeus fought.

The Middle East nations of Babylon, Assyria and the Hittite Empire remembered that enemy of the demons as the important "Storm or Sky God" (this is the god Crom, worshipped by that popular comic figure, "Conan the Barbarian"). The "Storm God" fighting a series of battles to destroy the demons and their leader the **"illuyanka"** Serpent. The single common factor in all these legends is that those wars were fought in order to release the waters which were held by the Serpent!

Through these ancient great battles, remembered by so many cultures as reflecting that ancient titanic worldwide war, is that central figure and saviour, that **Great Man**, the **Golden *"Lung"***, or the "king of gods".

THE LEGEND OF HUANG TI'S BATTLES WITH CH'IH YU

Do the Chinese legends contain any stories of a battle with demons and giants? The answer is "Yes". The Third World Emperor, Huang Ti, the **Golden *"Lung"***, fought a series of battles against giants and was nearly defeated by them!

Most enchanting of all the secrets is that ***"Lung"*** actually contains the ancient legend of the **Golden *"Lung"*** or Emperor Huang Ti's great efforts to bring peace to a disturbed ancient world! In China, the legend is that Huang Ti battled the race of giants led by the two-horned giant king, Ch'ih Yu, and brought peace to the entire world. Ch'ih Yu was leader of a race of giants. He appeared to be related in some way to Huang Ti because Huang Ti was supposed to be a half-brother of Shen Nung and Ch'ih Yu was a descendent of Shen Nung.

The Chinese word for **"Ch'ih Yu"** contains the sub-character for "mountain serpent". Vitra, the Dragon-Serpent leader of the demonic Rakhasas fighting against the devas-gods led by Indra, was also called the "serpent lying at the mountain." The evil of this giant leader was such that it must have given rise to the evil attached to the **Chiao Dragon**, a serpent believed found in marshes, including at the foothills.

YELLOW EMPEROR HUANG TI, the GOLDEN □*LUNG*□

DEFEATED CH'IH YOU, THE FIRST ARCH-REBEL AND LEADER OF THE GIANTS.

THE IDEOGRAM FOR "CH'IH YOU" INCLUDES THE SUB-CHARACTERS MEANING "MOUNTAIN SERPENT".

Of Ch'ih Yu's people, Walls and Walls (1984 p.43) write:

> **"All of them had two sharp horns on their heads, four eyes, six hands and hair growing erect behind their ears. Their feet were like hooves of an ox and they could walk as well as fly...They were skilled at making weapons — spears halberds, axes, shields and arrows. Above all they possessed superhuman strength."**

Hsu and Ward (1984) note that Ch'ih Yu was the inventor of iron weapons.

According to the legend, Huang Ti first divided the world into the four directions. It was after this that Ch'ih Yu managed to flee to the south and raise a revolt against Huang Ti. Ch'ih Yu led his giants, the forest and marsh monsters. Huang Ti organised "the spirits and gods from all directions and finally even bears, tigers, foxes, coyotes and other fierce animals". This is reminiscent of the Indian legend of Ramayana, where Rama and Hanuman the Monkey God led the gods and also animals against demonic and giant hordes of Ravanna the Demon King.

The giant Ch'ih Yu at first defeated Huang Ti, despite the latter calling forces from all over the world. Huang Ti was aided by a mysterious young man known as ***"Ying Lung"*** and a lady known as the Celestial Lady Ba (Walls and Walls 1984). ***"Ying Lung"***, who seemed able to control moisture and spread rainstorms, was apparently a great personnel of the East (likely the same person as Emperor Ta Yu, founder of the Hsia dynasty). Lady Ba on the other hand could also control rains for she could stop the rains and there would be drought where she goes. Huang Ti got further advice from a "Dark Lady" and he was able to defeat Ch'ih Yu. Ch'ih Yu was shackled and then executed and so ended a dark worldwide terror to the human race.

The Indians recorded the legend in the Ramayana. Among the

Teutonic cultures it was the Twilight of the Gods. In Greek mythology, it was the Gods led by Zeus against the Titans. The Bible recorded it as the legend of Nimrod and his Tower of Babel.

So began the legend of ***"Lung"***, the "chosen one of Heaven". Heaven only intervenes when there are serious troubles which humanity cannot solve or when demonic forces are too strong. During such times, Heaven would raise a "chosen one" to sweep away all the evil. The ***"Lung"*** is that "chosen one" whose caliber must be that of a leader of the people; who, for the Chinese, is the Emperor.

THE LEGEND OF HUANG TI AND THE FOUR DIRECTIONS

We have noted earlier the Chinese tradition that Emperor Huang Ti was the one responsible for assigning the directions of the Five Emperors (Wu, 1982; Walls and Walls, 1984).

Though Huang Ti appeared contemporary to Shen Nung, at least Fu Hsi was no longer alive around Huang Ti's time. Hence, the use of the **Five Emperors**' names must be symbolical — they likely represent some major racial or national differences. That is, the assignment of the different emperors to the different directions of the world is really another way of saying that the major races were assigned to different parts of the world. The legend indicates that Huang Ti must have managed to assume a powerful worldwide position, whereby Huang Ti could assign the races to different parts of the world. Huang Ti took and remained in the centre and he was the **Golden *"Lung"***.

Are there legends in other races that tell of a similar ancient division of races? Yes, in ancient Biblical history!:

> ***Now these are the generations of Noah, Shem, Ham and Japeth and unto them were sons born after the flood..By***

> ***these were the isles of the gentiles divided in their lands; every one after his tongue, after their families, to their nations..Out of that land went forth Asshur and builded Nineveh..the families of Canaanites spread abroad. And the border of the Canaanites was from Sidon..unto Gaza..even unto Lasha... And unto Eber were born two sons; the name of one was Peleg; for in his days was the earth divided; and his brother's name was Joktan....the sons of Joktan. And their dwelling was from Mesha as thou goest unto Sephar a mount of the east...These are the families of the sons of Noah after their generations in their nations and by these were the nations divided in the earth after the flood....*** (Genesis 10:1-32).

This remarkable Bible passage tells of the division of the earth according to the families of Noah. This incidence of division occurred during the time of Peleg, about 2246 to 2008 B.C. This period is not far from the contemporary period of Huang Ti (2688 B.C.).

The two incidents are one and the same ! A very important ancient world event occurred! One, the above Biblical passage, as remembered by the ancient Jewish people. The other as remembered by the ancient Chinese! Only someone very powerful and prestigious enough could arrange for such massive worldwide migrations. Someone like Noah or his sons.

In this division, the Chinese people were assigned the Eastern position, the position assumed by Emperor Fu Hsi, the **Azure *"Lung"***. While Huang Ti occupied the central position and appropriate for himself the symbol of the **Golden *"Lung"***. As Huang Ti, the **Golden *"Lung"***, is an acknowledged ancestor of the Chinese race, the central symbolism of ***"Lung"*** in Chinese culture would have been natural. However, Huang Ti is not the only ***"Lung"*** in Chinese culture.

THE EVOLUTION OF THE SYMBOLISM OF *"LUNG"*

China remembers; for the Emperor is always the "chosen one of Heaven". The legend of ***"Lung"*** thus involves two different great men, one the more ancient **Azure *"Lung"***, namely the World First Emperor and first man, Adam or Fu Hsi himself. The other and later is the **Golden *"Lung"***, who was the Third and last World Emperor Huang Ti himself. Huang Ti himself was associated with another ***"Lung"***; ***"Ying Lung"***, a celestial winged ***"Lung"***.

THE INITIAL SIGNIFICANCE

The primary axis of significance of ***"Lung"*** is formed by the line from Fu Hsi (the Biblical Adam) the First World Emperor to Huang Ti the Third World Emperor, being respectively the **Azure *"Lung"*** and **Golden *"Lung"***. This primary axis is infused with the august symbolism of sacredness, of guardian roles, of vigilance against evil and the very power of the **"flaming sword of *Lung*"**. This primary axis of significance is therefore one of divine power of Heaven. Various Emperors forming that line compose of two main lines:

- First of before the Flood, the **Nine Emperor Gods**, who are really the first nine patriarchs or kings who lived before the Noachian Flood. They are the Biblical Adam to Lamech the father of Noah. Noah was the 10th patriarch.

  Adam or Fu Hsi was the first ***"Lung"*** and Emperor God.

- Second, through the Flood, ***"Lung"*** passed through the **Five Emperors** symbolised by the various directions. Adam was Fu Hsi in the East and Huang Ti was in the centre. Noah is known as Emperor Shen Nung and occupied the south. Shao Hao and Chuan Hio who occupied the west and north were the son and grandson of Huang Ti.

These symbolisms of the emperors are in the first place of majestic divine Heaven power, of **Door Gods** and **"Double *Lungs*"** and the sacred ***"Lung*-phoenix"** significance against evil. In this primary axis significance, the emperor is also the King-Priest and is associated with the sacrificial fire to ***Shang Ti*** the Supreme God. Standing before the sacred sacrificial fire to ***Shang Ti*** the Supreme God, the emperor King-Priest must have appeared bathed by the roaring flames. His head must have seemed to be surrounded by the flames. Hence, the "lighted or crested head" of ***"Lung"***. Hence, the ancient graphs of ***"Wang"*** and ***"Huang"*** for the king — for the graphs also contain the symbolism of the "sacrificial fires and light".

In the very ancient graph for ***"Lung"***, "its head with four apparent horns" is also really the fire giving off light! The divine being with a shining halo! That long tail-like thing at the waist was the long sash.

The blue-green colour of **Azure *"Lung"*** is also an important clue. For this identified ***"Lung"*** as the green being; the four-faced Brahma in Indian Hinduism as well as in Buddhism. **Azure *"Lung"*** is also known as the Indian Indra and the Chinese Jade Emperor, both of whom are green and kings of the gods and thus are the equivalent of Neptune-Zeus-Jupiter. (Incidentally, Huang Ti is sometimes pictured as having Four-Faces — just like the Indian Brahma the Four-Faced God).

The ***"Lung"*** is a human being, not an animal!

THE LATER SIGNIFICANCE

It was later that the benevolent influences of water entered into the symbolism.

The First World Emperor Fu Hsi's era was one of hunting. Evidently irrigated agriculture was not required because it was said that Shen Nung, the Second World Emperor, invented agriculture and instituted irrigation. Something in the climate changed which led to the requirement of irrigation for agriculture. This something is the Noachian Flood, after which things were never the same.

It was during Shen Nung's time, that the emperors had to deal with the task of water regulation so crucial to the livelihood of millions. Emperors could even be deposed if they failed to secure the waters. That is when the later secondary significance of ***"Lung"*** came in. The ***"Lung"*** thus became associated with the ox which was used to plough the fields for irrigation.

The ancient graph of ***"Lung"*** eventually had an additional feature to symbolize that "water" as represented by three strokes beside the animal! These "three strokes" were mistaken for "wings" of the ***"Lung"*** by modern commentators but is actually to denote water!

By this time, owing to the additional association with water and clouds, Emperor Huang Ti became known in the Middle East as the "Storm or Sky God". It is possible that Huang Ti used some technology connected with water to defeat Ch'ih Yu as Huang Ti was aided by ***"Ying Lung"***, who was supposed to control rains.

"Lung" is thus first the symbol of divine power; it is only second and later that it come to symbolize the benevolent influences of water! Hence was born the Dragon Boat Festival occurring during the 5th Moon as the 4th Moon, the symbol month of Heaven and ***"Lung"***, faded away.

THE LEGEND LIVES ON

The Chinese people did not regard themselves to be the children of ***"Lung"*** just for these symbolism. They called themselves as **"children of *Lung*"** because they were direct physical descendants of both Adam-Fu Hsi, the **Azure *"Lung"***, and later Huang Ti, the **Golden *"Lung"***! That is, ***"Lungs"***, as the symbolic summation of the first Emperors, were indeed the true physical ancestors of the Chinese people!

These similarities all strongly point to the existence in that ancient past of at least two **Great Men** whose memory is commonly venerated by several cultures. These **Great Men** must have undertaken mighty exploits of international stature, so as to be remembered. The Chinese remember. It was not a dream nor an imagination. China remembers; as only a race of people who try to remember their ancestors could.

In all the nations today, only among the Chinese people does the legend of ***"Lung"*** truly live on. The ancient Chinese are particularly proud to be associated with ***"Lung"*** because of the illustrious great deeds of their majestic ancestors. The legend began in the early Middle East and was later brought later into China, which is now virtually the only nation which venerates the memory of the ***"Lung"***

So, as dim testimony to great exploits of ancient heroes, the great legends of the fabulous ***"Lung"*** live on.

CHAPTER 20

THE "CLOUD DRAGON", "*YING LUNG*"

THE "*LUNG*" OF THE 7TH MOON

The fifteenth day of the 7th Moon is, like the fifteenth day of the 1st Moon, also a day for putting up lanterns (Eberhard 1968 pp.247-248). The fifteenth day ceremony was to celebrate the dragon's ascension on the 1st Moon and to bid the dragon farewell on the 7th Moon. The lanterns are to guide the dragon into the waters; hence the lanterns are often water floating lanterns. They are also regarded as offerings to the souls of the dead.

The fifteenth day of the 1st Moon is associated with singing. The dragon would bring a scale for the singing girl. The dragon is thus a fertility symbol. The fifteenth day of the 7th Moon is also the festival of the dead, where sacrificial offerings are given for the souls of the dead.

THE "*LUNG*" OF THE 5TH MOON

In rain magic, the most important animal is the dragon, replicas of which are often made of clay. This dragon is the ***"Ying Lung"*** (Cloud Dragon), which had wings and could fly. In mythical times, it fought against the fire-god Ch'ih Po. This ***"Ying Lung"*** also used its tail to draw lines on the earth to give rise to rivers. Hence, this dragon makes waterways, so vital for the rice fields.

Emperor Ta Yu had problems with dragons, all in the Yangtze River (Eberhard 1968 pp.350-351). The real fight was against Hsiang-lu, a minister of Kung Kung, a water monster, and the enemy of Yellow Emperor Huang Ti. Hsiang-lu had a human face, but a snake-like body with nine heads. He was killed by Yu and his blood made the soil infertile. Emperor Ta Yu himself had a dragon called ***"Ying Lung"***. Hsiang-lu was supposed to be an eel and stopped the water with his body. ***"Ying Lung"*** waggled his tail in the muddy waters and thus helped Yu to control the floods.

"Ying Lung" was supposed to be the son of a ***Mao-tu***, i.e. hairy calf, an allusion to some form of water buffalo. Yu thus directed the waters and made the soils fertile. For this, Yu also because the earth god.

The ***Shan Hai King*** has a reference to the ***"Ying Lung"*** or winged dragon (Charles Gould 1822 p.238):

> **"In the north-east corner of the Great Desert are mountains called Hiung-li and T'u K'iu. The *Ying Lung* lived at the south extremity. He killed Tsz Yiu and Kwa Fu. He could not ascend to heaven. So, there is often drought. When there is a drought, the form of the *Ying* dragon is made and then there is much rain."**

"*YING LUNG*" AIDED HUANG TI AGAINST CH'IH YU

"Ying Lung" aided Yellow Emperor Huang Ti against Ch'ih Yu, leader of the giants (Yuan Ke 1993 p.44). He lived on Mount Xiongli in the distant southern border. ***"Ying Lung"*** was a water gatherer and could cause heavy rains. In the initial battles, Ch'ih Yu obtained the help of the Master of Wind and Master of Rain, causing strong winds and rains to batter Huang Ti's army.

However, the Lady Ba came to assist. She had the power to store great heat in her body. She walked onto the battlefield and radiated out her heat. The winds and rains disappeared. Seizing the opportunity, ***"Ying Lung"*** attacked and killed many of the Miao rebels, including a number of Ch'ih Yu's iron-headed brothers.

After the rebellion led by Ch'ih Yu was crushed, Huang Ti returned to heaven. But for some reasons, ***"Ying Lung"***, like the Lady Ba, was one of those left behind. ***"Ying Lung"*** went south to live among the cool mountain pools. Whenever there was drought, ***"Ying Lung"*** gave his gift of rains to overcome the drought.

CHAPTER 21

THE DRAGONS BEATEN BY THE MONKEY GOD AND NA CHA

INTRODUCTION

There are the well known stories of the Monkey God and Na Cha, the god who rides the twin fire wheels, defeating the sea dragons. What are the significance of ***"Lung"*** in these legends?

Na Cha (or Li No Cha) was the third son of Li Ching, a general of the tyrant Chou, last Shang Emperor, and canonised as Prime Minister of Heaven. He was the disciple of the Immortal T'ai Chen-jen. On a hot day during the 5th Moon, Na Cha was bathing in the river. The waters boiled into the Eastern Ocean and disturbed the water denizens, which rose to fight Na Cha. Na Cha defeated the water beings and killed Ao Ping the third son of the East Dragon King. He even defeated the Dragon King. Finally, Na-Cha, to prevent his parents from being blamed and punished, committed suicide. As the legend goes, Li Ching, infuriated, destroyed the temple to Na Cha, whereupon father and son become eternal enemies. Wen-chu T'ien-tsun gave Li Ching the magic pagoda to protect him against Na Cha's magic pole and twin-fire-wheels.

But in order to know the significance of the so-called ***"Lung"*** here, it is the legend of Monkey God that we should examine.

THE MONKEY GOD LEGEND

Sun Wu Kong was born out of a magic stone and soon gained

magical powers after being trained by the Taoist Immortal P'u-Ti Tsu-shih. He managed to obtain the magic pole of Yu by intimidating the Dragon King. He became the leader of the monkeys and assumed leadership among the animals of the earth. Not satisfied, Sun Wu Kong demanded and got positions from Heaven, including the title of "Great Sage Equaling to Heaven". Sun Wu Kong moved from one capricious act to another, including stealing and eating the peaches of immortality of the Queen of Heaven, until the host of heaven was sent to capture him. Though captured, the Monkey could not be destroyed by Heaven not even by Lao Tzu's furnace of the **Eight Diagrams**. However, the Goddess of Mercy was able to trick and trap Monkey under a magic mountain to await the coming of the priest, Hsuan Tsang, to fetch the Buddhist scriptures from India. What follows is the famous story where Monkey, along with the Pig God and the Mountain Hermit, assisted the priest to fetch the scriptures.

The tale **"Journey to the West"** of 100 chapters by Wu Cheng-En is a Ming tale of the Tang Emperor who commissioned a trip to the West to obtain the Sacred Buddhist Scriptures. The Ming tale is actually the merging of a collection of tales, some of which are known to exist long before the Tang dynasty. The historic event of the Tang mission to obtain the Buddhist Scriptures was used to thread the odd tales into a story.

The significance of the Monkey God is echoed in the famous Indian tale of the Ramayana where Hanuman, the Monkey King, aided Rama against the Ravanna the Demon King. The fight between Hanuman and Ravanna the Demon King finds parallel in the Chinese tale where Sun Wu Kong, the Monkey God, went into the ocean to force the Dragon King to yield to him the famous magic pole of Yu. Who exactly is the Monkey God?

THE REAL MONKEY GOD

The Monkey is most well known in Chinese fables as the

MONKEY GOD SUBDUIN
THE DRAGO

WITH THE "MAGIC POLE OF TA YU

IT IS THE STORY OF EMPEROR TA YU SUBDUING THE *CHIAO* DRAGON TO CONTRO THE FLOODS. *"TA YU"* ALSO MEANS "GREA APE"

mischievous but delightful Monkey God, Sun Wu Kong, although the story does not do full credit to the true significance of the Monkey God.

It is a symbol of ugliness and trickery. In **"Journey to the West"**, the Monkey is a symbol of human intelligence and of man's skill and resourcefulness. The nickname "Monkey King" is given to a cunning man. In **"Journey to the West"**, the Monkey is also adept in medicine. The Monkey holding the peach is a symbol of immortality. The Monkey is believed to control hobgoblins, witches, elves etc. Thus, it would confer health, protection and success through keeping off these evil spirits. The Monkey God may be worshipped to drive away evil influences from the spirits.

THE LINK BETWEEN THE MONKEY GOD AND EMPEROR TA YU

The Monkey God is also the "Great Sage Equal of Heaven" or the "Handsome White Monkey King" (Wu Cheng-An , Ming dynasty). The Song of the Ten Numbers quotes: "great king in the seventh heaven is the king of the monkeys" (Eberhard 1970 p.161).

Why is the Monkey God called the Great Sage King? This is a significant clue to the link between the Monkey God and Yu. It would reveal the true identity of the Monkey God, despite the caricature built around him due to the story **"Journey to the West"**.

For the "Yu", who used the magic pole of Yu to level the grounds when combating the ancient floods, is Ta Yu, the third and last of the Three Sage Emperors. Ta Yu is the founder of the legendary Hsia dynasty. Burkhardt (1982 p.172) mentions it was the Jade Emperor who placed the pole to gauge the tide.

In the ***Shan Hai Ching***, when Yu was taming the floods, he chained the water animal which was causing the damage. This animal had previously escaped from captivity at Tortoise Mountain. This water animal was said to be a monkey, or in other versions, the rhinoceros, water pig, or even the water buffalo. It is also said to be the ***Chiao*** Dragon. This animal was so fierce that Yu had to call in many helpers to capture it.

THE BIRTH OF THE MONKEY FROM A STONE

A most significant clue in the legend of the Monkey God is that he was born out of a stone. Chang (1983 pp. 10-11) records this legend about Yu's birth:

> **The Hsia dynasty... Yu, founder of the dynasty... the clan's ancestor appears to have been born out of a rock. Yu's father, Kun, charged with the task of stemming a great flood, "stole from the Supreme God the swelling mold...With this he tried to build dams which through their swelling would hold back the waters. When his efforts failed, the Supreme God angered by his theft had him executed. There his body remained for three years turning into a stone until somebody.. cut it open with a sword; thereupon Yu emerged from his father's belly." This story is more or less repeated to account as well for the birth of Yu's son: "While digging a passage through a certain mountain, Yu was changed ... into a bear. His wife, [the Lady of Tu Shan] seeing him, ran away and herself became changed to stone. She was pregnant at the time, and so when Yu pursued her and called out, "Give me my son!" the stone split open on its north side and a son, Ch'i came forth.**

Emperor Ta Yu, the founder of the Hsia dynasty, and his son are also supposed to be born out of stone! The very same origin for the Monkey God! It is evident that the story **"Journey to the West"** took the character of the Monkey God from this "Yu Monkey" and is a caricature based on the feats of the Sage Emperor Ta Yu. The Monkey God's title of "Great Sage Equal of Heaven" is an appropriation of the "Sage" title of Emperor Ta Yu.

Yu is also associated with the water animal, the Tortoise (Eberhard 1968 p.199). This water animal is also said to be a Bear. It is also interesting to note that Yu, or rather his father Kun, is also said to have a Pig form and connected to the one-eyed giant Fang-Seng (Eberhard 1968 pp.350-357); this could be the reason for the inclusion of the Pig God and the Mountain Hermit monster with the Monkey God in the story **"Journey to the West"**.

The Monkey God with the Magic Pole of Yu is Sage Emperor Ta Yu! Thus, the Monkey God fighting the Sea Dragon King is Ta Yu fighting the ***Chiao*** Dragon.

THE TRUTH ABOUT THE *CHIAO* DRAGON

The water animal defeated by Emperor Ta Yu, alias the Monkey God, is the ***Chiao*** Dragon which is sometimes confused with a river pig, water monkey, buffalo and even rhinoceros. The ***Chiao*** Dragon, a marsh creature and unlike the Sky Dragon, is often linked with evil aspects, including human sacrifices, in Chinese culture (Eberhard 1968). What is this ***Chiao*** Dragon?

"Lung", the Heraldic Animal of the East and Centre, is associated with the beneficial influences of water. What other animal is also associated with water?

The other animal also associated with water is the Heraldic Animal of the North, the Serpent! The North Serpent is also associated with water, but that of the evil influences of water, cold wind and the winter! Many cultures have depicted the Serpent with water!

Among the species of ***"Lungs"*** the ***Chiao*** Dragon is said to look like a snake (Williams 1931 p.110). The ***Chiao*** Dragon is actually a snake! The ***Chiao*** Dragon defeated by Na-Cha or Monkey God is the Serpent, not ***"Lung"***! The ***Chiao*** Dragon whom the Emperor Ta

Yu-Monkey God defeated was trying to cause water troubles and is the same Serpent which Huang Ti had to slay to release the waters. The ***Chiao*** Dragon-Serpent is connected in legends with the evil aspects of water. The **Golden *"Lung"*** acts against the Serpent or ***Chiao*** Dragon to release the beneficial influences of waters.

THE CONNECTION BETWEEN EMPEROR TA YU, MONKEY GOD AND *"YING LUNG"*

Emperor Ta Yu, alias Monkey God, is said to possess a dragon called the ***"Ying Lung"***. ***"Ying Lung"*** assisted **Golden *"Lung"*** Huang-Ti to kill that Serpent Chih Yu, leader of the giants. Emperor Ta Yu is the Indian Monkey God Hanuman who assisted Rama against that Dragon-Serpent King Ravanna and his giants. The Monkey God defeating the ***Chiao*** Dragon-Serpent is a universal legend in many cultures. The connections indicate that ***"Ying Lung"*** who assisted **Golden *"Lung"*** Huang Ti was none other than Emperor Ta Yu himself!

The story **"Journey to the West"** relates that the Monkey God was defeated by Hsien Yang, the "Great Immortal". Hsien Yang and the Monkey God then became sworn brothers. The name "Hsien Yang" is the name for Emperor Huang Ti. This shows that Emperor Huang Ti and the Monkey God (and therefore Emperor Ta Yu or ***"Ying Lung"***) were contemporaries.

Two animals are linked with water; one is ***"Lung"*** with the auspicious influences of water, and the Serpent with the evil aspects of water. The dragons defeated or slew by Na-Cha or Monkey God are not ***"Lungs"***, but ***Chiao*** Dragon-Serpents! Just as the Indian Buddhist Naga Serpent seeped into the significance of ***"Lung"***, so did the evil ***Chiao*** Dragon-Serpent do likewise. Too many persons, including Wu Cheng-An the author of **"Journey to the West"**, have confused ***"Lung"*** with the Serpent. The Serpent aspects contaminate the legend of the ***"Lung"***

CHAPTER 22

AUSPICIOUSNESS OF THE *"LUNG"* IN MAJOR FESTIVALS

THE LEGEND

The majestic Chinese ***"Lung"***, misunderstood by the West as the Chinese 'dragon', is thus the fabulous characteristic symbol of the Chinese culture. It is intimately associated with that other characteristic symbol of Chinese culture, viz. the ***Pakua***, or **Eight Diagrams**, which has close similarity with, and is possibly the same thing as, the **"*Lung*-pearl"**. The ***"Lung"*** casts the Chinese culture in an inspiring form as one of delightful industry, leadership and benevolence.

The ***"Lung"*** derives almost all its symbolism from the great exploits of the early emperors of the Chinese people before the period of 2000 B.C. These emperors include world first emperor Fu Hsi (**Azure *"Lung"***), world third emperor Yellow Emperor Huang Ti (**Golden *"Lung"***) and ***"Ying Lung"*** (the animal symbol for Emperor Ta Yu, founder of the Hsia dynasty and the last of the **"Three Sage Emperors"**). They reflect the original roles of the rulers as the guardians and protectors who cared immensely for the people.

Hence, ***"Lung"***, from the earliest times, is the symbol of what the ***I Ching***, the Chinese Classic of Changes, calls, the **Great Man**, the wise benevolent leader of the people.

Later, from Emperor Huang Ti's time onwards, the Chinese rulers had to be concerned with the water supplies for the crops and the people. Thus, the ***added*** roles of ***"Lung"*** include regulation of water. The ***added*** water roles are so prominent that the ***"Lung"*** has been virtually regarded, erroneously, as a water creature; its original non-water guardian roles almost forgotten.

This is why, the etymology of the Chinese word for ***"Lung"*** originally, at least before 1700 B.C., was that of a standing man, the priest. The symbols of the priest include the long sash, which later evolved into, and became confused as, the "tail of the modern dragon". This "tail", originally the priest's sash, with the added three strokes for "water" at around 300 B.C., became the right sub-character of the Chinese word for ***"Lung"***.

What many people today imagine of the ***"Lung"*** are the features represented by the right sub-character of the ideogram for ***"Lung"***, viz. the water regulation aspects. But, there is that left side of the ideogram which shows the standing priest with the halo from the altar fire.

This is also the reason why the earliest relics of ***"Lung"***, those of the Shang dynasty of 1700 to 1120 B.C., show the being as a half-man, half-fish being. The modern serpentine shape of the ***"Lung"*** was not the original form, but emerged from the time of the Han dynasty onwards due to Indian Buddhist concepts of the **Naga**-cobra. This is ironical, because the earliest legends show that Emperor Huang Ti and Emperor Ta Yu (respectively, **Golden *"Lung"*** and ***"Ying Lung"***) were the enemies of the "serpent". They fought a series of titanic battles against Ch'ih Yu, the first arch-rebel, dubbed the "mountain serpent".

The contest between the half-man, half-fish ***"Lung"*** against the serpent was also told in the legends of other cultures. There were the half-man, half-fish (or half-bull) beings, Ea and Marduk, kings of gods, who fought to destroy the monster serpent, Tiamat, in the Sumerian Babylonian legends. There was Feridun, the Persian bull being or the Indian Indra, who fought against the serpent monster, the Persian Azhi Dahaka or the Indian Vritra. The king of gods, Jupiter, was also a half-man, half-fish or bull being, who fought to destroy the serpent monster Typhon. In Egypt, the serpent was Set or Apop. Remarkably, all these legends show that one of the reasons the leaders of the gods fought the serpent was to snatch back the water held captive by the serpent and release the water to the people.

Which is what the Chinese legends say of Lao Chun, the Human Sovereign (pseudonym for Emperor Huang Ti), destroying the serpent in order to release the water for the people.

From ancient times, among the ancient cultures, the "dragon" had been associated with two different opposing forms, both involved with water: [1] the benevolent half-man, half-fish being, responsible for distributing the gainful water, and [2] the wicked serpent monster, infamous for holding back the water, as well as responsible for the ill effects of cold water. The Chinese has taken up the first form, the benevolent half-man, half-fish being, the ***"Lung"***, and developed its symbolism to permeate the whole Chinese culture.

As for the second serpentine form of the wicked serpent monster, the Chinese have always regarded ***"She"*** (the cobra) as the virtual symbol of evil. So, it is ironical that the picture of ***"Lung"*** evolved from the original half-man, half-fish form into the current modern serpentine form.

THE MAJOR FESTIVALS

The symbolism of ***"Lung"*** permeates the Chinese culture so much that the major festivals of the Chinese culture actually portray the story of the ancient exploits of the ***"Lung"***! The ancient Masters purposely enshrined the memory of ***"Lung"*** into the festivals to perpetuate the legend of ***"Lung"*** and to ensure that the positive delightful benevolent aspects of the ***"Lung"*** symbolism rub into the mind and soul of the Chinese people, making them the great people down the ages.

Although festivals today are celebrated in colourful gaity, the modern celebrations lack the serious and thoughtful significance attached to them as in ancient time (Legge 1967):

> **Besides "funeral rites, sacrifices, archery, chariot-driving, capping, marriages, audiences and friendly missions, Confucius particularly referred to the "seasons of Hsia."** (p. 368).

> **The *Li Yun* also notes: "The origin of all things being found in heaven and earth, they could be taken in hand, one after the other. The commencement of these being found in the two forces (of nature) their character and tendencies could be observed. The four seasons being used as a handle (the people) could be stimulated to the business of each. The sun and stars being constituted the measures of time, that business could be laid out in order. The moon being taken as the measures (of work to be done) that work could be accomplished successfully... The five elements being considered as giving substance (to things) what has been done could be repeated. Rules of propriety and righteousness being viewed as the instruments whatever was done would be completed** (pp. 383-384).

> **Yen Yen , disciple of Confucius, again asked, "Are the rules of Propriety indeed of such urgent importance?" Confucius said, "It was by those rules that the ancient kings sought to represent the ways of Heaven and to regulate the feelings of men. Therefore he who neglects or violates them may be (spoken of) as dead and he who observe them as alive."** (***Li Chi, The Li Yun***, section 4: p. 367).

The ancient Masters knew that the seasonal festivals have highly significant purposes and effects for the peace, prosperity and happiness of the nation and the people! Failure to observe them properly will result in individual failures as well as national disasters!

The ***Li Chi*** (Book of Rites) records that the Shang had five annual ceremonial rites and the Chou seven ceremonial rites, and the worship (or rather memorial) of the Kitchen God was one of them (Lai 1984 p. 85). The ***Li Chi***, in the "Royal Regulations", notes the ceremonies performed by the Emperor (Legge 1967 pp.216-218):

> **"In the second month he visited those on the East, going to the honoured mountain of Tai. There he burnt a great pile of wood and announced his arrival to Heaven.. sacrificed to the hills and rivers...**
>
> **In the seventh month the son of Heaven continued his tour, going to the south, to the mountain of that quarter, observing the same ceremonies as in the east. In the eight month, he went to the west, to the mountain of that quarter, observing the same ceremonies as in the south. In the eleventh month he went on to the north....**

It may amaze the Chinese that their major festivals are essentially very similar to Jewish festivals! The main basic features of the Chinese calendar may be summarised as follows (after Lagerway, 1987 pp.18-24):

24th day, 12th moon	Domestic gods leave home — return only on the 4th day of the New Year.
1st day, 1st moon	Chinese New Year (Heaven Festival) Worship of Tien-Kung (God of Heaven) early morning — repeated the next two days.

9th day, 1st moon	Worship of Tien-Kung.
10th day, 1st moon	Worship of Ti-Kung (Earth Deity).
15th day, 1st moon	Lantern Festival (Chap Goh Meh). [Jewish Passover - 1st Day of Festival of Unleavened Bread]
1st day, 7th moon	Gate of Hell open. [Jewish Feast of Trumpet]
15th day, 7th moon	Festival of Earth. [Jewish Feast of Tabernacle — 1st day]
1st to 15th day, 7th moon	Festival of Universal Salvation — feeding of hungry ghosts time — ***p'u tu***.
15th day, 10th moon	Festival of Water.
1st and 15th days, every moon	The Chinese also honour the domestic gods with offerings every 1st and 15th days of the month while the Jews offer on the 1st days.

Today's Chinese New Year, which is of the Chou dynasty, does not coincide with the Old Testament Jewish New Year although the periods are quite close. The Chinese New Year had been different during the different Chinese dynasties. In ancient times these New Years were likely at the same times. In 1990 the Chinese New Year is on 27th January while the Passover is on 10th of April — meaning the Jewish New Year would be end of March 1990 — two months after the present Chinese New Year.

The Jewish Mosaic New Year started with Nissan, which would be around March-April, and Passover was the fourteenth day of Nissan (Exodus 12). The Passover would be followed by a seven day Feast of Unleavened Bread. This is different from the Jewish civil new year which started in the month of Tishri, around September-October. The 1st and 7th months are also sacred in the Old Testament Jewish calendar. The only other Jewish sacred period not finding correspondence in the Chinese calendar is the Jewish Pentecost which occurred 50 days after the 7th Day of Unleavened Bread — falling around early of the 3rd moon.

Besides the above basic pattern of the Chinese calendar festivals there are also other days devoted to the several gods of the Chinese. But otherwise, in the basic pattern of the Chinese calendar, there is a great deal of overlapping similarities between the Chinese and Jewish calendar festivals both of which revolve mostly around the 1st and 7th months.

The evidence is that the Chinese festivals with ancient roots formed part of the universal system of festivals common in the ancient cultures all over the then world.

MEMORY OF *"LUNG"* IN MAJOR FESTIVALS

Not all the festivals were meant to be associated with the ***"Lung"***. However, at least four major festivals are linked to ***"Lung"***, illustrating much of benevolent symbolism of the ***"Lung"*** discussed in this book.

It will be remembered that the **Four Cardinal Directions** could be represented by the **Four Dragons**, viz. the **Azure *"Lung"*** at the East, **Red *"Lung"*** at the South, **White *"Lung"*** at the West and

Black *"Lung"* at the North, with **Golden *"Lung"*** in the Centre. The **Four Cardinal Directions** also represent the four seasons and the four major festivals associated with solstices and equinoxes, viz. Chinese New Year in spring in the East, the Dragon Boat Festival in summer solstice period in the South, Moon Cake Festival in autumn in the West and ***Tung-Chih*** in winter solstice period in the North.

CHINESE NEW YEAR

The **"Double *Lungs*"** characterise the Chinese New Year period. Linked to the **Twin Door Gods** and associated with the red cloth at the door, the **"Double *Lungs*"** prevent entry by the monster ***"Nien"*** Beast. The home is thus sealed against evil and only good blessings could enter the house.

During the Chinese New Year period is also the time of the dragon and lion dance. They are what remains of the ancient ***Fang Siang-Che*** ceremony performed to ward off great evil an ancient times. The dance is performed today to wish in good blessings. This ***Fang Siang-Che*** is also the **"Dance of Yu"**, indicating that the dragon dance is really the ancient memory of ***"Ying Lung's"*** assistance to the Yellow Emperor Huang Ti (**Golden *"Lung"***) in the destruction of the evil serpent.

In the ***Fang Siang-Che***, a person was dressed as a Bear and led twelve other animals from house to house to help destroy evil. Emperor Ta Yu, alias ***"Ying Lung"***, was in ancient times depicted as a bear in his works to regulate the water for irrigation of crops. This is why the ***Fang Siang-Che*** is also called the **"Dance of Yu"**

According to the ***I Ching***, the spring and East position is also the position of ***Chen***, the **"Arousing Thunder"**, which is the picture of the spring ***"Lung"***. The East position also symbolises the element of Wood and crop productivity in spring, which is naturally linked to the rain and water activities of the ***"Lung"***.

THE DRAGON BOAT OR SUMMER SOLSTICE FESTIVAL

The Dragon Boat Festival is the time when Lao Chun, Human Sovereign (Huang Ti or **Golden *"Lung"***), destroyed the serpent to release water for the people.

This is the time when people 'prayed to the ***"Lung"*** for rains'. This ***"Lung"*** is the ***"Ying Lung"***.

This is also the time to perform the **"Stork Dance"**. This stork dance aims at killing the serpent. This **"Stork Dance"** is also known as the **"Gait or Step of Yu"** and is also known to be the basis of the Taoist esoteric **Thunder Magic** ritual to destroy Mao Shan Black Magic (Ong, 1991, 1995). So, again, Emperor Ta Yu (***"Ying Lung"***) is involved, preserving further his role in assisting Huang Ti (**Golden *"Lung"***) to kill the serpent.

THE MOON CAKE OR MID-AUTUMN FESTIVAL

The Moon Cake Festival was the time after the summer harvest. It was a free time devoted to recreation, joy and happy marriages and the Moon Goddess Chang O. The **"*Lung*-phoenix"** pair is in particular the symbol of marriage.

The Moon Cake Festival, on the 15th day of the 8th Moon, is linked to the 7th Moon, which is the festival of the Seven Fairies. It tells of the great love between the seventh fairy and a mortal cowherd boy. The 7th Moon is also the time to bid farewell to ***"Ying Lung"***.

The 15th day of the 8th Moon was also the time when Emperor Ta Yu summoned the gods and vassals to Mao Shan mountain. This was known as the ***K'ui Chi*** meeting. One vassal, the giant Fang Feng, was late and Ta Yu ordered his execution. On this day, people drank chrysanthemum drinks to ward off evil.

There are some ill-understood links between the ***"Lung*-phoenix"** pair, reflecting the 8th Moon, and ***"Ying Lung's"*** roles in the 7th and also 8th Moon. According to Middle East legends, the Storm God (the Middle East equivalent of Huang Ti the **Golden *"Lung"*)**, in his fight against the serpent, was aided by the serpent goddess and her mortal lover. The love between ***"Ying Lung"*** and the seventh fairy must have some yet ill-understood roles in the destruction of the serpent.

TUNG-CHIH, THE WINTER SOLSTICE FESTIVAL

The cycle of festivals finally turns to ***Tung-Chih***, the Winter Solstice Festival. During this festival, the main theme is that of **Reunion**, whose symbol is the round ***Pakua***. In honour of the theme of **Reunion**, the five round fruits of grapes, orange, peach, apple and watermelon are considered sacred offerings on this day. The pious would make and eat the small round rice dumplings boiled in sweet syrup. These round dumplings would look like pearls of various colours shining in the liquid.

The Winter Solstice is the time with the longest night, when the light of day is at the shortest. It symbolises the coming of light to diminish the dark. Hence, the emperor and the people would celebrate ***Tung-Chih*** as the victory of light over darkness. There was a time when ***Tung-Chih*** was regarded as more important than the Chinese New Year and was in fact the ancient New Year.

The symbol is roundness, reflecting **Reunion**. It does not take much to see that this day commemorates that round symbol, the ***"Lung*-pearl"**! The ***"Lung*-pearl"**, which also shines light into the darkness.

A pearl features in the legend of Chang O the Moon Goddess. She stole the pearl of immortality from her husband, Shen I, the Divine Archer and flew to the Moon. However, according to the legends, Yellow Emperor Huang Ti also had a precious black pearl. Huang

Ti once lost this pearl, but it was recovered. It was then stolen and again recovered. There are undoubtedly some links, yet ill-understood, of these pearls with ***Tung-Chih***.

CENTRAL FIGURES OF HUANG TI AND TA YU

The cycle of the major festivals is actually the story of the ***"Lung"***! Each of the major festivals show intimate links with the Yellow Emperor Huang Ti (**Golden *"Lung"***) and Emperor Ta Yu (***"Ying Lung"***). The major festivals illustrate the efforts of the ***"Lungs"***, both Huang Ti the **Golden *"Lung"***, and Ta Yu, the ***"Ying Lung"***, were all directed towards **Reunion** of the whole country. From there to **Reunion** for the families of the people.

It is not a coincidence that, in astrology, Huang Ti the **Golden *"Lung"***, representing the Centre and Earth, also symbolises harmony.

Then only, the evil and wickedness of the serpent are finally exorcised. The festivals indicate that the serpent had pursued his evil on a policy of divide and rule. Symbolically, the evil of the serpent started around the Summer Solstice of the Dragon Boat Festival period. The serpent had caused family members to turn against each other. The serpent had used many stratagem in its evil, including theft of certain valuable things, called the **pearl** in the Chinese legends and the **"tablets of destiny"** in the Sumerian-Babylonian legends.

But the ***"Lungs"*** moved against the serpent. Through the Moon Cake Festival and ***Tung-Chih*** periods, they seized back the stolen precious things and marshalled up various allies. The final stages of the battles began at the Chinese New Year, when the **Dance of Yu"** was performed to ward off and destroy the evil. By the Summer Solstice Dragon Boat Festival the ***"Lungs"*** had effectively used the **"Dance of Yu"** to completely destroy the serpent.

HUANG TI, the GOLDEN □*LUNG*□, RIDING THE BIG DIPPER

THE CHINESE MAJOR FESTIVALS REVOLVE AROUND EXPLOITS OF HUANG TI, GOLDEN *"LUNG"*, AND EMPEROR TA YU, *"YING LUNG"*

A Han relief depicting the Yellow Emperor riding in his chariot, The Big Dipper.

THE MID-SEASON POSITIONS OF THE BIG DIPPER (URSA MAJOR) DETERMINE THE DATES OF THE CHINESE FESTIVALS. THIS IS WHY HUANG TI IS SHOWN RIDING THE BIG DIPPER. IN WESTERN LEGENDS, THE "WAIN" (URSA MAJOR) WAS THE CHARIOT OF KING ARTHUR.

We noted earlier that the **Four Cardinal Directions** representing the four seasons and major festivals could also be represented by the **Four Dragons.** The **Four Cardinal Directions** are also the mid-season positions of the star constellation of **Ursa Major**, the Big Bear, or the **Wain**, in the north. This **Ursa Major**, or **Wain**, is also the chariot of Huang Ti the **Golden "*Lung*"**. It is not surprising that the functions and activities reflected by the four major festivals should concern the Yellow Emperor Huang Ti the **Golden "*Lung*"**.

The **Ursa Major** or **Wain** is the chariot of Huang Ti the **Golden "*Lung*"**. The **"Tli"** dragon of the Hebrew Kabalic tradition, said to be confused with the lunar serpent-dragon, is also linked with the **Wain** and oriented in a north-south direction. They, Huang Ti the **Golden "*Lung*"** and the **"Tli"** dragon, are one and the same majestic being.

So, from common origins in the ancient cultures in the very ancient past, the majestic legend of the benevolent **"*Lung*"** lives on....

REFERENCES

Bilsky, Lewster James. 1975. The Ancient State Religion of Ancient China I. Asian Folklore and Social Life Monograph. Lou Tsu-k'uang, Editor. Volume 70. The Orient Cultural Service. 422 Fulin Road, Shihlin, Taipei, Taiwan, China.

*

Bord, Janet and Bord, Colin. 1980. Alien Animals. Book Club Associates. Bath, Britain.

*

Bowie, Henry P. 1952. On the Laws of Japanese Painting. Dover Publications, Inc. New York.

Bullinger Publication Trust. 1964. The Companion Bible. Zondervan Bible Publishers. Grand Rapids, Michigan.

Burkhardt, V.R. 1982. Chinese Creeds and Customs. A SCMP Publication. Hongkong.

*

Buttrick, George Arthur. Commentary Editor. 1954. The Interpreter's Bible. A Commentary in Twelve Volumes. Abingdon Press. Nashville, New York.

Chang, K.C. Art, Myth and Ritual, The Path to Political Authority in Ancient China. Harvard University Press. Cambridge, Massachusetts and London.

*

Chavannes, E. 1973. Five Happiness. Weatherhill. New York, Tokyo.

Cheu Hock Tong. 1988. The Nine Emperor Gods, A study of Chinese Spirit-Medium cults. Times Book International. Singapore, Kuala Lumpur.

Coyajee, J.C. 1929. Cults & Legends of Ancient Iran & China. Jehangir B. Karanis Sons. Bombay, India.

Denny, Nicholas, B. 1968. The Folklore of China and its affinity with the Aryan and Semitic races. Oriental Press. Amsterdam.

*

Derk Bodde (translator). 1965. Annual Customs and Festivals in Peking. by Tun Li-Chun, 1900. Hong Kong University Press. Hongkong.

Eberhard, W. 1968. The Local Cultures of South and East China. E.J. Brill. Leiden.

Eberhard, W. 1972. Chinese Festivals. The Orient Cultural Service Taipei, China.

*

Fleming, Kenneth C. 1981. God's Voice in the Stars. Loizeaux Brothers, Neptune, New Jersey.

Gorn, Walter. 1904. The Shu King, or the Chinese Historical Classic. The Theosophical Publishing Society, London and Benares, John Lane, New York.

Gould, Charles. 1882. Mythical Monsters, Facts or Fiction? Studio Editions Ltd. London.

Hirth, Friedrich. 1908. The Ancient History of China to the end of the Chou dynasty. The Columbia University Press, New York.

Huang, Tsai-kang. 1986. The Traditional Art of Chinese Woodblock Prints. Council for Cultural Planning and Development. Republic of China.

Hsu, C.H. and Ward, A.H.C. 1984. Ancient Chinese Society, An Epigraphical and Archaeological Interpretation. Yee Wan Publishing Co. San Francisco, California.

Ingersoll, Ernest. 1928. Dragons and Dragon Lore. Payson & Clarke Ltd. New York.

Jenner. see Wu Cheng-En.

Joel, C. Dobin, Rabbi. 1977. The Astrological Secrets of the Hebrew Sages. Inner Traditions International, Ltd. New York.

Keightley, David, N. (editor). 1983. The Origins of Chinese Civilisation. University of California Press, Berkeley and Los Angeles, California. A Berkeley Conference on Studies on China 1.

*

de Kermadec, Jean-Michel Huon. 1983. The Way to Chinese Astrology, the Four Pillars of Destiny. Unwin Paperbacks, London. translated by N. Derek Poulsen.

King James Version. The Holy Bible. Collins' Clear-Type Press. Glasglow, Toronto, Sydney and Auckland.

Kramer, Samuel Noah. 1961. Mythologies of the Ancient World. Anchor Books. Doubleday and Company, Inc. Garden City, New York.

*

Kwok Man-Ho. 1989. The Chinese Almanac 1990, The Year of the Horse. Bantam Books. Toronto, New York, London, Sydney, Auckland.

Lagerway, John. 1967. Taoist Ritual in Chinese Society and History. MacMillian Publishing Company. New York.

*

Lai Kuan Fook. 1984. The Hennessy Book of Chinese Festivals. Heinemann Educational Books (Asia) Ltd. Petaling Jaya, Malaysia.

*

Lee Siow-Mong. 1986. Spectrum of Chinese Culture. Pelanduk Publications. Petaling Jaya, Malaysia.

Legge, James. 1967. Li Chi, Book of Rites. University Books, New York Park, New York.

Levi, Eliphas. 1825. The Key of the Mysteries. Translated from French by Aleister Crowley, 1959. Rider, London, Melbourne, Auckland and Johannesburg.

*

Liang, Yin-Boone. 1979. Chinese Flower and Bird Painting. Wan Li Book Co. Ltd. Hongkong.

*

Low, C.C. and associates. (editors and translators) 1989. Canonisation of Deities. Canfonian Pte. Ltd. Singapore.

Lutin, Michael. 1988. 1988 Total Horoscope, SCORPIO. Jove Books, New York.

MacKenzie, D.A. 1926. The Migration of Symbols. AMS Press. New York.

*

Maspero, Henry. 1945. Taoism and Chinese Religion. Translated by Frank A Kierman Jr. 1981. The University of Massachusetts Press. Amherst.

Needham, Joseph. 1959. Astronomy. In Volume 3 of Science and Civilisation in China. At the University Press, Cambridge. Britain.

Ong, Hean-Tatt. 1991. The Chinese Pakua: An Expose. {Pelanduk Publications Sdn. Bhd., Petaling Jaya, Malaysia.

Ong, Hean-Tatt. 1994. Chinese Animal Symbolism. {Pelanduk Publications Sdn. Bhd., Petaling Jaya, Malaysia.

Ong Hean-Tatt. 1995. Chinese Black Magic: An Expose. Eastern Dragon Press, Kuala Lumpur, Malaysia.

Peloubet, Rev F. N. 1947. Peloubet Bible Dictionary. The John C. Winston Company. Great Britain.

Plopper, Clifford H. 1935. Chinese Religion seen through the Proverbs. Shanghai Modern Publishing House, Shanghai, China.

Saso, Michael. 1978. The Teaching of Taoist Master Chuang. Yale University Press, New Haven and London.

Seiss, Joseph A. 1972. The Gospel in the Stars. Kregel Publications, Grand Rapids, Michigan.

Sharf, A. 1876. The Universe of Shabbetai Donnolo. Aris & Phillips Ltd. Warminster, England.

Shumaker, Wayne. 1972. The Occult Sciences in the Renaissance. A Study in Intellectual Patterns. University of California Press, Berkeley, Los Angeles, London.

Skinner, Stephen. 1982. The Living Earth Manual of Feng-Shui. Graham Brash (Pte) Ltd. Singapore.

Strong, James, H. 1989. Strong's Exhaustative Concordance. Baker Book House, Grand Rapids, Michigan.

Thayer, Jospeh. H. 1977. Thayer's Greek-English Lexicon of the New Testament. Baker Book House, Grand Rapids, Michigan.

Vaccari, O. and E.E. Vaccari. 1950. Pictorial Chinese-Japanese Characters. A New and Fascinating Method to learn Ideograms. Vaccari's Language Institute, Tokyo.

Walls, Jan and Walls, Yvonne. 1984. Myths of Ancient China. Asiapac Books

& Educational Aids (S) Pte. Ltd. Singapore.

Waterbury, F. 1952. Bird-Deities in China. Artibus Asiae Publishers. Ascona, Switzerland.

Weiger, L.S.J. 1950. Chinese Characters. Their Origin, Etymology, History, Classification and Significance, A Thorough Study from Chinese Documents. Dover Publications Inc., New York.

Werner, E.T.C. 1922. Myths and Legends of China. George G. Harrap & Co. London, Toronto, Wellington, Sydney. 1958 edition.

Whittick, Arnold. 1960. Symbols, Signs and their Meanings. Leonard Hill Ltd. London.

Wilhelm, Richard. 1951. The I Ching or Book of Changes. rendered into English by Cary F. Baynes. 1980. Routledge & Kegan Paul. London and Henley.

Williams, C.A.S. 1920. Manual of Chinese Metaphors. AMS Press. New York.

Williams, C.A.S. 1931. Outlines of Chinese Symbolism. Customs College Press, Peiping, China.

*

Wing, R.L. 1982. The Illustrated I Ching. Doubleday Dolphin Book.

*

Wong, C.S. 1967. A Cycle of Chinese Festivals. Malaysia Publishing House Ltd. Singapore.

Wu, Cheng Eu. 1500-82, Ming dynasty. Journey to the West. Translated by W.J.F. Jenner. Foreign Language Press, Peiking.

Wu, Kuo Cheng. 1982. The Chinese Heritage. Crown Publishers, Inc. New York.

Xing, Qi. 1988. Folk Customs at Traditional Chinese Festivities. Foreign Language Press. Peiking.

Yuan Ke. 1993. Dragons and Dynasties. Penguin Books, England.